# ITIL® Continual Service Improvement

London: TSO

# ⊠ TSO

Published by TSO (The Stationery Office) and available from:

**Online**
www.tsoshop.co.uk

**Mail, Telephone, Fax & E-mail**
TSO
PO Box 29, Norwich, NR3 1GN
Telephone orders/General enquiries: 0870 600 5522
Fax orders: 0870 600 5533
E-mail: customer.services@tso.co.uk
Textphone 0870 240 3701

**TSO@Blackwell and other Accredited Agents**

**Customers can also order publications from:**
TSO Ireland
16 Arthur Street, Belfast BT1 4GD
Tel 028 9023 8451 Fax 028 9023 5401

First edition Crown Copyright 2007
Second edition Crown Copyright 2011

First published 2011

ISBN 9780113313082

Printed in the United Kingdom for The Stationery Office
Material is FSC certified and produced using ECF pulp.
Sourced from fully sustainable forests.

P002425506    c70   07/11

# Contents

List of figures       v

List of tables       vii

Foreword       viii

Preface       ix

Acknowledgements       x

1   Introduction       1

   1.1   Overview       3

   1.2   Context       6

   1.3   ITIL in relation to other publications in the Best Management Practice portfolio       8

   1.4   Why is ITIL so successful?       8

   1.5   Chapter summary       10

2   Service management as a practice       11

   2.1   Services and service management       13

   2.2   Basic concepts       20

   2.3   Governance and management systems       25

   2.4   The service lifecycle       27

3   Continual service improvement principles       33

   3.1   Continual service improvement approach       35

   3.2   CSI and organizational change       36

   3.3   Ownership       36

   3.4   CSI register       36

   3.5   External and internal drivers       37

   3.6   Service level management       37

   3.7   Knowledge management       38

   3.8   The Deming Cycle       38

   3.9   Service measurement       38

   3.10   IT governance       42

   3.11   Frameworks, models, standards and quality systems       42

   3.12   CSI inputs and outputs       44

4   Continual service improvement processes       45

   4.1   The seven-step improvement process       47

5   Continual service improvement methods and techniques       71

   5.1   Methods and techniques       73

   5.2   Assessments       74

   5.3   Benchmarking       79

   5.4   Service measurement       85

   5.5   Metrics       91

   5.6   Return on investment       106

   5.7   Service reporting       111

   5.8   CSI and other service management processes       112

   5.9   Summary       125

6   Organizing for continual service improvement       127

   6.1   Organizational development       129

   6.2   Functions       129

   6.3   Roles       129

   6.4   Customer engagement       138

   6.5   Responsibility model – RACI       138

   6.6   Competence and training       139

7   Technology considerations       143

   7.1   Tools to support CSI activities       145

   7.2   Summary       152

**8  Implementing continual service improvement**                                      **153**

   8.1  Critical considerations for implementing CSI                    155

   8.2  Where do I start?                       155

   8.3  Governance                              156

   8.4  CSI and organizational change           157

   8.5  Communication strategy and plan         162

   8.6  Summary                                  164

**9  Challenges, risks and critical success factors**                                 **165**

   9.1  Challenges                               167

   9.2  Critical success factors                 167

   9.3  Risks                                    167

   9.4  Summary                                  168

**Afterword**                                            **169**

**Appendix A: Related guidance**                         **173**

   A.1  ITIL guidance and web services          175

   A.2  Quality management system               175

   A.3  Risk management                          176

   A.4  Governance of IT                         176

   A.5  COBIT                                    176

   A.6  ISO/IEC 20000 service management series  177

   A.7  Environmental management and green/sustainable IT            177

   A.8  ISO standards and publications for IT    178

   A.9  ITIL and the OSI framework               178

   A.10 Programme and project management         179

   A.11 Organizational change                    179

   A.12 Skills Framework for the Information Age  180

   A.13 Carnegie Mellon: CMMI and eSCM framework  180

   A.14 Balanced scorecard                       180

   A.15 Six Sigma                                180

**Appendix B: Example of a continual service improvement register**                    **183**

**Appendix C: Risk assessment and management**                                         **187**

   C.1  Definition of risk and risk management  189

   C.2  Management of Risk (M_o_R)               189

   C.3  ISO 31000                                190

   C.4  ISO/IEC 27001                            191

   C.5  Risk IT                                  192

**Appendix D: Examples of inputs and outputs across the service lifecycle**            **195**

**Abbreviations and glossary**                          **199**

**Index**                                               **239**

# List of figures

| Figure 1.1 | The ITIL service lifecycle | 3 |
| Figure 1.2 | ITIL's relationship with other Best Management Practice guides | 9 |
| Figure 2.1 | Conversation about the definition and meaning of services | 14 |
| Figure 2.2 | Logic of value creation through services | 18 |
| Figure 2.3 | Sources of service management practice | 19 |
| Figure 2.4 | Examples of capabilities and resources | 21 |
| Figure 2.5 | Process model | 21 |
| Figure 2.6 | The service portfolio and its contents | 25 |
| Figure 2.7 | Architectural layers of an SKMS | 26 |
| Figure 2.8 | Plan-Do-Check-Act cycle | 27 |
| Figure 2.9 | Integration across the service lifecycle | 30 |
| Figure 2.10 | Continual service improvement and the service lifecycle | 31 |
| Figure 3.1 | Continual service improvement approach | 35 |
| Figure 3.2 | Knowledge management leads to better IT decisions | 38 |
| Figure 3.3 | Why do we measure? | 39 |
| Figure 3.4 | The seven-step improvement process | 40 |
| Figure 3.5 | Knowledge spiral – a gathering activity | 41 |
| Figure 3.6 | Enterprise governance (source: CIMA) | 42 |
| Figure 4.1 | From vision to measurements | 50 |
| Figure 4.2 | Monitoring and data collection procedures | 55 |
| Figure 4.3 | Common procedures for processing the data | 57 |
| Figure 4.4 | Service level achievement chart | 62 |
| Figure 4.5 | First- to fourth-order drivers | 64 |
| Figure 5.1 | The relationship of services, processes and systems | 77 |
| Figure 5.2 | The value of a process versus the maturity of a process | 79 |
| Figure 5.3 | Availability reporting | 86 |
| Figure 5.4 | Service measurement model | 88 |
| Figure 5.5 | Technology domain versus service management | 89 |
| Figure 5.6 | Service management model | 90 |
| Figure 5.7 | From vision to measurement | 92 |
| Figure 5.8 | Number of incidents opened by service desk over time | 96 |
| Figure 5.9 | Comparison of incidents opened and resolved on first contact by the service desk | 96 |
| Figure 5.10 | Deriving measurements and metrics from goals and objectives | 99 |
| Figure 5.11 | Reported outage minutes for a service | 100 |
| Figure 5.12 | IT balanced scorecard | 104 |
| Figure 5.13 | The expanded incident lifecycle | 114 |
| Figure 5.14 | Connecting business and service capacity management | 116 |
| Figure 5.15 | Business capacity growth model | 117 |
| Figure 5.16 | Connecting service and component capacity management | 117 |
| Figure 5.17 | Connecting businesses, service and component capacity management | 117 |
| Figure 5.18 | Capacity management activities | 120 |
| Figure 5.19 | Sources of knowledge | 123 |
| Figure 5.20 | Reasons for a risk management process | 124 |
| Figure 6.1 | Activities and skill levels needed for continual service improvement | 134 |

Figure 6.2    Service management roles and
              customer engagement                    139

Figure 7.1    The application of the
              architectural layers of the CMS        147

Figure 7.2    Service-centric view of the IT
              enterprise                             151

Figure 8.1    Process re-engineering changes
              everything                             157

Figure 8.2    Vision becomes blurred                 163

Figure 8.3    CSI roles and inputs                   164

Figure C.1    The M_o_R framework                    190

Figure C.2    ISO 31000 risk management
              process flow                           191

Figure C.3    ISACA Risk IT process
              framework                              193

# List of tables

| | | |
|---|---|---|
| Table 2.1 | The processes described in each core ITIL publication | 29 |
| Table 3.1 | CSI inputs and outputs by lifecycle stage | 43 |
| Table 4.1 | Policy template example | 49 |
| Table 4.2 | Monitoring and data collection procedures | 55 |
| Table 4.3 | Procedures for processing the data | 57 |
| Table 5.1 | Pros and cons of assessment approaches | 76 |
| Table 5.2 | Average results of over 100 process assessments before improvement | 84 |
| Table 5.3 | CMMI maturity model | 84 |
| Table 5.4 | Key performance indicators of the value of service management processes | 90 |
| Table 5.5 | High-level goals and key performance indicators | 91 |
| Table 5.6 | Examples of service quality metrics | 94 |
| Table 5.7 | Response times for three service desks | 97 |
| Table 5.8 | An example of a summary report format | 100 |
| Table 5.9 | Service report of outage minutes compared to goal | 101 |
| Table 5.10 | Percentage of incidents meeting target time for service restoration | 101 |
| Table 5.11 | Sample key performance indicators | 102 |
| Table 5.12 | Service desk balanced scorecard example | 105 |
| Table 5.13 | SWOT analysis | 107 |
| Table 5.14 | Sample SWOT analysis for CSI | 107 |
| Table 5.15 | Departmental requirements | 116 |
| Table 5.16 | Risk register | 125 |
| Table 6.1 | Skills involved in Step 1 – Identify the strategy for improvement | 135 |
| Table 6.2 | Skills involved in Step 2 – Define what you will measure | 135 |
| Table 6.3 | Skills involved in Step 3 – Gather the data | 135 |
| Table 6.4 | Skills involved in Step 4 – Process the data | 135 |
| Table 6.5 | Skills involved in Step 5 – Analyse the information and data | 136 |
| Table 6.6 | Skills involved in Step 6 – Present and use the information | 136 |
| Table 6.7 | Skills involved in Step 7 – Implement improvement | 136 |
| Table 6.8 | Comparison of CSI manager, service level manager, service owner and business relationship manager roles | 137 |
| Table 6.9 | An example of a simple RACI matrix | 140 |
| Table 8.1 | Eight steps that need to be implemented, and the main reasons why transformation efforts fail (from Kotter, 1996) | 158 |
| Table 8.2 | Table for sample communication plan | 163 |

# Foreword

Back in the 1980s no one truly understood IT service management (ITSM), although it was clear that it was a concept that needed to be explored. Hence a UK government initiative was instigated and ITIL® was born. Over the years, ITIL has evolved and, arguably, is now the most widely adopted approach in ITSM. It is globally recognized as the best-practice framework. ITIL's universal appeal is that it continues to provide a set of processes and procedures that are efficient, reliable and adaptable to organizations of all sizes, enabling them to improve their own service provision.

Having progressed a service from strategy to design through transition and then into live operation, where do we go then? Continual service improvement (CSI) is the answer.

One of the cornerstones of the ITIL service lifecycle is that we should always strive to improve, as to do otherwise leads to standing still, potentially followed by stagnation and ultimately death. Improvements can be a reduction in weaknesses or an enhancement of strengths, as well as adopting new approaches to existing activities. *ITIL Continual Service Improvement* offers guidance on ways to measure, review and act to identify and adopt improvements in service provision. If you have not started your IT service management journey then you may find that this publication is a good place to start, as you can use it to identify those areas where your organization will most benefit from applying service management practices.

The principles contained within *ITIL Continual Service Improvement* have been proven countless times in the real world. We encourage feedback from business and the ITSM community, as well as other experts in the field, to ensure that ITIL remains relevant. This practice of continual service improvement is one of the cornerstones of the ITIL framework and the fruits of this labour are here before you in this updated edition.

There is an associated qualification scheme so that individuals can demonstrate their understanding and application of the ITIL practices. So whether you are starting out or continuing along the ITIL path, you are joining a legion of individuals and organizations who have recognized the benefits of good quality service and have a genuine resolve to improve their service level provision.

ITIL is not a panacea to all problems. It is, however, a tried and tested approach that has been proven to work.

I wish you every success in your service management journey.

Frances Scarff

*Head of Best Management Practice*
*Cabinet Office*

# Preface

*'Learning is not compulsory … neither is survival.'*
W Edwards Deming

This is the fifth book in the series of five ITIL core publications containing advice and guidance around the activities and processes associated with the five stages of the service lifecycle. The primary purpose of the continual service improvement stage of the service lifecycle is to learn from experience and to apply that learning in order to continually improve the quality of IT services and to optimize costs.

Continual service improvement must permeate and become woven into every stage of the service lifecycle and into every process, function, activity, tool, supplier and member of staff. This will involve the establishment of appropriate monitoring, measurement, analysis, reporting and implementation of corrective actions to ensure that the IT services being provided, as well as the processes, tools and suppliers who deliver and operate them, remain fit for purpose or are updated as required. It should also ensure that the overall IT strategy itself remains robust, and that the knowledge, skills, qualifications and experience of IT staff are updated and maintained as required.

Continual service improvement is cyclical in nature; there are periods of stability followed by more improvements, then a new level of stability is followed by more improvements and so on.

*ITIL Continual Service Improvement* gives practical guidance on how to assess the overall health and maturity of an organization's IT service management capabilities, and explains how continual service improvement is closely akin to quality management. Both are aligned to a Plan-Do-Check-Act cycle, so should be used in conjunction to achieve ongoing service quality to continually meet required business outcomes.

## Contact information

Full details of the range of material published under the ITIL banner can be found at:

www.best-management-practice.com/IT-Service-Management-ITIL/

If you would like to inform us of any changes that may be required to this publication, please log them at:

www.best-management-practice.com/changelog/

For further information on qualifications and training accreditation, please visit

www.itil-officialsite.com

Alternatively, please contact:

APM Group – The Accreditor Service Desk
Sword House
Totteridge Road
High Wycombe
Buckinghamshire
HP13 6DG
UK

Tel: +44 (0) 1494 458948
Email: servicedesk@apmgroupltd.com

# Acknowledgements

## 2011 EDITION

### Authors and mentors

Vernon Lloyd (Fox IT)                           Author

David Wheeldon
(David Wheeldon IT Service Management)
                                                Mentor

Shirley Lacy (ConnectSphere)        Project mentor

Ashley Hanna (HP)        Technical continuity editor

### Other members of the ITIL authoring team

Thanks are due to the authors and mentors who have worked on all the publications in the lifecycle suite and contributed to the content in this publication and consistency across the suite. They are:

David Cannon (HP), Lou Hunnebeck (Third Sky), Anthony T. Orr (BMC Software), Stuart Rance (HP), Colin Rudd (IT Enterprise Management Services Ltd (ITEMS)) and Randy Steinberg (Migration Technologies Inc.).

### Project governance

Members of the project governance team included:

Jessica Barry, APM Group, project assurance (examinations); Marianna Billington, itSMFI, senior user; Emily Egle, TSO, team manager; Janine Eves, TSO, senior supplier; Phil Hearsum, Cabinet Office, project assurance (quality); Tony Jackson, TSO, project manager; Paul Martini, itSMFI, senior user; Richard Pharro, APM Group, senior supplier; Frances Scarff, Cabinet Office, project executive; Rob Stroud, itSMFI, senior user; Sharon Taylor, Aspect Group Inc., adviser to the project board (technical) and the ATO sub-group, and adviser to the project board (training).

For more information on the ATO sub-group see:

www.itil-officialsite.com/News/
ATOSubGroupAppointed.aspx

For a full list of acknowledgements of the ATO sub-group at the time of publication, please visit: www.itil-officialsite.com/Publications/
PublicationAcknowledgements.aspx

### Wider team

#### Change advisory board

The change advisory board (CAB) spent considerable time and effort reviewing all the comments submitted through the change control log and their hard work was essential to this project. Members of the CAB involved in this review included:

David Cannon, Emily Egle, David Favelle, Ashley Hanna, Kevin Holland, Stuart Rance, Frances Scarff and Sharon Taylor.

Once authors and mentors were selected for the 2011 update, a revised CAB was appointed and now includes:

Emily Egle, David Favelle, Phil Hearsum, Kevin Holland and Frances Scarff.

#### Reviewers

Claire Agutter, IT Training Zone; Deborah L. Anthony, HP; Nancy Arellano, Tata Consultancy Services; Ernest R. Brewster, Independent; David M. Brink, Solutions3; Jeroen Bronkhorst, HP; Tony Brough, DHL Supply Chain; Janaki Chakravarthy, Independent; Christiane Chung Ah Pong, NCS Pte Ltd, Singapore; Federico Corradi, Cogitek; Jenny Dugmore, Service Matters; Frank Eggert, MATERNA GmbH; David Favelle, UXC Consulting/ Lucid IT; Ryan Fraser, HP; Jenni Garvie; John Groom, WestGroom Consulting; Jabe Hickey, IBM; Kevin Holland, NHS Connecting for Health; Kai Holthaus, Third Sky; Steve Ingall, iCore-ltd; Brad Laatsch, HP; Chandrika Labru, Tata Consultancy Services; Reginald Lo, Third Sky; Brian McCabe, Hitachi Consulting; Jane McNamara, Lilliard Associates Ltd; Judit Pongracz, ITeal Consulting; Murali Ramakrishnan, Process-Symphony; Daniel Ramalho, Unilever Global IT Services; Devang Raval, Quint Wellington Redwood; Noel Scott, Symantec; Moira Shaw, Steria; Arun Simha, L-3 Communications

STRATIS; Helen Sussex, Logica; J.R. Tietsort, Micron Technology; Ken Turbitt, Service Management Consultancy (SMCG) Ltd; A.D. Williams, Cornell University; Neil Wilson, The Grey Matters Education Ltd

## 2007 EDITION

### Chief architect and authors

Thanks are still due to those who contributed to the 2007 edition of Continual Service Improvement, upon which this updated edition is based.

Sharon Taylor (Aspect Group Inc)     Chief architect

Gary Case (Pink Elephant)                      Author

George Spalding (Pink Elephant)             Author

All names and organizations were correct at publication in 2007.

For a full list of all those who contributed to the 2007 and 2011 editions of Service Strategy, Service Design, Service Transition, Service Operation and Continual Service Improvement, please go to

www.itil-officialsite.com/Publications/ PublicationAcknowledgements.aspx

# Introduction

1

# 1 Introduction

ITIL is part of a suite of best-practice publications for IT service management (ITSM).[1] ITIL provides guidance to service providers on the provision of quality IT services, and on the processes, functions and other capabilities needed to support them. ITIL is used by many hundreds of organizations around the world and offers best-practice guidance applicable to all types of organization that provide services. ITIL is not a standard that has to be followed; it is guidance that should be read and understood, and used to create value for the service provider and its customers. Organizations are encouraged to adopt ITIL best practices and to adapt them to work in their specific environments in ways that meet their needs.

ITIL is the most widely recognized framework for ITSM in the world. In the 20 years since it was created, ITIL has evolved and changed its breadth and depth as technologies and business practices have developed. ISO/IEC 20000 provides a formal and universal standard for organizations seeking to have their service management capabilities audited and certified. While ISO/IEC 20000 is a standard to be achieved and maintained, ITIL offers a body of knowledge useful for achieving the standard.

In 2007, the second major refresh of ITIL was published in response to significant advancements in technology and emerging challenges for IT service providers. New models and architectures such as outsourcing, shared services, utility computing, cloud computing, virtualization, web services and mobile commerce have become widespread within IT. The process-based approach of ITIL was augmented with the service lifecycle to address these additional service management challenges. In 2011, as part of its commitment to continual improvement, the Cabinet Office published this update to improve consistency across the core publications.

The ITIL framework is based on the five stages of the service lifecycle as shown in Figure 1.1, with a core publication providing best-practice guidance for each stage. This guidance includes

key principles, required processes and activities, organization and roles, technology, associated challenges, critical success factors and risks. The service lifecycle uses a hub-and-spoke design, with service strategy at the hub, and service design, transition and operation as the revolving lifecycle stages or 'spokes'. Continual service improvement (CSI) surrounds and supports all stages of the service lifecycle. Each stage of the lifecycle exerts influence on the others and relies on them for inputs and feedback. In this way, a constant set of checks and balances throughout the service lifecycle ensures that as business demand changes with business need, the services can adapt and respond effectively.

In addition to the core publications, there is also a complementary set of ITIL publications providing guidance specific to industry sectors, organization types, operating models and technology architectures.

## 1.1 OVERVIEW

*ITIL Continual Service Improvement* provides best-practice guidance for the CSI stage of the ITIL service lifecycle. Although this publication can be

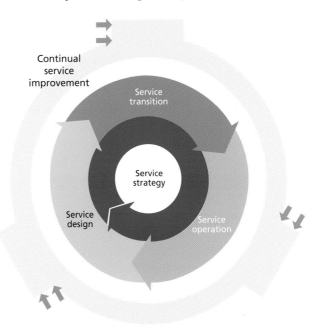

*Figure 1.1 The ITIL service lifecycle*

---

[1] ITSM and other concepts from this chapter are described in more detail in Chapter 2.

read in isolation, it is recommended that it is used in conjunction with the other core ITIL publications.

### 1.1.1 Purpose and objectives of CSI

The purpose of the CSI stage of the lifecycle is to align IT services with changing business needs by identifying and implementing improvements to IT services that support business processes. These improvement activities support the lifecycle approach through service strategy, service design, service transition and service operation. CSI is always seeking ways to improve service effectiveness, process effectiveness and cost effectiveness.

In order to identify improvement opportunities, the measurement of current performance is an important factor. Consider the following sayings about measurements and management:

*You cannot manage what you cannot control.*

*You cannot control what you cannot measure.*

*You cannot measure what you cannot define.*

If services and processes are not implemented, managed and supported using clearly defined goals, objectives and relevant measurements that lead to actionable improvements, the business will suffer. Depending upon the criticality of a specific IT service to the business, the organization could lose productive hours, experience higher costs, suffer loss of reputation or, perhaps, even risk business failure. Ultimately it could also lead to loss of customer business. That is why it is critically important to understand what to measure, why it is being measured and what the successful outcome should be.

The objectives of CSI are to:

- Review, analyse, prioritize and make recommendations on improvement opportunities in each lifecycle stage: service strategy, service design, service transition, service operation and CSI itself
- Review and analyse service level achievement
- Identify and implement specific activities to improve IT service quality and improve the efficiency and effectiveness of the enabling processes
- Improve cost effectiveness of delivering IT services without sacrificing customer satisfaction

- Ensure applicable quality management methods are used to support continual improvement activities
- Ensure that processes have clearly defined objectives and measurements that lead to actionable improvements
- Understand what to measure, why it is being measured and what the successful outcome should be.

### 1.1.2 Scope

*ITIL Continual Service Improvement* provides guidance in four main areas:

- The overall health of ITSM as a discipline
- The continual alignment of the service portfolio with the current and future business needs
- The maturity and capability of the organization, management, processes and people utilized by the services
- Continual improvement of all aspects of the IT service and the service assets that support them.

To implement CSI successfully it is important to understand the different activities that need to be applied. The following activities support CSI:

- Reviewing management information and trends to ensure that services are meeting agreed service levels
- Reviewing management information and trends to ensure that the output of the enabling processes are achieving the desired results
- Periodically conducting maturity assessments against the process activities and associated roles to demonstrate areas of improvement or, conversely, areas of concern
- Periodically conducting internal audits verifying employee and process compliance
- Reviewing existing deliverables for appropriateness
- Periodically proposing recommendations for improvement opportunities
- Periodically conducting customer satisfaction surveys
- Reviewing business trends and changed priorities, and keeping abreast of business projections
- Conducting external and internal service reviews to identify CSI opportunities

■ Measuring and identifying the value created by CSI improvements.

These activities do not happen automatically. They must be owned by individuals within the service provider organization who are empowered to make things happen. They must also be planned and scheduled on an ongoing basis. By default, 'improvement' becomes a process within ITSM with defined activities, inputs, outputs, roles and reporting levels. CSI must ensure that ITSM processes are developed and deployed in support of an end-to-end service management approach to business customers. It is essential to develop an ongoing continual improvement strategy for each of the processes as well as for the services that they support.

The deliverables of CSI must be reviewed on an ongoing basis to verify completeness, functionality and feasibility, and to ensure that they remain relevant and do not become stale and unusable. It is also important to ensure that monitoring of quality indicators and metrics will identify areas for process improvement.

Since any improvement initiative will more than likely necessitate changes, specific improvements will need to follow the defined change management process.

## 1.1.3 Usage

*ITIL Continual Service Improvement* provides access to proven best practice based on the skill and knowledge of experienced industry practitioners in adopting a standardized and controlled approach to service management. Although this publication can be used and applied in isolation, it is recommended that it is used in conjunction with the other core ITIL publications. All of the core publications need to be read to fully appreciate and understand the overall lifecycle of services and IT service management.

## 1.1.4 Value to business

Selecting and adopting the best practice as recommended in this publication will assist organizations in delivering significant benefits. It will help readers to set up CSI and the process that supports it, and to make effective use of the process to facilitate the effective improvement of service quality.

Adopting and implementing standard and consistent approaches for CSI will:

■ Lead to a gradual and continual improvement in service quality, where justified
■ Ensure that IT services remain continuously aligned to business requirements
■ Result in gradual improvements in cost effectiveness through a reduction in costs and/ or the capability to handle more work at the same cost
■ Use monitoring and reporting to identify opportunities for improvement in all lifecycle stages and in all processes
■ Identify opportunities for improvements in organizational structures, resourcing capabilities, partners, technology, staff skills and training, and communications.

## 1.1.5 Target audience

*ITIL Continual Service Improvement* is relevant to organizations involved in the development, delivery or support of services, including:

■ Service providers, both internal and external
■ Organizations that aim to improve services through the effective application of service management and service lifecycle processes to improve their service quality
■ Organizations that require a consistent managed approach across all service providers in a supply chain or value network
■ Organizations that are going out to tender for their services.

In addition, *ITIL Continual Service Improvement* is relevant to any professional involved in the management of services, particularly:

■ IT architects
■ IT managers and practitioners
■ CSI managers
■ Process owners
■ IT service owners
■ Business relationship managers
■ Any practitioner looking to improve their way of working and ultimately reduce costs.

## 1.2 CONTEXT

The context of this publication is the ITIL service lifecycle as shown in Figure 1.1.

The ITIL core consists of five lifecycle publications. Each provides part of the guidance necessary for an integrated approach as required by the ISO/IEC 20000 standard specification. The five publications are:

■ *ITIL Service Strategy*
■ *ITIL Service Design*
■ *ITIL Service Transition*
■ *ITIL Service Operation*
■ *ITIL Continual Service Improvement*

Each one addresses capabilities having direct impact on a service provider's performance. The core is expected to provide structure, stability and strength to service management capabilities, with durable principles, methods and tools. This serves to protect investments and provide the necessary basis for measurement, learning and improvement. The introductory guide, *Introduction to the ITIL Service Lifecycle*, provides an overview of the lifecycle stages described in the ITIL core.

ITIL guidance can be adapted to support various business environments and organizational strategies. Complementary ITIL publications provide flexibility to implement the core in a diverse range of environments. Practitioners can select complementary publications as needed to provide traction for the ITIL core in a given context, in much the same way as tyres are selected based on the type of vehicle, purpose and road conditions. This is to increase the durability and portability of knowledge assets and to protect investments in service management capabilities.

### 1.2.1 Service strategy

At the centre of the service lifecycle is service strategy. Value creation begins here with understanding organizational objectives and customer needs. Every organizational asset including people, processes and products should support the strategy.

*ITIL Service Strategy* provides guidance on how to view service management not only as an organizational capability but as a strategic asset. It describes the principles underpinning the practice of service management which are useful for developing service management policies,

guidelines and processes across the ITIL service lifecycle.

Topics covered in *ITIL Service Strategy* include the development of market spaces, characteristics of internal and external provider types, service assets, the service portfolio and implementation of strategy through the service lifecycle. Business relationship management, demand management, financial management, organizational development and strategic risks are among the other major topics.

Organizations should use *ITIL Service Strategy* to set objectives and expectations of performance towards serving customers and market spaces, and to identify, select and prioritize opportunities. Service strategy is about ensuring that organizations are in a position to handle the costs and risks associated with their service portfolios, and are set up not just for operational effectiveness but for distinctive performance.

Organizations already practising ITIL can use *ITIL Service Strategy* to guide a strategic review of their ITIL-based service management capabilities and to improve the alignment between those capabilities and their business strategies. *ITIL Service Strategy* will encourage readers to stop and think about why something is to be done before thinking of how.

### 1.2.2 Service design

For services to provide true value to the business, they must be designed with the business objectives in mind. Design encompasses the whole IT organization, for it is the organization as a whole that delivers and supports the services. Service design is the stage in the lifecycle that turns a service strategy into a plan for delivering the business objectives.

*ITIL Service Design* provides guidance for the design and development of services and service management practices. It covers design principles and methods for converting strategic objectives into portfolios of services and service assets. The scope of *ITIL Service Design* is not limited to new services. It includes the changes and improvements necessary to increase or maintain value to customers over the lifecycle of services, the continuity of services, achievement of service levels, and conformance to standards and regulations. It guides organizations on how to develop design capabilities for service management.

Other topics in *ITIL Service Design* include design coordination, service catalogue management, service level management, availability management, capacity management, IT service continuity management, information security management and supplier management.

### 1.2.3 Service transition

*ITIL Service Transition* provides guidance for the development and improvement of capabilities for introducing new and changed services into supported environments. It describes how to transition an organization from one state to another while controlling risk and supporting organizational knowledge for decision support. It ensures that the value(s) identified in the service strategy, and encoded in service design, are effectively transitioned so that they can be realized in service operation.

*ITIL Service Transition* describes best practice in transition planning and support, change management, service asset and configuration management, release and deployment management, service validation and testing, change evaluation and knowledge management. It provides guidance on managing the complexity related to changes to services and service management processes, preventing undesired consequences while allowing for innovation.

*ITIL Service Transition* also introduces the service knowledge management system, which can support organizational learning and help to improve the overall efficiency and effectiveness of all stages of the service lifecycle. This will enable people to benefit from the knowledge and experience of others, support informed decision-making, and improve the management of services.

### 1.2.4 Service operation

*ITIL Service Operation* describes best practice for managing services in supported environments. It includes guidance on achieving effectiveness and efficiency in the delivery and support of services to ensure value for the customer, the users and the service provider.

Strategic objectives are ultimately realized through service operation, therefore making it a critical capability. *ITIL Service Operation* provides guidance on how to maintain stability in service operation, allowing for changes in design, scale, scope and service levels. Organizations are provided with detailed process guidelines, methods and tools for use in two major control perspectives: reactive and proactive. Managers and practitioners are provided with knowledge allowing them to make better decisions in areas such as managing the availability of services, controlling demand, optimizing capacity utilization, scheduling of operations, and avoiding or resolving service incidents and managing problems. New models and architectures such as shared services, utility computing, web services and mobile commerce to support service operation are described.

Other topics in *ITIL Service Operation* include event management, incident management, request fulfilment, problem management and access management processes; as well as the service desk, technical management, IT operations management and application management functions.

### 1.2.5 Continual service improvement

*ITIL Continual Service Improvement* (this publication) provides guidance on creating and maintaining value for customers through better strategy, design, transition and operation of services. It combines principles, practices and methods from quality management, change management and capability improvement.

*ITIL Continual Service Improvement* describes best practice for achieving incremental and large-scale improvements in service quality, operational efficiency and business continuity, and for ensuring that the service portfolio continues to be aligned to business needs. Guidance is provided for linking improvement efforts and outcomes with service strategy, design, transition and operation. A closed loop feedback system, based on the Plan-Do-Check-Act (PDCA) cycle, is established. Feedback from any stage of the service lifecycle can be used to identify improvement opportunities for any other stage of the lifecycle.

Other topics in *ITIL Continual Service Improvement* include service measurement, demonstrating value with metrics, developing baselines and maturity assessments.

## 1.3 ITIL IN RELATION TO OTHER PUBLICATIONS IN THE BEST MANAGEMENT PRACTICE PORTFOLIO

ITIL is part of a portfolio of best-practice publications (known collectively as Best Management Practice or BMP) aimed at helping organizations and individuals manage projects, programmes and services consistently and effectively (see Figure 1.2). ITIL can be used in harmony with other BMP products, and international or internal organization standards. Where appropriate, BMP guidance is supported by a qualification scheme and accredited training and consultancy services. All BMP guidance is intended to be tailored for use by individual organizations.

BMP publications include:

- **Management of Portfolios (MoP™)** Portfolio management concerns the twin issues of how to do the 'right' projects and programmes in the context of the organization's strategic objectives, and how to do them 'correctly' in terms of achieving delivery and benefits at a collective level. MoP encompasses consideration of the principles upon which effective portfolio management is based; the key practices in the portfolio definition and delivery cycles, including examples of how they have been applied in real life; and guidance on how to implement portfolio management and sustain progress in a wide variety of organizations
Office of Government Commerce (2011). *Management of Portfolios*. TSO, London.

- **Management of Risk (M_o_R®)** M_o_R offers an effective framework for taking informed decisions about the risks that affect performance objectives. The framework allows organizations to assess risk accurately (selecting the correct responses to threats and opportunities created by uncertainty) and thereby improve their service delivery.
Office of Government Commerce (2010). *Management of Risk*: Guidance for Practitioners. TSO, London.

- **Management of Value (MoV™)** MoV provides a cross-sector and universally applicable guide on how to maximize value in a way that takes account of organizations' priorities, differing stakeholders' needs and, at the same time, uses resources as efficiently and effectively as

possible. It will help organizations to put in place effective methods to deliver enhanced value across their portfolio, programmes, projects and operational activities to meet the challenges of ever-more competitive and resource-constrained environments.
Office of Government Commerce (2010). *Management of Value*. TSO, London.

- **Managing Successful Programmes (MSP®)** MSP provides a framework to enable the achievement of high-quality change outcomes and benefits that fundamentally affect the way in which organizations work. One of the core themes in MSP is that a programme must add more value than that provided by the sum of its constituent project and major activities.
Cabinet Office (2011). *Managing Successful Programmes*. TSO, London.

- **Managing Successful Projects with PRINCE2®** PRINCE2 (PRojects IN Controlled Environments, V2) is a structured method to help effective project management via clearly defined products. Key themes that feature throughout PRINCE2 are the dependence on a viable business case confirming the delivery of measurable benefits that are aligned to an organization's objectives and strategy, while ensuring the management of risks, costs and quality.
Office of Government Commerce (2009). *Managing Successful Projects with PRINCE2*. TSO, London.

- **Portfolio, Programme and Project Offices (P3O®)** P3O provides universally applicable guidance, including principles, processes and techniques, to successfully establish, develop and maintain appropriate support structures. These structures will facilitate delivery of business objectives (portfolios), programmes and projects within time, cost, quality and other organizational constraints.
Office of Government Commerce (2008). *Portfolio, Programme and Project Offices*. TSO, London.

## 1.4 WHY IS ITIL SO SUCCESSFUL?

ITIL embraces a practical approach to service management – do what works. And what works is adapting a common framework of practices that unite all areas of IT service provision towards

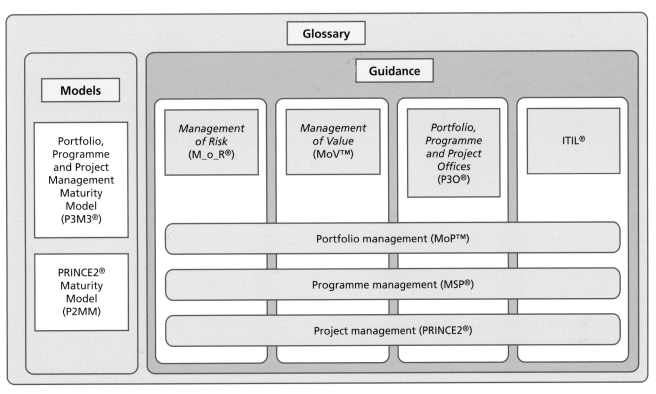

*Figure 1.2 ITIL's relationship with other Best Management Practice guides*

a single aim – that of delivering value to the business. The following list defines the key characteristics of ITIL that contribute to its global success:

■ **Vendor-neutral** ITIL service management practices are applicable in any IT organization because they are not based on any particular technology platform or industry type. ITIL is owned by the UK government and is not tied to any commercial proprietary practice or solution.

■ **Non-prescriptive** ITIL offers robust, mature and time-tested practices that have applicability to all types of service organization. It continues to be useful and relevant in public and private sectors, internal and external service providers, small, medium and large enterprises, and within any technical environment. Organizations should adopt ITIL and adapt it to meet the needs of the IT organization and their customers.

■ **Best practice** ITIL represents the learning experiences and thought leadership of the world's best-in-class service providers.

ITIL is successful because it describes practices that enable organizations to deliver benefits, return on investment and sustained success. ITIL is adopted by organizations to enable them to:

■ Deliver value for customers through services
■ Integrate the strategy for services with the business strategy and customer needs
■ Measure, monitor and optimize IT services and service provider performance
■ Manage the IT investment and budget
■ Manage risk
■ Manage knowledge
■ Manage capabilities and resources to deliver services effectively and efficiently
■ Enable adoption of a standard approach to service management across the enterprise
■ Change the organizational culture to support the achievement of sustained success
■ Improve the interaction and relationship with customers
■ Coordinate the delivery of goods and services across the value network
■ Optimize and reduce costs.

## 1.5 CHAPTER SUMMARY

*ITIL Continual Service Improvement* comprises:

- **Chapter 2 Service management as a practice**
  This chapter explains the concepts of service management and services, and describes how these can be used to create value. It also summarizes a number of generic ITIL concepts that the rest of the publication depends on.

- **Chapter 3 Continual service improvement principles**
  This chapter describes some of the key principles of CSI that will enable service providers to plan and implement best practice in CSI. These principles are the same irrespective of the organization; however, the approach may need to be tailored to circumstances, including the size of the organization, geographic distribution, culture and available resources. It concludes with a table showing the major inputs and outputs for the CSI lifecycle stage.

- **Chapter 4 Continual service improvement processes**
  Chapter 4 sets out the processes and activities on which effective CSI depends and how they integrate with the other stages of the lifecycle.

- **Chapter 5 Continual service improvement methods and techniques**
  Chapter 5 explores the various methods and techniques for continual improvement. It looks at ways of assessing organizations and explores benchmarking, the balanced scorecard, the PDCA cycle, and service measurement and reporting.

- **Chapter 6 Organizing for continual service improvement**
  This chapter identifies the organizational roles and responsibilities that should be considered to manage the CSI lifecycle stage and its related process. These roles are provided as guidelines and can be combined to fit into a variety of organization structures.

- **Chapter 7 Technology considerations**
  ITIL service management practices gain momentum when the right type of technical automation is applied. This chapter provides recommendations for the use of technology in CSI and the basic requirements a service provider will need to consider when choosing service management tools.

- **Chapter 8 Implementing continual service improvement**
  For organizations new to ITIL, or those wishing to improve their maturity and service capability, this chapter outlines effective ways to implement the CSI lifecycle stage.

- **Chapter 9 Challenges, risks and critical success factors**
  It is important for any organization to understand the challenges, risks and critical success factors that could influence their success. This chapter discusses typical examples of these for the CSI lifecycle stage.

- **Appendix A Related guidance**
  This contains a list of some of the many external methods, practices and frameworks that align well with ITIL best practice. Notes are provided on how they integrate into the ITIL service lifecycle, and when and how they are useful.

- **Appendix B Example of a continual service improvement register**
  This appendix provides an example of a CSI register.

- **Appendix C Risk assessment and management**
  This appendix contains basic information about several commonly used approaches to the assessment and management of risk.

- **Appendix D Examples of inputs and outputs across the service lifecycle**
  This appendix identifies some of the major inputs and outputs between each stage of the service lifecycle.

- **Abbreviations and glossary**
  This contains a list of abbreviations and a selected glossary of terms.

# Service management as a practice 2

# 2    Service management as a practice

## 2.1    SERVICES AND SERVICE MANAGEMENT

### 2.1.1    Services

Services are a means of delivering value to customers by facilitating the outcomes customers want to achieve without the ownership of specific costs and risks. Services facilitate outcomes by enhancing the performance of associated tasks and reducing the effect of constraints. These constraints may include regulation, lack of funding or capacity, or technology limitations. The end result is an increase in the probability of desired outcomes. While some services enhance performance of tasks, others have a more direct impact – they perform the task itself.

The preceding paragraph is not just a definition, as it is a recurring pattern found in a wide range of services. Patterns are useful for managing complexity, costs, flexibility and variety. They are generic structures useful to make an idea applicable in a wide range of environments and situations. In each instance the pattern is applied with variations that make the idea effective, economical or simply useful in that particular case.

> **Definition: outcome**
>
> The result of carrying out an activity, following a process, or delivering an IT service etc. The term is used to refer to intended results, as well as to actual results.

An outcome-based definition of service moves IT organizations beyond business–IT alignment towards business–IT integration. Internal dialogue and discussion on the meaning of services is an elementary step towards alignment and integration with a customer's business (Figure 2.1). Customer outcomes become the ultimate concern of business relationship managers instead of the gathering of requirements, which is necessary but not sufficient. Requirements are generated for internal coordination and control only after customer outcomes are well understood.

Customers seek outcomes but do not wish to have accountability or ownership of all the associated costs and risks. All services must have a budget when they go live and this must be managed. The service cost is reflected in financial terms such as return on investment (ROI) and total cost of ownership (TCO). The customer will only be exposed to the overall cost or price of a service, which will include all the provider's costs and risk mitigation measures (and any profit margin if appropriate). The customer can then judge the value of a service based on a comparison of cost or price and reliability with the desired outcome.

> **Definitions**
>
> *Service:* A means of delivering value to customers by facilitating outcomes customers want to achieve without the ownership of specific costs and risks.
>
> *IT service:* A service provided by an IT service provider. An IT service is made up of a combination of information technology, people and processes. A customer-facing IT service directly supports the business processes of one or more customers and its service level targets should be defined in a service level agreement. Other IT services, called supporting services, are not directly used by the business but are required by the service provider to deliver customer-facing services.

Customer satisfaction is also important. Customers need to be satisfied with the level of service and feel confident in the ability of the service provider to continue providing that level of service – or even improving it over time. The difficulty is that customer expectations keep shifting, and a service provider that does not track this will soon find itself losing business. *ITIL Service Strategy* is helpful in understanding how this happens, and how a service provider can adapt its services to meet the changing customer environment.

Services can be discussed in terms of how they relate to one another and their customers, and can be classified as core, enabling or enhancing.

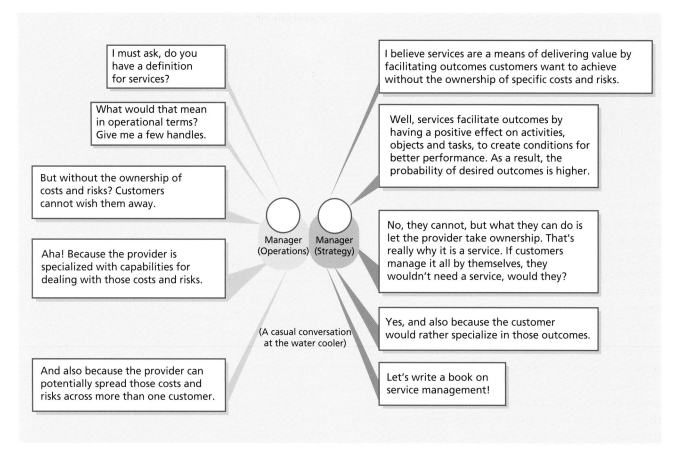

*Figure 2.1 Conversation about the definition and meaning of services*

*Core services* deliver the basic outcomes desired by one or more customers. They represent the value that the customer wants and for which they are willing to pay. Core services anchor the value proposition for the customer and provide the basis for their continued utilization and satisfaction.

*Enabling services* are services that are needed in order for a core service to be delivered. Enabling services may or may not be visible to the customer, but the customer does not perceive them as services in their own right. They are 'basic factors' which enable the customer to receive the 'real' (core) service.

*Enhancing services* are services that are added to a core service to make it more exciting or enticing to the customer. Enhancing services are not essential to the delivery of a core service, and are added to a core service as 'excitement' factors, which will encourage customers to use the core service more (or to choose the core service provided by one company over those of its competitors).

Services may be as simple as allowing a user to complete a single transaction, but most services are complex. They consist of a range of deliverables and functionality. If each individual aspect of these complex services were defined independently, the service provider would soon find it impossible to track and record all services.

Most service providers will follow a strategy where they can deliver a set of more generic services to a broad range of customers, thus achieving economies of scale and competing on the basis of price and a certain amount of flexibility. One way of achieving this is by using service packages. A service package is a collection of two or more services that have been combined to offer a solution to a specific type of customer need or to underpin specific business outcomes. A service package can consist of a combination of core services, enabling services and enhancing services.

Where a service or service package needs to be differentiated for different types of customer, one or more components of the package can be changed, or offered at different levels of utility and warranty, to create service options. These different service options can then be offered to customers and are sometimes called service level packages.

## 2.1.2 Service management

When we turn on a water tap, we expect to see water flow from it. When we turn on a light switch, we expect to see light fill the room. Not so many years ago, these very basic things were not as reliable as they are today. We know instinctively that the advances in technology have made them reliable enough to be considered a utility. But it isn't just the technology that makes the services reliable. It is how they are managed.

The use of IT today has become the utility of business. Business today wants IT services that behave like other utilities such as water, electricity or the telephone. Simply having the best technology will not ensure that IT provides utility-like reliability. Professional, responsive, value-driven service management is what brings this quality of service to the business.

Service management is a set of specialized organizational capabilities for providing value to customers in the form of services. The more mature a service provider's capabilities are, the greater is their ability to consistently produce quality services that meet the needs of the customer in a timely and cost-effective manner. The act of transforming capabilities and resources into valuable services is at the core of service management. Without these capabilities, a service organization is merely a bundle of resources that by itself has relatively low intrinsic value for customers.

**Definitions**

*Service management:* A set of specialized organizational capabilities for providing value to customers in the form of services.

*Service provider:* An organization supplying services to one or more internal or external customers.

Organizational capabilities are shaped by the challenges they are expected to overcome. An example of this is provided by Toyota in the 1950s when it developed unique capabilities to overcome the challenge of smaller scale and financial capital compared to its American rivals. Toyota developed new capabilities in production engineering, operations management and managing suppliers to compensate for its inability to afford large inventories, make components, produce raw materials or own the companies that produced them (Magretta, 2002).[2]

Service management capabilities are similarly influenced by the following challenges that distinguish services from other systems of value creation, such as manufacturing, mining and agriculture:

- Intangible nature of the output and intermediate products of service processes: they are difficult to measure, control and validate (or prove)
- Demand is tightly coupled with the customer's assets: users and other customer assets such as processes, applications, documents and transactions arrive with demand and stimulate service production
- High level of contact for producers and consumers of services: there is little or no buffer between the service provider's creation of the service and the customer's consumption of that service
- The perishable nature of service output and service capacity: there is value for the customer from assurance on the continued supply of consistent quality. Providers need to secure a steady supply of demand from customers.

Service management is more than just a set of capabilities. It is also a professional practice supported by an extensive body of knowledge, experience and skills. A global community of individuals and organizations in the public and private sectors fosters its growth and maturity. Formal schemes exist for the education, training and certification of practising organizations, and individuals influence its quality. Industry best practices, academic research and formal standards contribute to and draw from its intellectual capital.

The origins of service management are in traditional service businesses such as airlines, banks, hotels and phone companies. Its practice has grown with the adoption by IT organizations of a service-oriented approach to managing IT applications, infrastructure and processes. Solutions to business problems and support for business models, strategies and operations are increasingly in the form of services. The popularity of shared services and outsourcing has contributed to the increase in the number of organizations that behave as service providers, including internal IT organizations. This

² Magretta, J. (2002). *What Management Is: How it Works and Why it's Everyone's Business.* The Free Press, New York

in turn has strengthened the practice of service management while at the same time imposed greater challenges.

### 2.1.3 IT service management

Information technology (IT) is a commonly used term that changes meaning depending on the different perspectives that a business organization or people may have of it. A key challenge is to recognize and balance these perspectives when communicating the value of IT service management (ITSM) and understanding the context for how the business sees the IT organization. Some of these meanings are:

- IT is a collection of systems, applications and infrastructures which are components or sub-assemblies of a larger product. They enable or are embedded in processes and services.
- IT is an organization with its own set of capabilities and resources. IT organizations can be of various types such as business functions, shared services units and enterprise-level core units.
- IT is a category of services utilized by business. The services are typically IT applications and infrastructure that are packaged and offered by internal IT organizations or external service providers. IT costs are treated as business expenses.
- IT is a category of business assets that provide a stream of benefits for their owners, including, but not limited to, revenue, income and profit. IT costs are treated as investments.

Every IT organization should act as a service provider, using the principles of service management to ensure that they deliver the outcomes required by their customers.

**Definitions**

*IT service management (ITSM):* The implementation and management of quality IT services that meet the needs of the business. IT service management is performed by IT service providers through an appropriate mix of people, process and information technology.

*IT service provider:* A service provider that provides IT services to internal or external customers.

ITSM must be carried out effectively and efficiently. Managing IT from the business perspective enables organizational high performance and value creation.

A good relationship between an IT service provider and its customers relies on the customer receiving an IT service that meets its needs, at an acceptable level of performance and at a cost that the customer can afford. The IT service provider needs to work out how to achieve a balance between these three areas, and communicate with the customer if there is anything which prevents it from being able to deliver the required IT service at the agreed level of performance or price.

A service level agreement (SLA) is used to document agreements between an IT service provider and a customer. An SLA describes the IT service, documents service level targets, and specifies the responsibilities of the IT service provider and the customer. A single agreement may cover multiple IT services or multiple customers.

### 2.1.4 Service providers

There are three main types of service provider. While most aspects of service management apply equally to all types of service provider, other aspects such as customers, contracts, competition, market spaces, revenue and strategy take on different meanings depending on the specific type. The three types are:

- **Type I – internal service provider** An internal service provider that is embedded within a business unit. There may be several Type I service providers within an organization.
- **Type II – shared services unit** An internal service provider that provides shared IT services to more than one business unit.
- **Type III – external service provider** A service provider that provides IT services to external customers.

ITSM concepts are often described in the context of only one of these types and as if only one type of IT service provider exists or is used by a given organization. In reality most organizations have a combination of IT service providers. In a single organization it is possible that some IT units are dedicated to a single business unit, others provide shared services, and yet others have been outsourced or depend on external service providers.

Many IT organizations who traditionally provide services to internal customers find that they are dealing directly with external users because of the online services that they provide. *ITIL Service Strategy* provides guidance on how the IT organization interacts with these users, and who owns and manages the relationship with them.

### 2.1.5 Stakeholders in service management

Stakeholders have an interest in an organization, project or service etc. and may be interested in the activities, targets, resources or deliverables from service management. Examples include organizations, service providers, customers, consumers, users, partners, employees, shareholders, owners and suppliers. The term 'organization' is used to define a company, legal entity or other institution. It is also used to refer to any entity that has people, resources and budgets – for example, a project or business.

Within the service provider organization there are many different stakeholders including the functions, groups and teams that deliver the services. There are also many stakeholders external to the service provider organization, for example:

■ **Customers**   Those who buy goods or services. The customer of an IT service provider is the person or group who defines and agrees the service level targets. This term is also sometimes used informally to mean user – for example, 'This is a customer-focused organization.'
■ **Users**   Those who use the service on a day-to-day basis. Users are distinct from customers, as some customers do not use the IT service directly.
■ **Suppliers**   Third parties responsible for supplying goods or services that are required to deliver IT services. Examples of suppliers include commodity hardware and software vendors, network and telecom providers, and outsourcing organizations.

There is a difference between customers who work in the same organization as the IT service provider, and customers who work for other organizations. They are distinguished as follows:

■ **Internal customers**   These are customers who work for the same business as the IT

service provider. For example, the marketing department is an internal customer of the IT organization because it uses IT services. The head of marketing and the chief information officer both report to the chief executive officer. If IT charges for its services, the money paid is an internal transaction in the organization's accounting system, not real revenue.
■ **External customers**   These are customers who work for a different business from the IT service provider. External customers typically purchase services from the service provider by means of a legally binding contract or agreement.

### 2.1.6 Utility and warranty

The value of a service can be considered to be the level to which that service meets a customer's expectations. It is often measured by how much the customer is willing to pay for the service, rather than the cost to the service provider of providing the service or any other intrinsic attribute of the service itself.

Unlike products, services do not have much intrinsic value. The value of a service comes from what it enables someone to do. The value of a service is not determined by the provider, but by the person who receives it – because they decide what they will do with the service, and what type of return they will achieve by using the service. Services contribute value to an organization only when their value is perceived to be higher than the cost of obtaining the service.

From the customer's perspective, value consists of achieving business objectives. The value of a service is created by combining two primary elements: utility (fitness for purpose) and warranty (fitness for use). These two elements work together to achieve the desired outcomes upon which the customer and the business base their perceptions of a service.

Utility is the functionality offered by a product or service to meet a particular need. Utility can be summarized as 'what the service does' and can be used to determine whether a service is able to meet its required outcomes or is 'fit for purpose'. Utility refers to those aspects of a service that contribute to tasks associated with achieving outcomes. For example, a service that enables a business unit to process orders should allow sales people to access customer details, stock availability, shipping information etc. Any aspect of the service that improves the ability of sales people to improve the performance of the task of processing sales orders would be considered utility. Utility can therefore represent any attribute of a service that removes, or reduces the effect of, constraints on the performance of a task.

Warranty is an assurance that a product or service will meet its agreed requirements. This may be a formal agreement such as a service level agreement or contract, or a marketing message or brand image. Warranty refers to the ability of a service to be available when needed, to provide the required capacity, and to provide the required reliability in terms of continuity and security. Warranty can be summarized as 'how the service is delivered', and can be used to determine whether a service is 'fit for use'. For example, any aspect of the service that increases the availability or speed of the service would be considered warranty. Warranty can therefore represent any attribute of a service that increases the potential of the business to be able to perform a task. Warranty refers to any means by which utility is made available to the users.

Utility is *what* the service does, and warranty is *how* it is delivered.

Customers cannot benefit from something that is fit for purpose but not fit for use, and vice versa. The value of a service is therefore only delivered when both utility and warranty are designed and delivered. Figure 2.2 illustrates the logic that a service has to have both utility and warranty to create value. Utility is used to improve the performance of the tasks required to achieve an outcome, or to remove constraints that prevent the

task from being performed adequately (or both). Warranty requires the service to be available, continuous and secure and to have sufficient capacity for the service to perform at the required level. If the service is both fit for purpose and fit for use, it will create value.

It should be noted that the elements of warranty in Figure 2.2 are not exclusive. It is possible to define other components of warranty, such as usability, which refers to how easy it is for the user to access and use the features of the service to achieve the desired outcomes.

The warranty aspect of the service needs to be designed at the same time as the utility aspect in order to deliver the required value to the business. Attempts to design warranty aspects after a service has been deployed can be expensive and disruptive.

Information about the desired business outcomes, opportunities, customers, utility and warranty of the service is used to develop the definition of a service. Using an outcome-based definition helps to ensure that managers plan and execute all aspects of service management from the perspective of what is valuable to the customer.

### 2.1.7 Best practices in the public domain

Organizations benchmark themselves against peers and seek to close gaps in capabilities. This enables them to become more competitive by improving their ability to deliver quality services that meet the needs of their customers at a price their customers can afford. One way to close such gaps is the adoption of best practices in wide industry use.

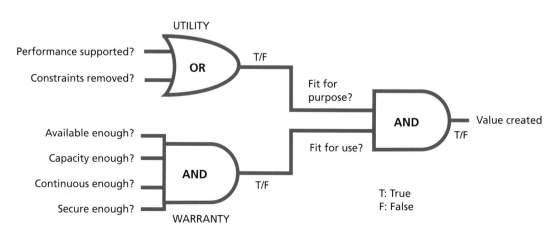

**Figure 2.2  Logic of value creation through services**

There are several sources for best practice including public frameworks, standards and the proprietary knowledge of organizations and individuals (Figure 2.3). ITIL is the most widely recognized and trusted source of best-practice guidance in the area of ITSM.

Public frameworks and standards are attractive when compared with proprietary knowledge for the following reasons:

■ Proprietary knowledge is deeply embedded in organizations and therefore difficult to adopt, replicate or even transfer with the cooperation of the owners. Such knowledge is often in the form of tacit knowledge which is inextricable and poorly documented.

■ Proprietary knowledge is customized for the local context and the specific needs of the business to the point of being idiosyncratic. Unless the recipients of such knowledge have matching circumstances, the knowledge may not be as effective in use.

■ Owners of proprietary knowledge expect to be rewarded for their investments. They may make such knowledge available only under commercial terms through purchases and licensing agreements.

■ Publicly available frameworks and standards such as ITIL, LEAN, Six Sigma, COBIT, CMMI, PRINCE2, PMBOK®, ISO 9000, ISO/IEC 20000 and ISO/IEC 27001 are validated across a diverse set of environments and situations rather than the limited experience of a single organization. They are subject to broad review across multiple organizations and disciplines, and vetted by diverse sets of partners, suppliers and competitors.

■ The knowledge of public frameworks is more likely to be widely distributed among a large community of professionals through publicly available training and certification. It is easier for organizations to acquire such knowledge through the labour market.

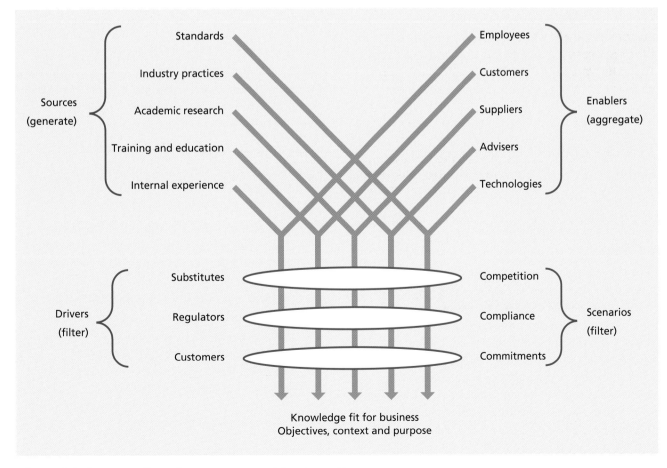

**Figure 2.3 Sources of service management best practice**

Ignoring public frameworks and standards can needlessly place an organization at a disadvantage. Organizations should cultivate their own proprietary knowledge on top of a body of knowledge based on public frameworks and standards. Collaboration and coordination across organizations become easier on the basis of shared practices and standards. Further information on best practice in the public domain is provided in Appendix A.

## 2.2 BASIC CONCEPTS

### 2.2.1 Assets, resources and capabilities

The service relationship between service providers and their customers revolves around the use of assets – both those of the service provider and those of the customer. Each relationship involves an interaction between the assets of each party.

Many customers use the service they receive to build and deliver services or products of their own and then deliver them on to their own customers. In these cases, what the service provider considers to be the customer asset would be considered to be a service asset by their customer.

Without customer assets, there is no basis for defining the value of a service. The performance of customer assets is therefore a primary concern for service management.

**Definitions**

*Asset:* Any resource or capability.

*Customer asset:* Any resource or capability used by a customer to achieve a business outcome.

*Service asset:* Any resource or capability used by a service provider to deliver services to a customer.

There are two types of asset used by both service providers and customers – resources and capabilities. Organizations use them to create value in the form of goods and services. Resources are direct inputs for production. Capabilities represent an organization's ability to coordinate, control and deploy resources to produce value. Capabilities are typically experience-driven, knowledge-intensive, information-based and firmly embedded within an organization's people, systems, processes and technologies. It is relatively easy to acquire

resources compared to capabilities (see Figure 2.4 for examples of capabilities and resources).

Service providers need to develop distinctive capabilities to retain customers with value propositions that are hard for competitors to duplicate. For example, two service providers may have similar resources such as applications, infrastructure and access to finance. Their capabilities, however, differ in terms of management systems, organization structure, processes and knowledge assets. This difference is reflected in actual performance.

Capabilities by themselves cannot produce value without adequate and appropriate resources. The productive capacity of a service provider is dependent on the resources under its control. Capabilities are used to develop, deploy and coordinate this productive capacity. For example, capabilities such as capacity management and availability management are used to manage the performance and utilization of processes, applications and infrastructure, ensuring service levels are effectively delivered.

### 2.2.2 Processes

**Definition: process**

A process is a structured set of activities designed to accomplish a specific objective. A process takes one or more defined inputs and turns them into defined outputs.

Processes define actions, dependencies and sequence. Well-defined processes can improve productivity within and across organizations and functions. Process characteristics include:

- **Measurability** We are able to measure the process in a relevant manner. It is performance-driven. Managers want to measure cost, quality and other variables while practitioners are concerned with duration and productivity.
- **Specific results** The reason a process exists is to deliver a specific result. This result must be individually identifiable and countable.
- **Customers** Every process delivers its primary results to a customer or stakeholder. Customers may be internal or external to the organization, but the process must meet their expectations.

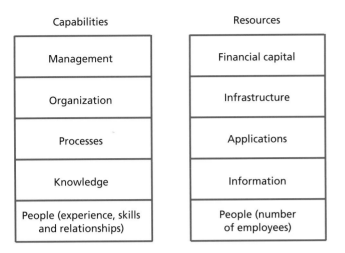

Figure 2.4  *Examples of capabilities and resources*

■ **Responsiveness to specific triggers**   While a process may be ongoing or iterative, it should be traceable to a specific trigger.

A process is organized around a set of objectives. The main outputs from the process should be driven by the objectives and should include process measurements (metrics), reports and process improvement.

The output produced by a process has to conform to operational norms that are derived from business objectives. If products conform to the set norm, the process can be considered effective (because it can be repeated, measured and managed, and achieves the required outcome). If the activities of the process are carried out with a minimum use of resources, the process can also be considered efficient.

Inputs are data or information used by the process and may be the output from another process.

A process, or an activity within a process, is initiated by a trigger. A trigger may be the arrival of an input or other event. For example, the failure of a server may trigger the event management and incident management processes.

A process may include any of the roles, responsibilities, tools and management controls required to deliver the outputs reliably. A process may define policies, standards, guidelines, activities and work instructions if they are needed.

Processes, once defined, should be documented and controlled. Once under control, they can be

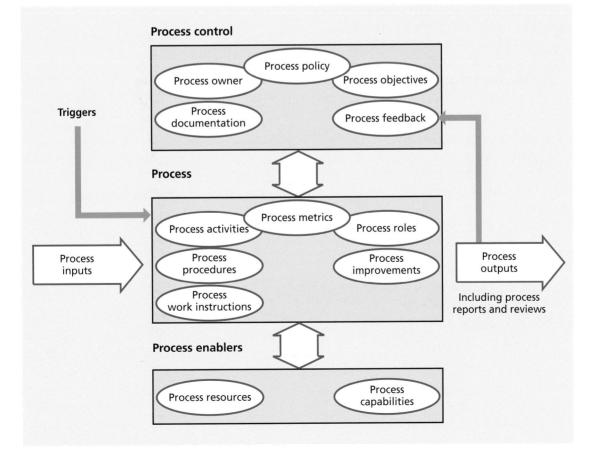

Figure 2.5  *Process model*

repeated and managed. Process measurement and metrics can be built into the process to control and improve the process as illustrated in Figure 2.5. Process analysis, results and metrics should be incorporated in regular management reports and process improvements.

### 2.2.3 Organizing for service management

There is no single best way to organize, and best practices described in ITIL need to be tailored to suit individual organizations and situations. Any changes made will need to take into account resource constraints and the size, nature and needs of the business and customers. The starting point for organizational design is strategy. Organizational development for service management is described in more detail in *ITIL Service Strategy* Chapter 6.

#### 2.2.3.1 Functions

A function is a team or group of people and the tools or other resources they use to carry out one or more processes or activities. In larger organizations, a function may be broken out and performed by several departments, teams and groups, or it may be embodied within a single organizational unit (e.g. the service desk). In smaller organizations, one person or group can perform multiple functions – for example, a technical management department could also incorporate the service desk function.

For the service lifecycle to be successful, an organization will need to clearly define the roles and responsibilities required to undertake the processes and activities involved in each lifecycle stage. These roles will need to be assigned to individuals, and an appropriate organization structure of teams, groups or functions will need to be established and managed. These are defined as follows:

- **Group** A group is a number of people who are similar in some way. In ITIL, groups refer to people who perform similar activities – even though they may work on different technologies or report into different organizational structures or even different companies. Groups are usually not formal organizational structures, but are very useful in defining common processes across the organization – for example, ensuring that all

people who resolve incidents complete the incident record in the same way.

- **Team** A team is a more formal type of group. These are people who work together to achieve a common objective, but not necessarily in the same organizational structure. Team members can be co-located, or work in multiple locations and operate virtually. Teams are useful for collaboration, or for dealing with a situation of a temporary or transitional nature. Examples of teams include project teams, application development teams (often consisting of people from several different business units) and incident or problem resolution teams.
- **Department** Departments are formal organizational structures which exist to perform a specific set of defined activities on an ongoing basis. Departments have a hierarchical reporting structure with managers who are usually responsible for the execution of the activities and also for day-to-day management of the staff in the department.
- **Division** A division refers to a number of departments that have been grouped together, often by geography or product line. A division is normally self-contained.

*ITIL Service Operation* describes the following functions in detail:

- **Service desk** The single point of contact for users when there is a service disruption, for service requests, or even for some categories of request for change. The service desk provides a point of communication to users and a point of coordination for several IT groups and processes.
- **Technical management** Provides detailed technical skills and resources needed to support the ongoing operation of IT services and the management of the IT infrastructure. Technical management also plays an important role in the design, testing, release and improvement of IT services.
- **IT operations management** Executes the daily operational activities needed to manage IT services and the supporting IT infrastructure. This is done according to the performance standards defined during service design. IT operations management has two sub-functions that are generally organizationally distinct. These are IT operations control and facilities management.

■ **Application management** Is responsible for managing applications throughout their lifecycle. The application management function supports and maintains operational applications and also plays an important role in the design, testing and improvement of applications that form part of IT services.

The other core ITIL publications do not define any functions in detail, but they do rely on the technical and application management functions described in *ITIL Service Operation*. Technical and application management provide the technical resources and expertise to manage the whole service lifecycle, and practitioner roles within a particular lifecycle stage may be performed by members of these functions.

### 2.2.3.2 Roles

A number of roles need to be performed during the service lifecycle. The core ITIL publications provide guidelines and examples of role descriptions. These are not exhaustive or prescriptive, and in many cases roles will need to be combined or separated. Organizations should take care to apply this guidance in a way that suits their own structure and objectives.

> **Definition: role**
>
> A role is a set of responsibilities, activities and authorities granted to a person or team. A role is defined in a process or function. One person or team may have multiple roles – for example, the roles of configuration manager and change manager may be carried out by a single person.

Roles are often confused with job titles but it is important to realize that they are not the same. Each organization will define appropriate job titles and job descriptions which suit their needs, and individuals holding these job titles can perform one or more of the required roles.

It should also be recognized that a person may, as part of their job assignment, perform a single task that represents participation in more than one process. For example, a technical analyst who submits a request for change (RFC) to add memory to a server to resolve a performance problem is participating in activities of the change management process at the same time as taking part in activities of the capacity management and problem management processes.

See Chapter 6 for more details about the roles and responsibilities described in *ITIL Continual Service Improvement*.

### 2.2.3.3 Organizational culture and behaviour

Organizational culture is the set of shared values and norms that control the service provider's interactions with all stakeholders, including customers, users, suppliers, internal staff etc. An organization's values are desired modes of behaviour that affect its culture. Examples of organizational values include high standards, customer care, respecting tradition and authority, acting cautiously and conservatively, and being frugal.

High-performing service providers continually align the value network for efficiency and effectiveness. Culture through the value network is transmitted to staff through socialization, training programmes, stories, ceremonies and language.

Constraints such as governance, capabilities, standards, resources, values and ethics play a significant role in organizational culture and behaviour. Organizational culture can also be affected by structure or management styles resulting in a positive or negative impact on performance. Organizational structures and management styles contribute to the behaviour of people, process, technology and partners. These are important aspects in adopting service management practices and ITIL.

Change related to service management programmes will affect organizational culture and it is important to prepare people with effective communication plans, training, policies and procedures to achieve the desired performance outcomes. Establishing cultural change is also an important factor for collaborative working between the many different people involved in service management. Managing people through service transitions is discussed at more length in Chapter 5 of *ITIL Service Transition*.

### 2.2.4 The service portfolio

The service portfolio is the complete set of services that is managed by a service provider and it represents the service provider's commitments and investments across all customers and market spaces. It also represents present contractual commitments, new service development, and ongoing service improvement plans initiated by continual service improvement. The portfolio may include third-party services, which are an integral part of service offerings to customers.

The service portfolio represents all the resources presently engaged or being released in various stages of the service lifecycle. It is a database or structured document in three parts:

- **Service pipeline** All services that are under consideration or development, but are not yet available to customers. It includes major investment opportunities that have to be traced to the delivery of services, and the value that will be realized. The service pipeline provides a business view of possible future services and is part of the service portfolio that is not normally published to customers.
- **Service catalogue** All live IT services, including those available for deployment. It is the only part of the service portfolio published to customers, and is used to support the sale and delivery of IT services. It includes a customer-facing view (or views) of the IT services in use, how they are intended to be used, the business processes they enable, and the levels and quality of service the customer can expect for each service. The service catalogue also includes information about supporting services required by the service provider to deliver customer-facing services. Information about services can only enter the service catalogue after due diligence has been performed on related costs and risks.
- **Retired services** All services that have been phased out or retired. Retired services are not available to new customers or contracts unless a special business case is made.

Service providers often find it useful to distinguish customer-facing services from supporting services:

- **Customer-facing services** IT services that are visible to the customer. These are normally services that support the customer's business processes and facilitate one or more outcomes desired by the customer.
- **Supporting services** IT services that support or 'underpin' the customer-facing services. These are typically invisible to the customer, but are essential to the delivery of customer-facing IT services.

Figure 2.6 illustrates the components of the service portfolio, which are discussed in detail in *ITIL Service Strategy*. These are important components of the service knowledge management system (SKMS) described in section 2.2.5.

## 2.2.5 Knowledge management and the SKMS

Quality knowledge and information enable people to perform process activities and support the flow of information between service lifecycle stages and processes. Understanding, defining, establishing and maintaining information is a responsibility of the knowledge management process.

Implementing an SKMS enables effective decision support and reduces the risks that arise from a lack of proper mechanisms. However, implementing an SKMS can involve a large investment in tools to store and manage data, information and knowledge. Every organization will start this work in a different place, and have their own vision of where they want to be, so there is no simple answer to the question 'What tools and systems are needed to support knowledge management?' Data, information and knowledge need to be interrelated across the organization. A document management system and/or a configuration management system (CMS) can be used as a foundation for implementation of the SKMS.

Figure 2.7 illustrates an architecture for service knowledge management that has four layers including examples of possible content at each layer. These are:

- **Presentation layer** Enables searching, browsing, retrieving, updating, subscribing and collaboration. The different views onto the other layers are suitable for different audiences. Each view should be protected to ensure that only authorized people can see or modify the underlying knowledge, information and data.
- **Knowledge processing layer** Is where the information is converted into useful knowledge which enables decision-making.
- **Information integration layer** Provides integrated information that may be gathered from data in multiple sources in the data layer.
- **Data layer** Includes tools for data discovery and data collection, and data items in unstructured and structured forms.

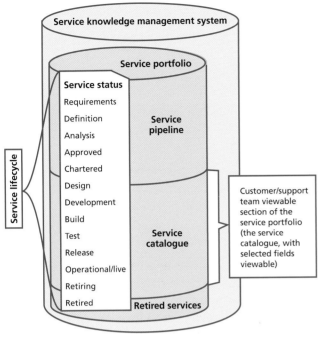

**Figure 2.6   The service portfolio and its contents**

In practice, an SKMS is likely to consist of multiple tools and repositories. For example, there may be a tool that provides all four layers for the support of different processes or combinations of processes. Various tools providing a range of perspectives will be used by different stakeholders to access this common repository for collaborative decision support.

This architecture is applicable for many of the management information systems in ITIL. A primary component of the SKMS is the service portfolio, covered in section 2.2.4. Other examples include the CMS, the availability management information system (AMIS) and the capacity management information system (CMIS).

## 2.3   GOVERNANCE AND MANAGEMENT SYSTEMS

### 2.3.1   Governance

Governance is the single overarching area that ties IT and the business together, and services are one way of ensuring that the organization is able to execute that governance. Governance is what defines the common directions, policies and rules that both the business and IT use to conduct business.

Many ITSM strategies fail because they try to build a structure or processes according to how they would like the organization to work instead of working within the existing governance structures.

> **Definition: governance**
>
> Ensures that policies and strategy are actually implemented, and that required processes are correctly followed. Governance includes defining roles and responsibilities, measuring and reporting, and taking actions to resolve any issues identified.

Governance works to apply a consistently managed approach at all levels of the organization – first by ensuring a clear strategy is set, then by defining the policies whereby the strategy will be achieved. The policies also define boundaries, or what the organization may not do as part of its operations.

Governance needs to be able to evaluate, direct and monitor the strategy, policies and plans. Further information on governance and service management is provided in Chapter 5 of *ITIL Service Strategy*. The international standard for corporate governance of IT is ISO/IEC 38500, described in Appendix A.

### 2.3.2   Management systems

A system is a number of related things that work together to achieve an overall objective. Systems should be self-regulating for agility and timeliness. In order to accomplish this, the relationships within the system must influence one another for the sake of the whole. Key components of the system are the structure and processes that work together.

A systems approach to service management ensures learning and improvement through a big-picture view of services and service management. It extends the management horizon and provides a sustainable long-term approach.

By understanding the system structure, the interconnections between all the assets and service components, and how changes in any area will affect the whole system and its constituent parts over time, a service provider can deliver benefits such as:

■ Ability to adapt to the changing needs of customers and markets
■ Sustainable performance
■ Better approach to managing services, risks, costs and value delivery

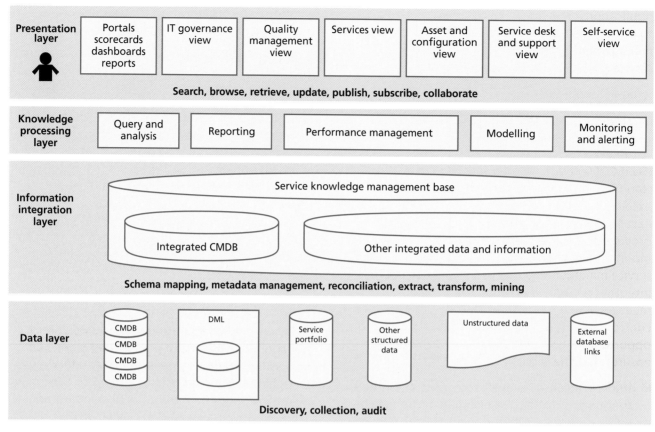

**Figure 2.7 Architectural layers of an SKMS**

- Effective and efficient service management
- Simplified approach that is easier for people to use
- Less conflict between processes
- Reduced duplication and bureaucracy.

Many businesses have adopted management system standards for competitive advantage and to ensure a consistent approach in implementing service management across their value network. Implementation of a management system also provides support for governance (see section 2.3.1).

**Definition: management system (ISO 9001)**

The framework of policy, processes, functions, standards, guidelines and tools that ensures an organization or part of an organization can achieve its objectives.

A management system of an organization can adopt multiple management system standards, such as:

- A quality management system (ISO 9001)
- An environmental management system (ISO 14000)

- A service management system (ISO/IEC 20000)
- An information security management system (ISO/IEC 27001)
- A management system for software asset management (ISO/IEC 19770).

Service providers are increasingly adopting these standards to be able to demonstrate their service management capability. As there are common elements between such management systems, they should be managed in an integrated way rather than having separate management systems. To meet the requirements of a specific management system standard, an organization needs to analyse the requirements of the relevant standard in detail and compare them with those that have already been incorporated in the existing integrated management system. Appendix A provides further information on these standards.

ISO management system standards use the Plan-Do-Check-Act (PDCA) cycle shown in Figure 2.8. The ITIL service lifecycle approach embraces and enhances the interpretation of the PDCA cycle. You will see the PDCA cycle used in the structure of the guidance provided in each of the core ITIL publications. This guidance recognizes the need to drive governance, organizational design and management systems from the business strategy, service strategy and service requirements.

> **Definition: ISO/IEC 20000**
>
> An international standard for IT service management.

ISO/IEC 20000 is an internationally recognized standard that allows organizations to demonstrate excellence and prove best practice in ITSM. Part 1 specifies requirements for the service provider to plan, establish, implement, operate, monitor, review, maintain and improve a service management system (SMS). Coordinated integration and implementation of an SMS, to meet the Part 1 requirements, provides ongoing control, greater effectiveness, efficiency and opportunities for continual improvement. It ensures that the service provider:

- Understands and fulfils the service requirements to achieve customer satisfaction
- Establishes the policy and objectives for service management
- Designs and delivers changes and services that add value for the customer
- Monitors, measures and reviews performance of the SMS and the services

- Continually improves the SMS and the services based on objective measurements.

Service providers across the world have successfully established an SMS to direct and control their service management activities. The adoption of an SMS should be a strategic decision for an organization.

One of the most common routes for an organization to achieve the requirements of ISO/IEC 20000 is by adopting ITIL service management best practices and using the ITIL qualification scheme for professional development.

Certification to ISO/IEC 20000-1 by an accredited certification body shows that a service provider is committed to delivering value to its customers and continual service improvement. It demonstrates the existence of an effective SMS that satisfies the requirements of an independent external audit. Certification gives a service provider a competitive edge in marketing. Many organizations specify a requirement to comply with ISO/IEC 20000 in their contracts and agreements.

## 2.4 THE SERVICE LIFECYCLE

Services and processes describe how things change, whereas structure describes how they are connected. Structure helps to determine the correct behaviours required for service management.

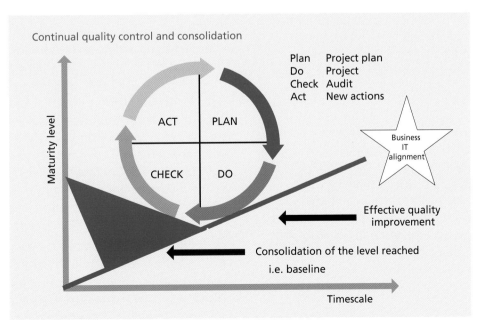

*Figure 2.8 Plan-Do-Check-Act cycle*

Structure describes how process, people, technology and partners are connected. Structure is essential for organizing information. Without structure, our service management knowledge is merely a collection of observations, practices and conflicting goals. The structure of the service lifecycle is an organizing framework, supported by the organizational structure, service portfolio and service models within an organization. Structure can influence or determine the behaviour of the organization and people. Altering the structure of service management can be more effective than simply controlling discrete events.

Without structure, it is difficult to learn from experience. It is difficult to use the past to educate for the future. We can learn from experience but we also need to confront directly many of the most important consequences of our actions.

See Chapter 1 for an introduction to each ITIL service lifecycle stage.

### 2.4.1 Specialization and coordination across the lifecycle

Organizations need a collaborative approach for the management of assets which are used to deliver and support services for their customers.

Organizations should function in the same manner as a high-performing sports team. Each player in a team and each member of the team's organization who are not players position themselves to support the goal of the team. Each player and team member has a different specialization that contributes to the whole. The team matures over time taking into account feedback from experience, best practice, current process and procedures to become an agile high-performing team.

Specialization and coordination are necessary in the lifecycle approach. Specialization allows for expert focus on components of the service but components of the service also need to work together for value. Specialization combined with coordination helps to manage expertise, improve focus and reduce overlaps and gaps in processes. Specialization and coordination together help to create a collaborative and agile organizational architecture that maximizes utilization of assets.

Coordination across the lifecycle creates an environment focused on business and customer outcomes instead of just IT objectives and projects. Coordination is also essential between functional groups, across the value network, and between processes and technology.

Feedback and control between organizational assets helps to enable operational efficiency, organizational effectiveness and economies of scale.

### 2.4.2 Processes through the service lifecycle

Each core ITIL lifecycle publication includes guidance on service management processes as shown in Table 2.1.

Service management is more effective if people have a clear understanding of how processes interact throughout the service lifecycle, within the organization and with other parties (users, customers, suppliers).

Process integration across the service lifecycle depends on the service owner, process owners, process practitioners and other stakeholders understanding:

- The context of use, scope, purpose and limits of each process
- The strategies, policies and standards that apply to the processes and to the management of interfaces between processes
- Authorities and responsibilities of those involved in each process
- The information provided by each process that flows from one process to another; who produces it; and how it is used by integrated processes.

Integrating service management processes depends on the flow of information across process and organizational boundaries. This in turn depends on implementing supporting technology and management information systems across organizational boundaries, rather than in silos. If service management processes are implemented, followed or changed in isolation, they can become a bureaucratic overhead that does not deliver value for money. They could also damage or negate the operation or value of other processes and services.

As discussed in section 2.2.2, each process has a clear scope with a structured set of activities that transform inputs to deliver the outputs reliably. A process interface is the boundary of the process.

**Table 2.1 The processes described in each core ITIL publication**

| Core ITIL lifecycle publication | Processes described in the publication |
|---|---|
| *ITIL Service Strategy* | Strategy management for IT services |
| | Service portfolio management |
| | Financial management for IT services |
| | Demand management |
| | Business relationship management |
| *ITIL Service Design* | Design coordination |
| | Service catalogue management |
| | Service level management |
| | Availability management |
| | Capacity management |
| | IT service continuity management |
| | Information security management |
| | Supplier management |
| *ITIL Service Transition* | Transition planning and support |
| | Change management |
| | Service asset and configuration management |
| | Release and deployment management |
| | Service validation and testing |
| | Change evaluation |
| | Knowledge management |
| *ITIL Service Operation* | Event management |
| | Incident management |
| | Request fulfilment |
| | Problem management |
| | Access management |
| *ITIL Continual Service Improvement* | Seven-step improvement process |

Process integration is the linking of processes by ensuring that information flows from one process to another effectively and efficiently. If there is management commitment to process integration, processes are generally easier to implement and there will be fewer conflicts between processes.

Stages of the lifecycle work together as an integrated system to support the ultimate objective of service management for business value realization. Every stage is interdependent as shown in Figure 2.9. See Appendix D for examples of inputs and outputs across the service lifecycle.

The SKMS, described in section 2.2.5, enables integration across the service lifecycle stages. It provides secure and controlled access to the knowledge, information and data that are needed to manage and deliver services. The

service portfolio represents all the assets presently engaged or being released in various stages of the lifecycle.

Chapter 1 provides a summary of each stage in the service lifecycle but it is also important to understand how the lifecycle stages work together.

Service strategy establishes policies and principles that provide guidance for the whole service lifecycle. The service portfolio is defined in this lifecycle stage, and new or changed services are chartered.

During the service design stage of the lifecycle, everything needed to transition and operate the new or changed service is documented in a service design package. This lifecycle stage also designs everything needed to create, transition

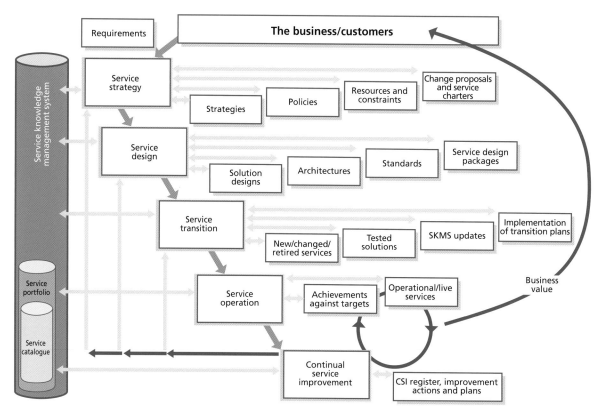

*Figure 2.9  Integration across the service lifecycle*

and operate the services, including management information systems and tools, architectures, processes, measurement methods and metrics.

The activities of the service transition and service operation stages of the lifecycle are defined during service design. Service transition ensures that the requirements of the service strategy, developed in service design, are effectively realized in service operation while controlling the risks of failure and disruption.

The service operation stage of the service lifecycle carries out the activities and processes required to deliver the agreed services. During this stage of the lifecycle, the value defined in the service strategy is realized.

Continual service improvement acts in tandem with all the other lifecycle stages. All processes, activities, roles, services and technology should be measured and subjected to continual improvement.

Most ITIL processes and functions have activities that take place across multiple stages of the service lifecycle. For example:

■ The service validation and testing process may design tests during the service design stage and perform these tests during service transition.

■ The technical management function may provide input to strategic decisions about technology, as well as assisting in the design and transition of infrastructure components.

■ Business relationship managers may assist in gathering detailed requirements during the service design stage of the lifecycle, or take part in the management of major incidents during the service operation stage.

■ All service lifecycle stages contribute to the seven-step improvement process.

Appendix D identifies some of the major inputs and outputs between each stage of the service lifecycle. Chapter 3 of each core ITIL publication provides more detail on the inputs and outputs of the specific lifecycle stage it describes.

The strength of the service lifecycle rests upon continual feedback throughout each stage of the lifecycle. This feedback ensures that service optimization is managed from a business perspective and is measured in terms of the value the business derives from services at any point in time during the service lifecycle. The service lifecycle is non-linear in design. At every point in the service lifecycle, the process of monitoring, assessment and feedback between each stage

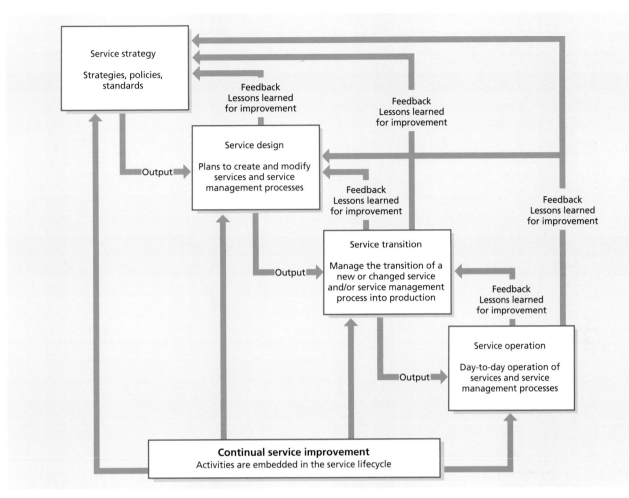

*Figure 2.10 Continual service improvement and the service lifecycle*

drives decisions about the need for minor course corrections or major service improvement initiatives.

Figure 2.10 illustrates some examples of the continual feedback system built into the service lifecycle.

Adopting appropriate technology to automate the processes and provide management with the information that supports the processes is also important for effective and efficient service management.

# Continual service improvement principles

**3**

# 3 Continual service improvement principles

Service improvement must focus on increasing the efficiency, maximizing the effectiveness and optimizing the cost of services and the underlying IT service management (ITSM) processes. The only way to do this is to ensure that improvement opportunities are identified throughout the entire service lifecycle.

## 3.1 CONTINUAL SERVICE IMPROVEMENT APPROACH

Figure 3.1 shows an overall approach to continual service improvement (CSI) and illustrates a continual cycle of improvement. This approach to improvement can be summarized as follows:

■ Embrace the vision by understanding the high-level business objectives. The vision should align the business and IT strategies.

■ Assess the current situation to obtain an accurate, unbiased snapshot of where the organization is right now. This baseline assessment is an analysis of the current position in terms of the business, organization, people, process and technology.

■ Understand and agree on the priorities for improvement based on a deeper development of the principles defined in the vision. The full vision may be years away but this step provides specific goals and a manageable timeframe.

■ Detail the CSI plan to achieve higher quality service provision by implementing or improving ITSM processes.

■ Verify that measurements and metrics are in place and that the milestones were achieved, process compliance is high, and business objectives and priorities were met by the level of service.

■ Finally, the approach should ensure that the momentum for quality improvement is maintained by assuring that changes become embedded in the organization.

### 3.1.1 Business questions for CSI

The business needs to be involved with CSI in decision-making on what improvement initiatives make sense and add the greatest value back to the business. There are some key questions that

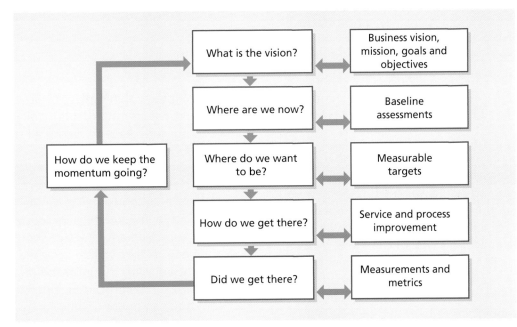

*Figure 3.1 Continual service improvement approach*

will assist the business in making decisions about whether a CSI initiative is warranted or not.

The CSI approach will enable the correct questions to be asked from both a business and an IT perspective. Not understanding some of these questions can lead to challenges, perceived poor service or in some cases actual poor service:

■ What is the vision?  The question should be asked by the IT service provider to understand what the ultimate and long term aims are.
■ Where are we now?  This is a question every business should start out asking as this creates a baseline of data for services currently being delivered.
■ Where do we want to be?  This is often expressed as business requirements.
■ How do we get there?  What improvement initiatives are required in the short, medium and long term? These initiatives should be logged in the CSI register (see section 3.4).
■ Did we get there?  This is documented through monitoring, reporting and reviewing of service level achievements and actual performance against targets identified by the business requirements.

There is a common belief that CSI activities cannot improve a service that doesn't yet exist and that the service has to be operational to identify improvement opportunities. However, CSI can add value in designing a new service by bringing the knowledge and experience from improving existing services. CSI can proactively prevent the potential flaws in the new service. CSI activities can be executed within service strategy, service design, service transition and service operation.

## 3.2 CSI AND ORGANIZATIONAL CHANGE

Improving service management is to embark upon an organizational change programme. Many organizational change programmes fail to achieve the desired results. Successful ITSM requires understanding the way in which work is done and putting in place a programme of change within the IT organization. This type of change is, by its very nature, prone to difficulties. It involves people and the way they work. People generally do not like to change; the benefits must be explained to everyone to gain their support and to ensure that they break out of old working practices.

One approach to managing organizational change is that of John P. Kotter. His eight-step approach to transforming an organization is discussed in detail in section 8.4.

## 3.3 OWNERSHIP

The principle of ownership is fundamental to any improvement strategy. CSI is a best practice and one of the keys to successful implementation is to ensure that a specific manager, a CSI manager, is accountable for ensuring the best practice is adopted and sustained throughout the organization. The CSI manager is the chief advocate and owns all CSI issues. The CSI manager is accountable for the success of CSI in the organization. This ownership responsibility extends beyond ensuring the CSI practices are embedded in the organization but also to ensuring there are adequate resources (including people and technology) to support and enable CSI. Also included are ongoing CSI activities such as monitoring, analysing, evaluating trends and reporting as well as project-based service improvement activities – activities that are fundamental to the ITIL framework. Improvement will be difficult without clear and unambiguous accountability.

While the CSI manager is responsible and accountable for CSI, the CSI manager is not accountable for improvements to specific services. Specific service improvements are the responsibility of the appropriate service owner working within the CSI framework.

## 3.4 CSI REGISTER

It is likely that several initiatives or possibilities for improvement are identified. It is recommended that a CSI register is kept to record all the improvement opportunities and that each one should be categorized into small, medium or large undertakings. Additionally they should be categorized into initiatives that can be achieved quickly, or in the medium term or longer term. Each improvement initiative should also show the benefits that will be achieved by its implementation. With this information a clear prioritized list can be produced. One failing that has been observed is when something has been identified as a lower priority. It never makes its way higher up the list for a further consideration, so automated raising of priorities over time may be a useful addition to the register.

The CSI register contains important information for the overall service provider and should be held and regarded as part of the service knowledge management system (SKMS).

The CSI register will introduce a structure and visibility to CSI ensuring that all initiatives are captured and recorded, and benefits realized. Additionally the benefits will be measured to show that they have given the desired results. In forecasting the benefits of each proposed improvement we should also try to quantify the benefit in terms of aspirational key performance indicator (KPI) metrics. This will assist in prioritizing those changes that deliver the most significant incremental benefit to the business.

The CSI register provides a coordinated, consistent view of the potentially numerous improvement activities. It is important to define the interface from the CSI register of initiatives with strategic initiatives and with processes such as problem management, capacity management and change management. In particular the service review meeting is likely to result in a number of requirements for improvement.

The CSI manager should have accountability and responsibility for the production and maintenance of the CSI register.

Appendix B shows a simple example of what a CSI register could look like. Each organization should evaluate its own requirements and amend the register to suit their own purposes.

## 3.5 EXTERNAL AND INTERNAL DRIVERS

There are two major areas within every organization driving improvement: aspects that are external to the organization such as regulation, legislation, competition, external customer requirements, market pressures and economics; and aspects that are internal to the organization such as organizational structures, culture, new knowledge, new technologies, new skills, existing and projected staffing levels, union rules etc. In some cases these aspects may serve to hinder improvement rather than drive it forward. A SWOT analysis (examining strengths, weaknesses, opportunities and threats), discussed in section 5.5.9, may be helpful in illuminating significant

opportunities for improvement. The strengths and weaknesses focus on the internal aspects of the organization while the opportunities and threats focus on aspects external to the organization.

## 3.6 SERVICE LEVEL MANAGEMENT

Adopting the service level management (SLM) process is a key principle of CSI. While in the past many IT organizations viewed SLM as merely a smattering of isolated agreements around system availability or service desk calls, this is no longer true. SLM is no longer optional. Today's business demands that IT be driven by service requirements and outcomes. This service orientation of IT toward the business becomes the foundation for the trusted partnership that IT must endeavour to create. Today IT is a core enabler of every critical business process. It cannot be overemphasized that IT organizations can no longer afford to operate with a technology-only bias, but rather must consistently strive to be included in every conceivable channel of communication and level of decision-making all the way to the boardroom.

SLM involves a number of steps:

- Involving the business and determining its service level requirements (SLRs)
- Identifying internal relationships in IT organizations, negotiating the terms and responsibilities of the internal relationships, and codifying them with operational level agreements (OLAs)
- Identifying existing contractual relationships with external vendors; working with the supplier manager to verify that these underpinning contracts (UCs) meet the revised business requirements
- Using the service catalogue as the baseline to negotiate service level agreements (SLAs) with the business
- Reviewing service achievement and identifying where improvements are required, feeding them into CSI.

Once the IT organization and the business begin working together through SLM, IT management soon realizes that the old definitions of 'successful IT' are beginning to fall by the wayside. A high network availability percentage or great ratings in a customer satisfaction survey are no longer the end goal but merely positive metrics rolling towards the achievement of a service level and the required business outcomes. IT management understands that with the adoption of SLM a fundamental shift has taken place. The definition of success in IT is both the agreed service level achieved and the resulting business outcomes achieved. IT is then structured, managed, staffed, funded and operated to meet or exceed the service levels. The service level rules and everything else are just details. The SLM process is fully defined in *ITIL Service Design*.

## 3.7 KNOWLEDGE MANAGEMENT

*'Those who cannot remember the past are condemned to repeat it.'* George Santayana

Knowledge management is explained fully in ITIL Service Transition but it plays a key role in CSI. Within each service lifecycle stage, data should be captured to enable knowledge gain and an understanding of what is actually happening, thus enabling wisdom. This is often referred to as the Data-to-Information-to-Knowledge-to-Wisdom (DIKW) structure (see Figure 3.2). All too often an organization will capture the appropriate data but fail to process the data into information, synthesize the information into knowledge, and then combine that knowledge with others to bring wisdom. Wisdom will lead to better decisions around improvement.

This applies both when looking at the IT services themselves and when drilling down into each individual IT process. Knowledge management is a mainstay of any improvement process.

## 3.8 THE DEMING CYCLE

W. Edwards Deming is best known for his management philosophy leading to higher quality, increased productivity, and a more competitive position. As part of this philosophy he formulated 14 points of attention for managers. Some of them are more appropriate to service management than others. For quality improvement he proposed the Deming Cycle or Circle. This cycle is particularly applicable in CSI. As already mentioned in section 2.3.2, the four key stages of the cycle are Plan, Do, Check and Act, after which a phase of consolidation prevents the circle from rolling back down the hill (see Figure 2.8). Our goal in using the Deming Cycle (or the PDCA cycle, as it is

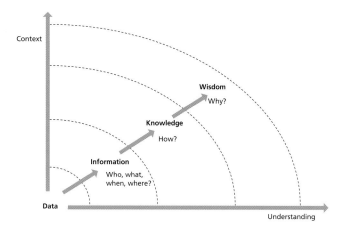

**Figure 3.2 Knowledge management leads to better IT decisions**

now more commonly known) is steady, ongoing improvement. It is a fundamental tenet of CSI.

The PDCA cycle is critical at two points in CSI: implementation of CSI, and for the application of CSI to services and service management processes. At implementation, all four stages of the PDCA cycle are used. With ongoing improvement, CSI draws on the check and act stages to monitor, measure, review and implement initiatives.

The seven-step improvement process fully described in Chapter 4 can be viewed as an example of an implementation of the PDCA cycle, with each of the steps falling within one of the phases of the cycle: Plan, Do, Check, Act.

The cycle is underpinned by a process-led approach to management where defined processes are in place, the activities are measured for compliance to expected values and outputs are audited to validate and improve the process.

It should be noted that the PDCA cycle is a fundamental part of many quality standards including ISO/IEC 20000.

## 3.9 SERVICE MEASUREMENT

### 3.9.1 Baselines

An important beginning point for highlighting improvement is to establish baselines as markers or starting points for later comparison. Baselines are also used to establish an initial data point to determine if a service or process needs to be improved. As a result, it is important that baselines are documented, recognized and accepted throughout the organization. Baselines must be established at each level: strategic goals and objectives, tactical process maturity, and operational metrics and KPIs.

If a baseline is not initially established the first measurement efforts will become the baseline. That is why it is essential to collect data at the outset, even if the integrity of the data is in question. It is better to have data to question than to have no data at all.

## 3.9.2 Why do we measure?

As shown in Figure 3.3 there are four reasons to monitor and measure:

- **To validate**   Monitoring and measuring to validate previous decisions
- **To direct**   Monitoring and measuring to set the direction for activities in order to meet set targets; this is the most prevalent reason for monitoring and measuring
- **To justify**   Monitoring and measuring to justify, with factual evidence or proof, that a course of action is required
- **To intervene**   Monitoring and measuring to identify a point of intervention including subsequent changes and corrective actions.

The four basic reasons to monitor and measure lead to three key questions: 'Why are we monitoring and measuring?', 'When do we stop?' and 'Is anyone using the data?' To answer these questions, it is important to identify which of the above reasons is driving the measurement effort. Too often, we continue to measure long after the need has passed. Every time you produce a report you should ask: 'Do we still need this?'

## 3.9.3 The seven-step improvement process

Fundamental to CSI is the concept of measurement. CSI uses the seven-step improvement process shown in Figure 3.4. The seven-step improvement process is a crucial part of CSI and is described in detail in section Chapter 4 – but it is briefly introduced here so it can be seen alongside the other key principles.

### 3.9.3.1 Which steps support CSI?

It is obvious that all the activities of the improvement process assist CSI in some way. It is relatively simple to identify what takes place but more difficult to understand exactly how this will

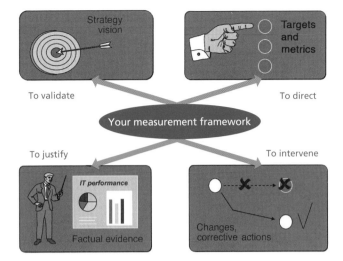

**Figure 3.3  Why do we measure?**

happen. The improvement process spans not only the management organization but the entire service lifecycle. This is a cornerstone of CSI, the main steps of which are as follows:

1 **Identify the strategy for improvement**
   Identify the overall vision, business need, the strategy and the tactical and operational goals.

2 **Define what you will measure**
   Service strategy and service design should have identified this information early in the lifecycle. CSI can then start its cycle all over again at 'Where are we now?' and 'Where do we want to be?' This identifies the ideal situation for both the business and IT. CSI can conduct a gap analysis to identify the opportunities for improvement as well as answering the question 'How do we get there?'

3 **Gather the data**
   In order to properly answer the question 'Did we get there?', data must first be gathered (usually through service operations). Data can be gathered from many different sources based on goals and objectives identified. At this point the data is raw and no conclusions are drawn.

4 **Process the data**
   Here the data is processed in alignment with the critical success factors (CSFs) and KPIs specified. This means that timeframes are coordinated, unaligned data is rationalized and made consistent, and gaps in the data are identified. The simple goal of this step is to process data from multiple disparate sources to give it context that can be compared. Once we have rationalized the data we can begin analysis.

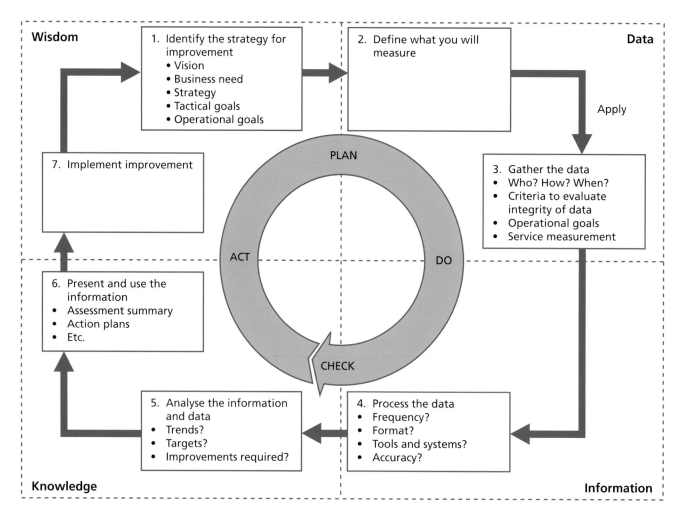

*Figure 3.4 The seven-step improvement process*

**5 Analyse the information and data**

As we bring the data more and more into context, it evolves from raw data into information with which we can start to answer questions about who, what, when, where and how as well as trends and the impact on the business. It is the analysing step that is most often overlooked or forgotten in the rush to present data to management.

**6 Present and use the information**

Here the answer to 'Did we get there?' is formatted and communicated in whatever way necessary to present to the various stakeholders an accurate picture of the results of the improvement efforts. Knowledge is presented to the business in a form and manner that reflects their needs and assists them in determining the next steps.

**7 Implement improvement**

The knowledge gained is used to optimize, improve and correct services and processes. Issues have been identified and now solutions are implemented – wisdom is applied to the knowledge. The improvements that need to be taken to improve the service or process are communicated and explained to the organization. Following this step the organization establishes a new baseline and the cycle begins anew.

While these seven steps appear to form a circular set of activities, in fact, they constitute a knowledge spiral (see Figure 3.5). In practice, knowledge gathered and wisdom derived from the knowledge at one level of the organization becomes a data input to the next.

People often believe data, information, knowledge and wisdom to be synonymous or at least broadly similar in meaning. This view is incorrect. There is

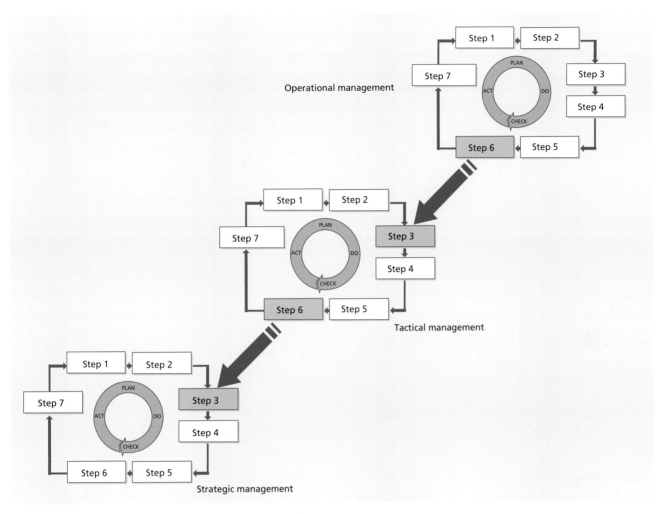

Operational management

Tactical management

Strategic management

***Figure 3.5 Knowledge spiral – a gathering activity***

a significant difference between each of the four items.

Data is quantitative. Data is defined as numbers, characters, images or other outputs from devices to convert physical quantities into symbols, in a very broad sense. Essentially it can be defined as a collection of facts, whereas information is the result of processing and organizing data in a way that adds to the knowledge of the person receiving it. Raw data is a relative term; data processing commonly occurs by stages, and the 'processed data' from one stage may be considered the 'raw data' of the next. For example, the service desk and incident management may collect data on an average of 12,000 incidents per month. Data can also be qualitative such as comments in a customer satisfaction survey.

Data can be defined as a collection of facts in context from which conclusions may be drawn. Information is the result of processing and organizing data in a way that adds to the knowledge of the person receiving it.

By processing data into information it is possible to know the breakdown of which customers are using the service desk and the specific issues that are incidents or service requests. For example, further processing of the data into information may show that 32% of all contacts to the service desk are 'How to' questions, and that 18% of all contacts are service incidents with the organization's email system.

Knowledge can be defined as information combined with experience, context, interpretation and reflection. For example, based on the data and information, and an understanding of who uses the service, and their reasons for using the service, the impact to the business can be determined.

Wisdom is defined as the ability to make correct judgements and decisions. It consists of making the best use of available knowledge. For example, knowledge about the customer impact of incidents can lead to identifying improvement opportunities such as training programmes or initiating a service improvement plan (SIP) for improving the email service.

## 3.10 IT GOVERNANCE

IT governance is only part of an organization's corporate governance, but it is an important part. Governance is important for all organizations and will provide an environment within which CSI can operate and thrive. With the exposure of high-level corporate fraud in the early years of this century, IT was forced to comply with new legislation and an ever-increasing number of external regulations. External auditors are now commonplace in large IT organizations.

Chapter 5 of *ITIL Service Strategy* includes a detailed description of governance and how it should be applied to ITSM.

The Chartered Institute of Management Accountants (CIMA) has a framework for enterprise governance as shown in Figure 3.6, which covers the corporate governance and the business management aspects of the organization.

> **IT governance**
>
> *'IT governance is the responsibility of the board of directors and executive management. It is an integral part of enterprise governance and consists of the leadership, organizational structures and processes that ensure that the organization's IT sustains and extends the organization's strategies and objectives.'* IT Governance Institute (2003). *Board Briefing on IT Governance*, 2nd edition.

IT governance touches nearly every area detailed in Figure 3.6. On the one hand, IT organizations must now comply with new rules and legislation and continually demonstrate their compliance through successful independent audits by external organizations. On the other hand, IT organizations are increasingly being called on to do more with less and create additional value while maximizing the use of existing resources.

These increasing pressures dovetail perfectly with the basic premise of ITIL: IT is a service business. Existing internal IT organizations must transform themselves into effective and efficient IT service providers or they will cease to be relevant to

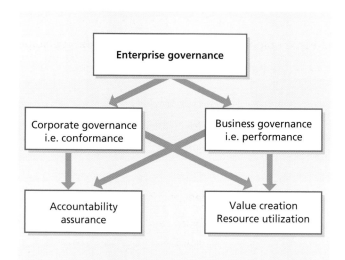

*Figure 3.6 Enterprise governance (source: CIMA)*

the business and, soon after, cease to exist. This continual and unceasing drive toward greater business value with greater internal efficiency is at the heart of CSI.

## 3.11 FRAMEWORKS, MODELS, STANDARDS AND QUALITY SYSTEMS

Appendix A gives a detailed description of related guidance and outlines the frameworks, models, standards and quality systems that an organization may choose to use in support of ITSM. As well as ITIL itself this includes:

- Quality management system ISO 9000
- Total Quality Management (TQM)
- Risk management
- Control OBjectives for Information and related Technology (COBIT)
- ISO/IEC 20000 and other ISO standards for IT
- ISO 14001 – Environmental management standard
- Programme and project management including PRINCE2
- Skills Framework for the Information Age (SFIA)
- Capability Maturity Model Integration (CMMI)
- ISO/IEC 27001 – Information security management system.

### 3.11.1 Which one should I choose?

Experience has shown that while each may be complete unto itself, none provides a total answer for IT management. Indeed, there is a good deal of overlap between them but, for the most

**Table 3.1 CSI inputs and outputs by lifecycle stage**

| Lifecycle stage | CSI inputs (from the lifecycle stages in the first column) | CSI outputs (to the lifecycle stages in the first column) |
| --- | --- | --- |
| Service strategy | Vision and mission<br><br>Service portfolio<br><br>Policies<br><br>Strategies and strategic plans<br><br>Priorities<br><br>Financial information and budgets<br><br>Patterns of business activity<br><br>Achievements against metrics, KPIs and CSFs<br><br>Improvement opportunities logged in the CSI register | Results of customer and user satisfaction surveys<br><br>Input to business cases and the service portfolio<br><br>Feedback on strategies and policies<br><br>Financial information regarding improvement initiatives for input to budgets<br><br>Data required for metrics, KPIs and CSFs<br><br>Service reports<br><br>Requests for change (RFCs) for implementing improvements |
| Service design | Service catalogue<br><br>Service design packages including details of utility and warranty<br><br>Knowledge and information in the SKMS<br><br>Achievements against metrics, KPIs and CSFs<br><br>Design of services, measurements, processes, infrastructure and systems<br><br>Design for the seven-step improvement process and procedures<br><br>Improvement opportunities logged in the CSI register | Results of customer and user satisfaction surveys<br><br>Input to design requirements<br><br>Data required for metrics, KPIs and CSFs<br><br>Service reports<br><br>Feedback on service design packages<br><br>RFCs for implementing improvements |
| Service transition | Test reports<br><br>Change evaluation reports<br><br>Knowledge and information in the SKMS<br><br>Achievements against metrics, KPIs and CSFs<br><br>Improvement opportunities logged in the CSI register | Results of customer and user satisfaction surveys<br><br>Input to testing requirements<br><br>Data required for metrics, KPIs and CSFs<br><br>Input to change evaluation and change advisory board meetings<br><br>Service reports<br><br>RFCs for implementing improvements |
| Service operation | Operational performance data and service records<br><br>Proposed problem resolutions and proactive measures<br><br>Knowledge and information in the SKMS<br><br>Achievements against metrics, KPIs and CSFs<br><br>Improvement opportunities logged in the CSI register | Results of customer and user satisfaction surveys<br><br>Service reports and dashboards<br><br>Data required for metrics, KPIs and CSFs<br><br>RFCs for implementing improvements |

part, they are not competitive or exclusive but complementary. In fact, many organizations use a combination to manage and improve IT more effectively.

It should be emphasized that ISO/IEC 20000 (the IT service management standard) is most closely aligned with ITIL and is specifically aimed at IT service providers.

ISACA, in conjunction with the Office of Government Commerce (OGC), created a briefing paper entitled 'Aligning COBIT, ITIL and ISO17799 for Business Benefit'. Other organizations have combined ITIL, CMMI and Six Sigma as their formula for success.

Some organizations have doubts about which frameworks, models, standards or quality system to choose, not wishing to go down the wrong path. The decision is not 'Which one should I choose?' but rather 'What should I improve first?'

An effective CSI practice will be integrated within all stages of the service lifecycle. The greatest value to the business and IT will be realized by having a continuous monitoring and feedback loop as the service and ITSM processes move through the service lifecycle. Look for improvement opportunities within service strategy, service design, service transition and service operation. It is imperative that the concept of continual improvement be woven into the day-to-day fabric of the organization.

## 3.12 CSI INPUTS AND OUTPUTS

Table 3.1 shows the major CSI inputs and outputs, by lifecycle stage. Appendix D provides a summary of the major inputs and outputs between each stage of the service lifecycle.

# Continual service improvement processes

# 4 Continual service improvement processes

Many activities have to be completed to ensure continual service improvement (CSI) across the service lifecycle. Some of them could be regarded as processes in their own right but in order that readers get the full picture they have been pulled together into a single contiguous process: the seven-step improvement process.

## 4.1 THE SEVEN-STEP IMPROVEMENT PROCESS

Chapter 3 introduced the seven-step improvement process shown in Figure 3.4 and its interaction with the Plan-Do-Check-Act (PDCA) cycle and the CSI approach. The PDCA cycle provides steady, ongoing improvement, which is a fundamental tenet of CSI.

Figure 3.4 also shows how the cycle fits into the Data-to-Information-to-Knowledge-to-Wisdom (DIKW) structure of knowledge management. The integration of the PDCA cycle and the seven-step improvement process is as follows:

- Plan
  1. Identify the strategy for improvement
  2. Define what you will measure
- Do
  3. Gather the data
  4. Process the data
- Check
  5. Analyse the information and data
  6. Present and use the information
- Act
  7. Implement improvement.

### 4.1.1 Purpose and objectives

The purpose of the seven-step improvement process is to define and manage the steps needed to identify, define, gather, process, analyse, present and implement improvements.

The objectives of the seven-step improvement process are to:

- Identify opportunities for improving services, processes, tools etc.

- Reduce the cost of providing services and ensuring that IT services enable the required business outcomes to be achieved. A clear objective will be cost reduction, but this is not the only criterion. If service delivery or quality reduces as a result the overall impact may be neutral or even negative.
- Identify what needs to be measured, analysed and reported to establish improvement opportunities.
- Continually review service achievements to ensure they remain matched to business requirements; continually align and re-align service provision with outcome requirements.
- Understand what to measure, why it is being measured and carefully define the successful outcome.

It is important to note that improvements in quality should not be implemented if there is a cost associated with the improvement and if this cost has not been justified. Every potential improvement opportunity will have to have a business case justification to show that the business will have an overall benefit. For small initiatives the business case does not have to be a full blown report but could be a simple justification. The seven-step improvement process is not free-standing and will only achieve its desired outcomes when applied to technology, services, processes, organization or partners.

### 4.1.2 Scope

The seven-step improvement process includes analysis of the performance and capabilities of services, processes throughout the lifecycle, partners and technology. It includes the continual alignment of the portfolio of IT services with the current and future business needs as well as the maturity of the enabling IT processes for each service. It also includes making best use of the technology that the organization has and looks to exploit new technology as it becomes available where there is a business case for doing so. Also within the scope are the organizational structure, the capabilities of the personnel, and asking whether people are working in appropriate functions and roles, and if they have the required skills.

### 4.1.3 Value to business

The value of the seven-step improvement process is that by monitoring and analysing the delivery of services it will ensure the current and future business outcome requirements can be met. The seven-step improvement process enables continual assessment of the current situation against business needs and identifies opportunities to improve service provision for customers.

### 4.1.4 Policies, principles and basic concepts

The seven-step improvement process puts a structure in place to enable continual assessment of the current situation against business needs and looks for opportunities to improve service provision, thus enabling the overall business to be more successful.

#### 4.1.4.1 Policies

Many of the policies that support the seven-step improvement process are often found as a part of other processes such as service level management (SLM), availability management and capacity management. Examples of some of these policies are:

- Monitoring requirements must be defined and implemented
- Data must be gathered and analysed and its integrity checked on a consistent basis
- Trend reporting must be provided on a consistent basis
- Service level achievement reports must be provided on a consistent basis
- Internal and external service reviews must be completed on a consistent basis (internal is within IT and external is with the business)
- Services must have either clearly defined service levels or service targets that can be used to determine if there are gaps in the services provided
- Service management processes must have critical success factors (CSFs) and key performance indicators (KPIs) to determine if there are gaps between the expected outcome and the real outcome.

On a regular basis means that the activity is not done *ad hoc* but on scheduled dates such as monthly or quarterly. Most organizations review service achievement and service management process results on a monthly basis.

If a new service is being introduced, it is recommended to monitor, report and review much sooner than after a month. You may want to review the new service daily, as part of early life support, for a period of time, before changing to weekly and finally monthly reviews.

The following are additional CSI policies that an IT service provider should implement:

- All improvement initiatives must use the formal change management process
- All functional groups within IT have a responsibility for CSI activities. This might be only one person in the group, but the intent here is that CSI is not usually a functional group within an organization but that everyone has a hand in supporting CSI activities
- Roles and responsibilities will be documented, communicated and filled within IT.

When defining the CSI policies you may want to use a consistent template. The template in Table 4.1 is an example that documents the policy statement, reason for the policy and a definition of the benefits of the policy. If an organization has difficulty defining the reason for and benefits of a policy it should consider whether the policy is needed. If compliance to a policy cannot be monitored then the value of the policy must be in doubt.

#### 4.1.4.2 Principles

Many service providers operate in a competitive environment and they need to continually assess their services against market expectations to ensure they remain competitive. Also, new delivery mechanisms (e.g. cloud computing) can introduce service efficiencies and need to be reviewed. The following activities should be regularly performed:

- Services must be checked against competitive service offerings to ensure they continue to add true business value to the client, and the service provider remains competitive in its delivery of such services.
- Services must be reviewed in the light of new technological advances (e.g. cloud deployment

**Table 4.1 Policy template example**

| Title | Monitoring services, systems and components |
|---|---|
| Policy statement | IT and the business must agree on what to monitor and collect data for each service. This data should be aligned with the service level agreements (SLAs), operational level agreements (OLAs) and contracts. |
| Reason for policy | Provides input into CSI activities to identify gaps and improvement opportunities. |
| Benefits | Ensures agreement on defining what to monitor (work with SLM). |
| | Defines monitoring requirements for new services and/or existing services to support CSI activities. |
| | Identifies trends and gaps. |
| | Supports prioritization of improvement projects. |

architectures) to ensure they are delivering the most efficient services to the customer.

### 4.1.4.3 Basic concepts

CSI is often viewed as an *ad hoc* activity within IT services. The activity is only triggered when someone in IT management flags up that there is a problem. This is not the right way to address CSI. Often these reactionary events are not even providing continual improvement, but simply stopping a single failure from occurring again.

CSI takes a commitment from everyone in IT working throughout the service lifecycle to be successful at improving services and service management processes. It requires ongoing attention, a well-thought-out plan, and consistent attention to monitoring, analysing and reporting results with an eye toward improvement. Improvements can be incremental in nature but also require a huge commitment to implement a new service or meet new business requirements.

This section spells out the seven steps of improvement, each of which needs attention. There is no reward for taking a short cut or not addressing each step in a sequential nature. If any step is missed, there is a risk of not being efficient and effective in meeting the goals of CSI.

IT services must ensure that proper staffing and tools are identified and implemented to support CSI activities. It is also important to understand the difference between what should be measured and what can be measured. Start small – don't expect to measure everything at once. Understand the organizational capability to gather and process the data. Be sure to spend time analysing data as this is where the real value comes in. Without analysis of the data, there is no real opportunity

to truly improve services or service management processes. Think through the strategy and plan for reporting and using the data. Reporting is partly a marketing activity. It is important that IT managers focus on the value added to the organization as well as reporting on issues and achievements. In order for steps 5 to 7 to be carried out correctly, it is imperative that the target audience is considered when packaging the information.

An organization can find improvement opportunities throughout the entire service lifecycle. An IT organization does not need to wait until a service or service management process is transitioned into the operations area to begin identifying improvement opportunities.

### 4.1.5 Process activities, methods and techniques

The seven-step improvement process is shown in Figure 3.4 and is discussed at the start of section 4.1.

Figure 4.1 shows the trail from metrics to KPI to CSF, all the way back to the vision where appropriate. Elements from this trail are used at points throughout the seven-step improvement process.

These are the seven steps.

### 4.1.5.1 Step 1 – Identify the strategy for improvement

Before any further activity can be started it is imperative that the overall vision is identified. What are we trying to achieve for the business as a whole? The questions we need to ask are: What initiatives does the business have that could be undermined by poor IT service provision? Or, more positively: How can improvements in IT enable the business vision to be achieved? The answers to

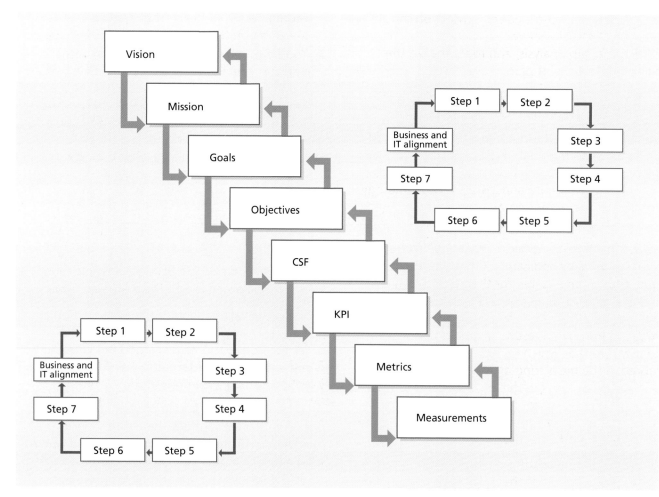

*Figure 4.1 From vision to measurements*

these questions will come from stepping through the seven-step improvement process.

What are the business and IT strategy and plans for the coming months and years? Why do we want to measure for improvement? The overall strategy should be assessed and analysed to see where we need to focus our measurements, for example. The technical and operational goals as well as the strategic goals need to be identified and assessed. The vision should not be to have state-of-the-art servers and desk-top computers, but to have state-of-the-art services that ensure and enable the overall business to perform as well as possible so it is not in any way constrained by the quality or cost of the IT services.

Like all the steps in the process, this should be revisited to reassess the potentially changing vision and goals. When revisiting this process we would apply any wisdom gained from previous iterations.

One of the potential sources for a revisit would be one or more initiatives raised and documented in the CSI register. Inputs for this step are:

- Business plans and strategy
- Service review meetings
- Vision and mission statements
- Corporate, divisional and departmental goals and objectives
- Legislative requirements
- Governance requirements
- Customer satisfaction surveys
- CSI initiatives as logged in the CSI register.

### 4.1.5.2 Step 2 – Define what you will measure

This step is directly related to the strategic, tactical and operational goals that have been defined for measuring services and service management processes as well as the existing technology and capability to support measuring and CSI activities.

In this step you need to define what you should measure; define what you can actually measure; carry out a gap analysis; and then finalize the actual measurement plan.

As stated previously, measurement will take place at service, process and technology levels.

Step 2 is iterative during the rest of the activities. Depending on the goals and objectives to support service improvement activities, an organization may have to purchase and install new technology to support the gathering and processing of the data and/or hire staff with the required skills sets.

Effective service measures concentrate on a few vital, meaningful indicators that are economical, quantitative and usable for the desired results. If there are too many measures, organizations may become too intent on measurement and lose focus on improving results. A guiding principle is to measure that which matters most. IT has never lacked in the measuring area. In fact, many IT organizations measure far too many things that have little or no value. There is often no thought or effort given to aligning measures to the business and IT goals and objectives.

As part of the measuring process it is important to confirm regularly that the data being collected and collated is still required and that measurements are being adjusted where necessary. This responsibility falls on the owner of each report or dashboard. They are the individuals designated to keep the reports useful and to make sure that effective use is being made of the results.

The overall step is too often ignored because:

- The process does not include this step. Too often people start gathering information without asking what should be collected in the first place and if we have the capabilities to do the measurements. Often what is going to done with the data later is not considered. This is common but poor practice.
- The IT organization thinks it knows better. When it comes to data, IT believes, incorrectly, that they know the needs of their customers. The reality is that neither the customer nor the IT organization sits down together to discuss what should be measured or to identify the purpose of the data in the first place. Even in organizations where SLAs have been signed, they often include measurement and reporting

requirements that cannot be met. This always leads to significant customer dissatisfaction.
- Tools are very sophisticated and can gather myriads of data points. IT organizations get lulled into a false sense of security in the knowledge that the data will be there when they need it. Too often the tool is too powerful for the needs of the organization. It is like hammering a small finishing nail using a sledgehammer.

When the data is finally presented (Step 6) without going through the rest of the steps, the results appear incorrect or incomplete. People blame each other, the vendor, the tools, anyone but themselves. This step is crucial. A dialogue must take place between IT and the customer. Goals and objectives of the target audience must be identified in order to properly identify what should be measured and what can be measured.

Based on the goals of the target audience (operational, tactical or strategic) the service owners need to define what they should measure in a perfect world by:

- Mapping the activities or elements of the service or service management processes that need to be measured
- Considering what measurements would indicate that each service and service management activity is being performed consistently to determine the health of the service.

Identify the measurements that can be provided based on existing toolsets, organizational culture and process maturity. Note there may be a gap in what can be measured compared with what should be measured. Quantify the cost and business risk of this gap to validate any expenditures for tools. The actual definition of what you will measure will come from this analysis.

When initially implementing service management processes do not try to measure everything; rather be selective of what measures will help to understand the health of a process. Chapter 5 will discuss the use of CSFs, KPIs and activity metrics. A major mistake many organizations make is trying to do too much in the beginning. Be smart about what you choose to measure.

*Question: What do you actually want to measure?*

*Answer:* Talk to the business, the customers and IT management. Use the service catalogue as your starting point as well as the service level requirements (SLRs) of the different customers. This is the place where you start with the end in mind. What you should measure is that which is important to the business.

Compile a list of what you should measure driven by business requirements. Don't try to cover every single eventuality or possible metric in the world. Make it simple. The number of items you should measure can grow rapidly. So too can the number of metrics and measurements.

Identify and link the following items:

- Corporate vision, mission, goals and objectives
- IT vision, mission, goals and objectives
- CSFs, KPIs, metrics and measurements
- Service level targets
- Service provider personnel.

Inputs include (note some of these can also be input into other steps):

- SLRs and targets
- Service review meeting
- Service portfolio and the service catalogue
- Vision and mission statements
- Corporate, divisional and departmental goals and objectives
- Legislative requirements
- Governance requirements
- Budget cycle
- Measurement results and reports, e.g. balanced scorecard
- Customer satisfaction surveys
- Service operation plan
- Service models
- Service design package
- Budgeting and accounting requirements
- Benchmark data
- Baseline data
- Risk assessments and risk mitigation plans.

Every organization may find that they have limitations on what can actually be measured. If you cannot measure something, then it should not appear in an SLA.

*Question: What can you actually measure?*

*Answer:* Start by listing the tools you currently have in place. These tools will include service management tools, monitoring tools, reporting tools, investigation tools and others. Compile a list of what each tool can currently measure without any configuration or customization.

*Question: Where do you actually find the information?*

*Answer:* The information is found within each service, process, procedure and work instruction. The tools are merely a way to collect and provide the data. Look at existing reports and databases. What data is currently being collected and what data is being reported on? (These two things are often not the same although of course they should be.)

To produce the final definition of what you will measure perform a gap analysis between the data collected and the data being reported on. Report the gap analysis information back to the business, the customers and IT management. It is possible that new tools are required or that configuration or customization is required to be able to measure what is needed.

The following are some other potential areas for measurement:

- **Service levels** As well as normal SLAs targets we may need to collect availability management measures such as mean time to repair (MTTR) and mean time to restore service (MTRS), which are also used by problem management.
- **Customer satisfaction** Surveys are conducted on a continual basis to measure and track how satisfied customers are with the IT organization.
- **Business impact** Measure what actions are invoked for any disruption in service that adversely affects the customer's business operation, processes or its own customers.
- **Supplier performance** Whenever an organization has entered into a supplier relationship where some services or parts of services have been outsourced or co-sourced it is important to measure the performance of the supplier.
- **Market performance** This ensures the services remain aligned with those being delivered by other service providers in the IT service delivery community.

One of CSI's key sets of activities is to measure, analyse and report on IT services and IT service management (ITSM) results. Measurements produce data, which should be analysed over time to produce a trend. This will tell a story that may be good or bad. It is essential that measurements of this kind have ongoing relevance. What was important to know last year may no longer be pertinent this year.

### 4.1.5.3 Step 3 – Gather the data

> **Key message**
>
> Gathering the data is synonymous with service measurement (see section 5.4).

Gathering data requires having monitoring in place. Monitoring could be executed using technology such as application, system and component monitoring tools as used in the event management process (documented in service operation) or even be a manual process for certain tasks. The accuracy and integrity of the data should always be maintained.

Quality is the key objective of monitoring for CSI. Monitoring will therefore focus on the effectiveness and efficiency of a service, process, tool, organization or configuration item (CI). The emphasis is not on assuring real-time service performance; rather it is on identifying where improvements can be made to the existing level of service, or IT performance. Monitoring for CSI will therefore tend to focus on detecting exceptions and resolutions. For example, CSI is not as interested in whether an incident was resolved, but whether it was resolved within the agreed time, and whether future incidents can be prevented.

CSI is not only interested in exceptions, though. If an SLA is consistently met over time, CSI will also be interested in determining whether that level of performance can be sustained at a lower cost or whether it needs to be upgraded to an even better level of performance because of changing business requirements. CSI may therefore also need access to regular performance reports.

However since CSI is unlikely to need, or be able to cope with, the vast quantities of data that are produced by all monitoring activity, they will most likely focus on a specific subset of monitoring at any given time. This could be determined by input from the business or improvements to technology.

When a new service is being designed or an existing one changed, this is a perfect opportunity to ensure that what CSI needs to monitor is designed into the service requirements (see *ITIL Service Design*).

This has two main implications:

■ Monitoring for CSI will change over time. They may be interested in monitoring the messaging service one quarter, and then move on to look at human resources (HR) systems in the next quarter.
■ This means that service operation and CSI need to build a process which will help them to agree on what areas need to be monitored and for what purpose.

It is important to remember that there are three types of metrics that an organization will need to collect to support CSI and other process activities:

■ **Technology metrics** These are often associated with component and application-based metrics such as performance, availability etc.
■ **Process metrics** These are captured in the form of CSFs, KPIs and activity metrics for the service management processes. These metrics can help determine the overall health of a process. KPIs can help answer key questions on quality, performance, value and compliance in following the process. CSI would use these metrics as input in identifying improvement opportunities for each process.
■ **Service metrics** These are the results of the end-to-end service. Technology metrics are normally used to help compute the service metrics.

*Question: What needs to be gathered?*

*Answer:* You gather whatever data has been identified as both needed and measurable. Not all data is gathered automatically so manual procedures will have to be implemented as well. A lot of data is entered manually by people. It is important to ensure that policies are in place to drive the right behaviour.

As much as possible, you need to standardize the data structure through policies and published standards. For example, how do you enter names in your tools – John Smith; Smith, John; or J. Smith? These can be the same or different individuals. Having three different ways of entering the same name would slow down trend analysis and severely impede any CSI initiative.

*Question: Where do you actually find the information?*

*Answer:* IT service management tools, monitoring tools, reporting tools, investigation tools, existing reports and other sources.

Gathering data is defined as the act of monitoring and data collection. This activity needs to clearly define:

■ Who is responsible for monitoring and gathering the data?
■ How will the data be gathered?
■ When and how often is the data gathered?
■ Criteria to evaluate the integrity of the data.

The answers will be different for every organization.

Service monitoring allows weak areas to be identified, so that remedial action can be taken (if there is a justifiable business case), thus improving future service quality. Service monitoring also can show where customer actions are causing the fault and thus lead to identifying where working efficiency and/or training can be improved.

Service monitoring should also address both internal and external suppliers since their performance must be evaluated and managed as well.

Service management monitoring helps determine the health and welfare of service management processes in the following manner:

■ **Process compliance**   Are the processes being followed? Process compliance seeks to monitor the compliance of the IT organization to the new or modified service management processes and also the use of the authorized service management tool that was implemented.
■ **Quality**   How well are the processes working? Monitor the individual or key activities as they relate to the objectives of the end-to-end process.
■ **Performance**   How fast or slow? Monitor the process efficiency such as throughput or cycle times.
■ **Value**   Is this making a difference? Monitor the effectiveness and perceived value of the process to the stakeholders and the IT staff executing the process activities.

■ **Volume**   To determine the loading and throughput on the service management processes (e.g. number of incidents or number of changes).

Monitoring is often associated with automated monitoring of infrastructure components for performance such as availability or capacity etc., but monitoring should also be used for monitoring staff behaviour such as adherence to process activities and use of authorized tools, as well as project schedules and budgets.

Exceptions and alerts need to be considered during the monitoring activity as they can serve as early warning indicators that services are failing. Sometimes the exceptions and alerts will come from tools, but they will often come from those who are using the service or service management processes. These alerts should not be ignored.

Inputs to gathering the data include:

■ New business requirements
■ Existing SLAs
■ Existing monitoring and data capture capability
■ Plans from other processes, e.g. availability management and capacity management
■ The CSI register and existing service improvement plans (SIPs)
■ Previous trend analysis reports
■ List of what you should measure
■ List of what you can measure
■ Gap analysis report
■ List of what to measure
■ Customer satisfaction surveys.

Figure 4.2 and Table 4.2 show the common procedures to follow in monitoring.

*Note:* Monitoring and event management solutions become, by definition, services in their own right and hence require continual assessment, effectiveness reviews, provisioning and change processes etc.

Outputs from gathering the data include:

■ Updated availability and capacity plans
■ Monitoring procedures
■ Identified tools to use
■ Monitoring plan
■ Input on IT capability
■ Collection of data
■ Agreement on the integrity of the data.

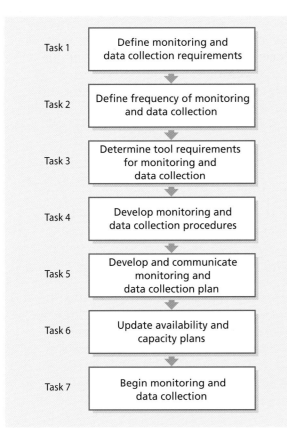

**Figure 4.2 Monitoring and data collection procedures**

It is also important in this activity to look at the data that was collected and ask whether it makes any sense.

### 4.1.5.4 Step 4 – Process the data

This step is to convert the data into the required format and for the required audience. Follow the trail from metric to KPI to CSF, all the way back to the vision if necessary (see Figure 4.1).

Report-generating technologies are typically used at this stage as various amounts of data are condensed into information for use in the analysis activity. The data is also typically put into a format that provides an end-to-end perspective on the overall performance of a service. This activity begins the transformation of raw data into packaged information. Use the information to develop insight into the performance of the service and/or processes. Process the data into information (by creating logical groupings), which provides a better means to analyse the information and data – the next step in CSI.

**Table 4.2 Monitoring and data collection procedures**

| Tasks | Procedures |
|---|---|
| Task 1 | Based on service improvement strategies, goals and objectives plus the business requirements, determine what services, systems, applications and/or components as well as service management process activities will require monitoring. |
| | Specify monitoring requirements. |
| | Define data collection requirements, changes in budgets. |
| | Document the outcome. |
| | Get agreement with internal IT, customers, suppliers as appropriate. |
| Task 2 | Determine frequency of monitoring and data gathering. |
| | Determine method of monitoring and data gathering. |
| Task 3 | Define tools required for monitoring and data gathering. |
| | Build, purchase or modify tools for monitoring and data gathering. |
| | Test the tool. |
| | Install the tool. |
| Task 4 | Write monitoring procedures and work instructions when required for monitoring and data collection. |
| Task 5 | Produce and communicate monitoring and data collection plan. |
| | Get approval from internal IT and external vendors who may be impacted. |
| Task 6 | Update availability and capacity plans if required. |
| Task 7 | Begin monitoring and data collection. |
| | Process data into a logical grouping and report format. |
| | Review data to ensure the data makes sense. |

**Example of poor data management**

An organization that was developing some management information activities asked a consultant to review the data they had collected. The data was for incident management and the service desk. It was provided in a spreadsheet format and when the consultant opened the spreadsheet it showed that for the month the organization had opened approximately 42,000 new incidents and 65,000 incidents were closed on the first contact. It is hard to close more incidents than were opened – in other words the data did not make sense.

However, all is not lost. Even if the data did not make any sense, it provides insight into the ability to monitor and gather data, the tools that are used to support monitoring and data gathering, and the procedures for processing the raw data into a report that can be used for analysis. When investigating the example above, it was discovered that it was a combination of how data was pulled from the tools plus human error in inputting the data into a spreadsheet. There was no check and balance before the data was actually processed and presented to key people in the organization.

The output of logical groupings could be in spreadsheets, reports generated directly from the service management tool suite, system monitoring and reporting tools, or telephony tools such as an automatic call distribution tool.

Processing the data is an important CSI activity that is often overlooked. While monitoring and collecting data on a single infrastructure component is important, it is also important to understand that component's impact on the larger infrastructure and IT service. Knowing that a server was up 99.99% of the time is one thing; knowing that no one could access the server is another. An example of processing the data is taking the data from monitoring of individual components, such as the mainframe, applications, WAN, LAN, servers etc., and processing it into a structure of an end-to-end service from the customer's perspective.

Key questions that need to be addressed in the processing activity are:

- What is the frequency of processing the data? This could be hourly, daily, weekly or monthly. When introducing a new service or service management process it is a good idea to monitor and process in shorter intervals than longer intervals. How often analysis and trend investigation activities take place will drive how often the data is processed.
- What format is required for the output? This is also driven by how analysis is carried out and ultimately how the information is used.
- What tools and systems can be used for processing the data?
- How do we evaluate the accuracy of the processed data?

There are two aspects to processing data. One is automated and the other is manual. While both are important and contribute greatly to the measuring process, accuracy is a major differentiator between the two types. The accuracy of the automated data gathering and processing is not the issue here. Nearly all CSI-related data will be gathered by automated means. Human data gathering and processing is the issue. It is important for staff to properly document their compliance activities, to update logs and records. Common excuses are that people are too busy, that this is not important or that it is not their job. Ongoing communication about the benefits of performing administrative tasks is of utmost importance. Tying these administrative tasks to job performance is one way to alleviate this issue.

Inputs to processing data include:

- Data collected through monitoring
- Reporting requirements
- SLAs
- OLAs
- Service catalogue
- List of metrics, KPI, CSF, objectives and goals
- Report frequency
- Report template.

Figure 4.3 and Table 4.3 show common procedures for processing data.

A flow diagram is nice to look at and gracefully summarizes the procedure but it does not contain all the required information. It is important to

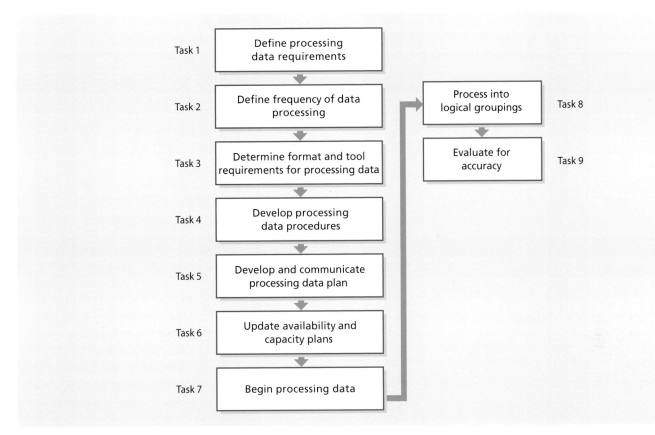

*Figure 4.3  Common procedures for processing the data*

**Table 4.3 Procedures for processing the data**

| Tasks | Procedures |
|---|---|
| Task 1 | Based on strategy, goals and SLAs, define the data processing requirements. |
| Task 2 | Determine frequency of processing the data. |
| | Determine method of processing the data. |
| Task 3 | Identify and document the format of logical grouping of data elements. |
| | Define tools required for processing data. |
| | Build, purchase or modify tools for measuring. |
| | Test tool. |
| | Install tool. |
| Task 4 | Develop processing data procedures. |
| | Train people on procedures. |
| Task 5 | Develop and communicate monitoring plan. |
| | Get approval from internal IT and external vendors who may be impacted. |
| Task 6 | Update availability and capacity plans if required. |
| Task 7 | Begin the data processing. |
| Task 8 | Process into logical groupings. |
| Task 9 | Evaluate processed data for accuracy. |

translate the flow diagram in a more meaningful way so that people can understand the procedure with the appropriate level of detail, including roles and responsibilities, timeframes, inputs and outputs, and more.

While it is important to identify the outputs of each activity such as data and decisions, it is even more important to determine the output of the procedure, the level of detail, the quality, the format etc.

Examples of outputs of processing data from procedures include:

■ Updated availability and capacity plans
■ Reports
■ Logical groupings of data ready for analysis.

### 4.1.5.5 Step 5 – Analyse the information and data

Your organization's service desk has a trend of reduced call volumes consistently over the last four months. Even though this is a trend, you need to ask yourself the question: 'Is this a good trend or a bad trend?' You don't know if the call reduction is because you have reduced the number of recurring errors in the infrastructure by good problem management activities or if the customers feel that the service desk doesn't provide any value and have started bypassing the service desk and going directly to second-level support groups.

Data analysis transforms the information into knowledge of the events that are affecting the organization. More skill and experience is required to perform data analysis than data gathering and processing. Verification against goals and objectives is expected during this activity. This verification validates that objectives are being supported and value is being added. It is not sufficient to simply produce graphs of various types but to document the observations and conclusions.

*Question: What do you actually analyse?*

*Answer:* Once the data is processed into information, you can then analyse the results, looking for answers to questions such as:

■ Are there any clear trends?
■ Are they positive or negative trends?
■ Are changes required?
■ Are we operating according to plan?
■ Are we meeting targets?

■ Are improvements required?
■ Are there underlying structural problems?

In this step you apply knowledge to your information. Without this, you have nothing more than sets of numbers showing metrics that are meaningless. It is not enough to simply look at this month's figures and accept them without question, even if they meet SLA targets. You should analyse the figures to stay ahead of the game. Without analysis you merely have information. With analysis you have knowledge. If you find anomalies or poor results, then look for ways to improve.

It is interesting to note the number of job titles for IT professionals that contain the word 'analyst' and even more surprising to discover that few of these professionals actually analyse anything. This step takes time. It requires concentration, knowledge, skills, experience etc. One of the major assumptions is that the automated processing, reporting, monitoring tool has actually done the analysis. Too often people simply point at a trend and say, 'Look, numbers have gone up over the last quarter.' However, key questions need to be asked, such as:

■ Is this good?
■ Is this bad?
■ Is this expected?
■ Is this in line with targets?
■ Are there any side effects (whether positive or negative) on any other process, component of the system, or service?

Combining multiple data points on a graph may look nice but it is important to know what it means. There is a saying 'A picture is worth a thousand words'; in analysing the data one needs to ask, 'Which thousand words?' To transform this data into knowledge, compare the information from Step 3 against the requirements from Step 2 and what could realistically be measured from this step.

Be sure also to compare the information with the clearly defined objectives with measurable targets that were set in the service design, transition and operations lifecycle stages. Seek confirmation that these objectives and the milestones were reached. If not, have improvement initiatives been implemented? If so, then the CSI activities start again by gathering data, processing data and analysing data to identify if the desired improvement in service quality has been achieved.

At the completion of each significant stage or milestone, conduct a review to ensure the objectives have been met. It is possible here to use the post-implementation review (PIR) from the change management process. The PIR will include a review of supporting documentation and the general awareness among staff of the refined processes or service. A comparison is required of what has been achieved against the original goals.

During the analysis activity, but after the results are compiled and the trends analysed and evaluated, it is recommended that internal meetings be held within IT managers to review the results and collectively identify improvement opportunities. It is important to have these internal meetings before you begin presenting and using the information, which is the next activity of CSI. IT is a key player in determining how the results and any actions items are presented to the business.

This puts IT in a better position to formulate a plan of presenting the results and any action items to the business and senior IT management. Throughout this publication the terms 'service' and 'service management' have been used extensively. IT is too often focused on managing the various systems used by the business, often (but incorrectly) equating service and system. A service is actually made up of systems as well as other entities such as people and suppliers. Therefore if an IT service provider wants to be perceived as a key player, it must move from a systems-based organization to a service-based organization. This transition will force the improvement of communication between the different IT silos that exist in many IT organizations.

Performing proper analysis on the data also places the business in a position to make strategic, tactical and operational decisions about whether there is a need for service improvement. Unfortunately, the analysis activity is often not performed. Whether this is because of lack of people with the right skills and/or simply a lack of time is unclear. What is clear is that without proper analysis, errors will continue to occur and mistakes will continue to be repeated. There will be little improvement.

Data analysis transforms the information into knowledge of the events that are affecting the organization. As an example, a sub-activity of capacity management is workload management. This involves analysing the data to determine which customers use what resource, how they use the resource, when they use the resource and how this impacts the overall performance of the resource. You will also be able to see if there is a trend on the usage of the resource over a period of time. From an incremental improvement process this could lead to some focus on demand management, or influencing the behaviour of customers.

Consideration must be given to the skills required to analyse from both a technical viewpoint and from an interpretation viewpoint.

When analysing data, it is important to seek answers to questions such as:

- Are operations running according to plan? This could be a project plan, financial plan, availability plan, capacity plan or even an IT service continuity management (ITSCM) plan.
- Are targets defined in SLAs or the service catalogue being met?
- Are there underlying structural problems that can be identified?
- Are improvements required?
- Are there any trends? If so, what are the trends showing? Are they positive trends or negative trends?
- What is leading to or causing the trends?

Reviewing trends over a period of time is another important task. It is not good enough to see a 'snapshot' of a data point at a specific moment in time, but to look at the data points over a period of time. How did we do this month compared with last month, this quarter compared with last quarter, this year compared with last year?

It is not enough only to look at the results; one needs to look at what led to the results for the current period. If we had a bad month, was it because of an anomaly? Is this a demonstrable trend or simply a one-off?

Trends are an indicator that more analysis is needed to understand what is causing it. When a trend goes up or down it is a signal that further investigation is needed to determine if it is positive or negative.

Without analysis the data is merely information. With analysis come improvement opportunities.

**Example of the benefits of trend analysis**

When one organization started performing trend analysis activities around incident management, it discovered that the number of incidents increased for a one month period every three months. When staff investigated the cause, they found it was tied directly to a quarterly release of an application change. This provided statistical data for them to review the effectiveness of their change management and release and deployment management processes as well as understand the impact each release would have on the service desk with the number of increased call volumes. The service desk was also able to begin identifying key skill sets needed to support this specific application.

**Example of different ways of interpreting trends**

A change manager communicates that the change management process is doing well because the volume of requests for changes has steadily decreased. Is this positive or negative? If problem management is working well, it could be positive as recurring incidents are removed, therefore fewer changes are required as the infrastructure is more stable. However, if users have stopped submitting requests for changes because the process is not meeting expectations, the trend is negative.

Throughout CSI, assessment should identify whether targets were achieved and, if so, whether new targets (and therefore new KPIs) need to be defined. If targets were achieved but the perception has not improved, then new targets may need to be set and new measures put in place to ensure that these new targets are being met.

When analysing the results from process metrics keep in mind that a process will only be as efficient as its limited bottleneck activity. So if the analysis shows that a process activity is not efficient and continually creates a bottleneck then this would be a logical place to begin looking for a process improvement opportunity.

Inputs include:

- Results of the monitored data
- Existing KPIs and targets
- Perceptions from customer satisfaction surveys etc.

### 4.1.5.6 Step 6 – Present and use the information

**Key message**

Presenting the information is synonymous with service reporting (see section 5.7)

The sixth step is to take our knowledge, which is represented in the reports, monitors, action plans, reviews, evaluations and opportunities, and present it to the target audience in a clear, digestible and timely way. Consider the target audience; make sure that you identify exceptions to the service, benefits that have been revealed, or can be expected. Data gathering occurs at the operational level of an organization. Format this data into knowledge that all levels can appreciate and gain insight into their needs and expectations.

This stage involves presenting the information in a format that is understandable, at the right level, provides value, notes exceptions to service, identifies benefits that were revealed during the time period, and allows those receiving the information to make strategic, tactical and operational decisions. In other words, present the information in the manner that makes it the most useful for the target audience.

Most organizations create reports and present information to some extent or another; however, it is often not done well. Many organizations simply take the gathered raw data (often straight from the tool) and report it to everyone, without necessarily processing or analysing the data. The report should emphasize and ideally highlight areas where the recipient needs to take action.

The other issue often associated with presenting and using information is that it is overdone. Managers at all levels are bombarded with too many emails, too many meetings, too many reports. The reality is that the managers often don't need this information or, at the very least, not in that format. It is often unclear what role the manager has in making decisions and providing guidance on improvement programmes.

As we have discussed, CSI is an ongoing activity of monitoring and gathering data, processing the data into logical groupings, and analysing it in order to meet targets, and identify trends and improvement opportunities. There is no value in all the work done to this point if we don't do a good job of presenting our findings and then using them to make decisions that will lead to improvements.

Begin with the end in mind is habit number 2 in Stephen Covey's *The Seven Habits of Highly Effective People*.[3] Even though the book is about personal leadership, the habit holds true with presenting and using information. In addition to understanding the target audience, it is also important to understand the purpose of any information being presented. If the purpose and value cannot be articulated, then it is important to question if it is needed at all.

There are usually four distinct audiences:

- **The customers**   Their real need is to understand whether IT delivered the service they promised at the levels they promised and, if not, what improvements are being implemented to improve the situation.
- **Senior IT management**   This group is often focused on the results surrounding CSFs and KPIs, such as customer satisfaction, actual versus plan, and costing and revenue targets. Information provided at this level helps determine strategic and tactical improvements on a larger scale. Senior IT management often wants this type of information provided in the form of a balanced scorecard or IT scorecard format to see the big picture at one glance.
- **Internal IT**   This group is often interested in KPIs and activity metrics that help them plan, coordinate, schedule and identify incremental improvement opportunities.
- **Suppliers**   This group will be interested in KPIs and activity metrics related to their own services and performance. Suppliers may also be targeted with improvement initiatives.

Often there is a gap between what IT reports and what is of interest to the business. IT is famous for reporting availability in percentages such as '99.85% available'. In most cases this is not calculated from an end-to-end perspective but only considers mainframe or server availability or application availability; it often doesn't take into consideration LAN/WAN or desktop downtime. In reality, most people in IT don't know the difference between 99.95% and 99.99% availability, let alone other people in the business. Yet reports continue to show availability achievements in percentages.

What the business really wants to understand is the number of outages that occurred and the duration of the outages with an analysis describing the impact on the business processes, in essence, unavailability expressed in a commonly understood measure – time. Of course what the business is really interested in is what the service provider is going to do to prevent it happening again.

Now more than ever, IT managers must invest the time to understand specific business goals and translate IT metrics to reflect an impact against these goals. Businesses invest in tools and services that affect productivity, and support should be one of those services. The major challenge, and one that can be met, is to communicate effectively the business benefits of a well-run IT support group. The starting point is a new perspective on goals, measures, reporting and how IT actions affect business results. You will then be prepared to answer the question: 'How does IT help to generate value for your company?'

Although most reports tend to concentrate on areas where things are not going as well as hoped for, do not forget to report on the good news as well. A report showing improvement trends is IT services' best marketing vehicle. It is vitally important that reports show whether CSI has actually improved the overall service provision and, if it has not, the actions taken to rectify the situation.

Figure 4.4 is an example of an SLA monitoring chart that provides a visual representation of an organization's ability to meet defined targets over a period of months.

These are some of the common problems associated with the presenting and reporting activity:

- Everyone (business, senior management and IT managers) gets the same report.
- The format is not what people want. It is important to understand the audience and how they like to receive information. Some like the information in text format, some in graphs, some in pie charts etc. It is hard to please everyone, but getting agreement on the report format is a step in the right direction.

This is why many organizations are moving to a balanced scorecard or IT scorecard concept. This concept can start at the business level, then

---

[3] Covey, S. (1989). *The Seven Habits of Highly Effective People*. Free Press, New York.

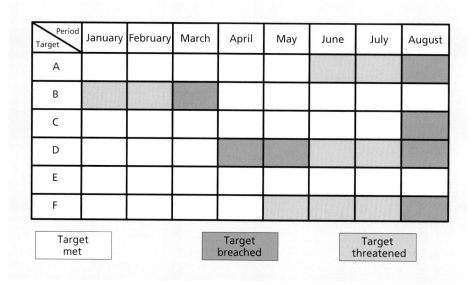

*Figure 4.4 Service level achievement chart*

the IT level, and then functional groups and/or services within IT.

■ Lack of an executive summary – the executive summary should discuss the current results, what led to the results and what actions have or will be taken to address any issues.

■ Reports are not linked to any baseline, IT scorecard or balanced scorecard.

■ Too much supporting data is provided.

■ Reports are presented in terms that are not understandable. For example, availability is reported in percentages when the business often is interested in knowing the number, duration and impact of outages.

The resources required to produce, verify and distribute reports should not be underestimated. Even with automation, this can be a time-consuming activity.

When measuring and reporting, IT managers need to shift from their normal way of reporting to a more business view that the business can really understand. As discussed above, the traditional IT approach on measuring and reporting availability is to present the results in percentages, but these are often at a component level and not at the service level. Availability when measured and reported should reflect the experience of the customer. Below are the common measurements that are meaningful to a customer:

■ Number of outages on each service, e.g. there were two outages this month on Service 1

■ Duration of outages for each service, e.g. Service 1 outages lasted 179 minutes

■ The impact of the outages to each business, e.g. Business 1 uses five services; there were 11 outages, whose total duration was 1,749 minutes. During this time the business was unable to generate revenue.

Inputs include:

■ Collated information
■ Format details and templates etc.
■ Stakeholder contact details.

*Note:* The results from Step 6 may indicate the need for improvement initiatives. In all such cases use the CSI register to document the requirements and initiatives.

### 4.1.5.7 Step 7 – Implement improvement

Use the knowledge gained and combine it with previous experience to make informed decisions about optimizing, improving and correcting services. Managers need to identify issues and present solutions.

This stage may include any number of activities such as approval of improvement activities, prioritization and submitting a business case, integration with change management, integration with other lifecycle stages, and guidance on how to manage an ongoing improvement project successfully, and on checking whether the improvement actually achieved its objective.

**Example of poor advice**

An organization hired an expensive consulting firm to assess the maturity of the processes against the ITIL framework. The report from the consulting organization had the following observation and recommendation about the incident management process:

*'The help desk is not doing incident management the way ITIL does. Our recommendation is that you must implement incident management.'*

The reaction from the customer was simple. They fired the consulting organization.

CSI identifies many opportunities for improvement, but organizations cannot afford to implement all of them. As discussed earlier, an organization needs to prioritize improvement activities for its goals, objectives, return on investment (ROI), types of service breaches etc., and document them in the CSI register. Improvement initiatives can also be externally driven by regulatory requirements, changes in competition, or even political decisions.

If organizations were implementing improvement according to CSI, there would be no need for this publication. Improvement often takes place in reaction to a single event that caused a (severe) outage to part or all of the organization. At other times, minor problems are noticed and specific improvements are implemented in no relation to the priorities of the organization, thus taking valuable resources away from real emergencies. This is common practice but obviously not best practice.

After a decision to improve a service and/or service management process is made, then the service lifecycle continues. A new service strategy may be defined, service design builds the changes, service transition implements the changes into production and then service operation manages the day-to-day operations of the service and/or service management processes. Keep in mind that CSI activities continue through each stage of the service lifecycle.

Each service lifecycle stage requires resources to build or modify the services and/or service management processes, potential new technology or modifications to existing technology, potential changes to KPIs and other metrics, and possibly even new or modified OLAs or underpinning contracts (UCs) to support SLAs. Communication,

training and documentation are required to move a new or improved service, tool or service management process into production.

**Example of improvement being implemented**

A financial organization with a strategically important website continually failed to meet its operational targets, especially with regard to the quality of service delivered by the site. The prime reason for this was its lack of focus on the monitoring of operational events, service availability and response. This situation was allowed to develop until senior business managers demanded action from the senior IT management. There were major repercussions, and reviews were undertaken to determine the underlying cause of the failure to meet an acceptable quality of service. After considerable pain and disruption, an operations group was identified to monitor this particular service. A part of the requirement was the establishment of weekly internal reviews and weekly reports on operational performance. Operational events were immediately investigated whenever they occurred and were individually reviewed after resolution. An improvement team was established, with representation from all areas, to implement the recommendations from the reviews and the feedback from the monitoring group. This eventually resulted in considerable improvement in the quality of service delivered to the business and its customers.

Often steps are forgotten or are taken for granted, or someone assumes that someone else has completed the step. This indicates a breakdown in the process and a lack of understanding of roles and responsibilities. The harsh reality is that some steps are overdone while others are incomplete or overlooked.

There are various levels of management in an organization; when implementing improvements it is important to understand which level to focus their activities on. Managers need to show overall performance and improvement. Directors need to show that quality and performance targets are being met, while risk is being minimized. Overall, senior management need to know what is going on so they can make informed choices and exercise judgement. Each level has its own perspective. Understanding these perspectives is where maximum value of information is leveraged.

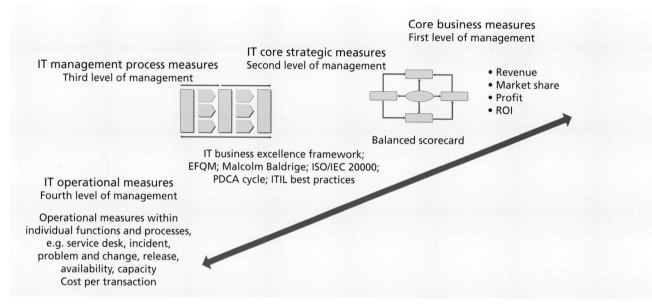

**Figure 4.5 First- to fourth-order drivers**

Understanding the level your intended audience occupies and their drivers helps you present the issues and benefits of your process in the correct manner. At the highest level of the organization are the strategic thinkers. Reports need to be short, quick to read and aligned to their drivers. Discussions about risk avoidance, protecting the image or brand of the organization, profitability and cost savings are compelling reasons to support your improvement efforts.

The second level of management consists of vice presidents and directors. Reports can be more detailed, but need to summarize findings over time. Identifying how processes support the business objectives, early warning around issues that place the business at risk, and alignment to existing measurement frameworks that they use are strong methods you can use to sell the process benefits to them.

The third level of management consists of managers and high level supervisors. Compliance to stated objectives, overall team and process performance, insight into resource constraints and continual improvement initiatives are their drivers. Measurements and reports need to market how these are being supported by the process outputs.

Lastly at the fourth level of the hierarchy are the staff members and team leaders. At a personal level, the personal benefits need to be emphasized. Therefore metrics that show their individual performance, provide recognition of

their skills (and gaps in skills) and identify training opportunities are essential in getting these people to participate in the processes willingly.

The four levels of management are shown in Figure 4.5.

Inputs include:

■ Knowledge gained from presenting and using the information
■ Agreed implementation plans (from Step 6)
■ A CSI register for those initiatives that have been initiated from other sources.

*Note:* Implementing improvement is also discussed in section 5.1.2 and assessments are discussed in section 5.2.

### 4.1.6 Triggers, inputs, outputs and interfaces

Monitoring to identify improvement opportunities is and must be an ongoing process. New incentives may trigger additional measurement activity such as changing business requirements, poor performance with a process or spiralling costs.

Many inputs and outputs to the process are documented within the steps discussed earlier but examples of key inputs include:

■ Service catalogue
■ SLRs
■ The service review meeting
■ Vision and mission statements

- Corporate, divisional and departmental goals and objectives
- Legislative requirements
- Governance requirements
- Budget cycle
- Customer satisfaction surveys
- The overall IT strategy
- Market expectations (especially in relation to competitive IT service providers)
- New technology drivers (e.g. cloud based delivery and external hosting)
- Flexible commercial models (e.g. low capital expenditure and high operational expenditure commercial models, and rental models).

### 4.1.6.1 Interfaces

In order to support improvement activities it is important to have CSI integrated within each lifecycle stage including the underlying processes residing in each lifecycle stage. Each step of the CSI lifecycle will be involved in every one of the other lifecycle stages.

Examples include monitoring the progress of strategies, standards, policies and architectural decisions that have been made and implemented. Service strategy will also analyse results associated with implemented strategies, policies and standards.

Within the service design stage, monitoring and gathering data are associated with creating and modifying services and service management processes. This part of the service lifecycle also measures against the effectiveness and ability to measure CSFs and KPIs that were defined through gathering business requirements. It is during service design that the definition of what should be measured is produced. Service design analyses current results of design and project activities. Trends are also noted with results compared against the design goals. Service design also identifies improvement opportunities and analyses the effectiveness and ability to measure CSFs and KPIs that were defined when gathering business requirements.

Service transition develops and tests the monitoring procedures and criteria to be used during and after implementation. Service transition monitors and gathers data on the actual release into production of services and service management processes. Service transition develops

the monitoring procedures and criteria to be used during and after implementation.

It is during the service operation lifecycle stage that the actual monitoring of services in the live environment takes place. People working in the service operation functions will play a large part in the processing activity. Service operation staff provide input into what can be measured and processed into logical groupings, and then process the data. Service operation staff would also be responsible for taking the component data and processing it in the format to provide a better end-to-end perspective of the service achievements. Service operation staff analyse current results as well as trends over a period of time. Service operation staff also identify both incremental and large-scale improvement opportunities, providing input into what can be measured and processed into logical groupings. They also perform the actual data processing.

The seven-step improvement process receives and collects the data as an input. If there is a CSI functional group within an organization, it can be the single point for combining all analysis, trend data and comparison of results to targets. This group could then review all proposed improvement opportunities and help prioritize the opportunities and finally make a consolidated recommendation to senior management. For smaller organizations, this may fall to an individual or smaller group acting as a coordinating point and owning CSI. This is a key point. Too often data is gathered in the various technical domains never to be heard of again. Designating a CSI group provides a single place in the organization for all the data to reside and be analysed.

### 4.1.7 Role of other processes in gathering and processing the data (Steps 3 and 4)

All the ITIL processes have responsibility for continual improvement of the process itself. The process metrics will indicate where improvements or cost reductions can be made. Some of the key processes related to general improvement are documented below.

### 4.1.7.1 Service level management

The SLM process is fully documented in *ITIL Service Design*. It is important the CSI is involved in the design of SLM and has a constant interface with the SLM team to ensure that measurable targets are created from which to identify potential service improvements.

The SLM process plays a key role in CSI activities and supports the seven-step improvement process by helping to drive what to measure and monitoring requirements, and by reporting service level achievements. This provides input into CSI activities and helps prioritize improvement projects.

SLM is essential in any organization so that the levels of IT service needed to support the business can be determined and monitoring can be initiated to identify whether the required service levels are being achieved.

If an organization is outsourcing its service provision to a third party, the issue of service improvement should be discussed at the outset and covered (and budgeted for) in the contract, otherwise there is no incentive during the lifetime of the contract for suppliers to improve service targets if they are already meeting contractual obligations and additional expenditure is needed to make the improvements.

SLM plays a key role in the data gathering activity as SLM is responsible for defining not only business requirements but also IT's capabilities to achieve them:

■ SLM needs to look at what is happening with the monitoring data to ensure that end-to-end service performance is being monitored and analysed.

■ SLM should also identify who gets the data, whether any analysis takes place on the data before it is presented, and if any trend evaluation is undertaken to understand the performance over a period of time. This information will be helpful in following CSI activities.

■ Through the negotiation process with the business, SLM would define what to measure and which aspects to report. This would in turn drive the monitoring and data collection requirements. If there is no capability to monitor and/or collect data on an item then it should not appear in the SLA. SLM should be a part of the review process to monitor results.

■ SLM is responsible for developing and getting agreement on OLAs and external UCs that require internal or external monitoring.

SLM supports the CSI data processing activity by:

■ Ensuring that the SLAs only incorporate measurements that truly can be measured and reported on

■ Negotiating and documenting OLAs and UCs that define the required measurements

■ Reviewing the results of the processed data from an end-to-end approach

■ Helping define the reporting frequency of processing and reporting formats.

### 4.1.7.2 Availability management and capacity management

Availability management and capacity management support the data processing activities of CSI by:

■ Providing significant input into existing monitoring and data collection capabilities and tool requirements to meet new data collection requirements, and ensuring the availability and capacity plans are updated to reflect new or modified monitoring and data collection requirements

■ Being accountable for the actual infrastructure monitoring and data collection activities that take place; therefore roles and responsibilities need to be defined and the roles filled with properly skilled and trained staff

■ Being accountable for ensuring tools are in place to gather data

■ Being accountable for ensuring that the actual monitoring and data collection activities are consistently performed

■ Being responsible for processing the data at a component level and then working with SLM to provide service level data

■ Processing data on KPIs such as availability or performance measures

■ Utilizing the agreed reporting formats

■ Analysing processed data for accuracy.

### 4.1.7.3 Event management, incident management and service desk

Event management, incident management and the service desk support the data processing activities of CSI:

- Through incident management defining monitoring requirements to support event and incident detection through automation; incident management also has the ability to automatically open incidents and/or auto-escalate incidents
- Through event management automatically monitoring events and producing alerts, some of which may require CSI activities to correct
- Through event and incident monitoring identifying abnormal situations and conditions, which helps with predicting and pre-empting situations and conditions thereby avoiding possible service and component failures
- By monitoring the response times, repair times, resolution times and incident escalations
- By monitoring telephony items such as call volumes, average speed of answer, call abandonment rates etc. so that immediate action can be taken when there is an increase in contacts to the service desk; this is important for the service desk as a single point of contact; it also applies to those service desks that provide support via email and the web
- By processing data on incidents and service requests such as who is using the service desk and what is the nature of the incidents
- By collecting and processing data on KPIs such as MTRS and percentage of incidents resolved within service targets
- By processing data for telephony statistics at the service desk such as number of inbound/outbound calls, average talk time, average speed of answer, abandoned calls etc.
- By utilizing the agreed reporting format
- By analysing processed data for accuracy.

### 4.1.7.4 Information security management

Information security management contributes to monitoring and data collection by:

- Defining security monitoring and data collection requirements
- Monitoring, verifying and tracking the levels of security according to the organizational security policies and guidelines
- Assisting in determining effects of security measures on the data monitoring and collection from the confidentiality (accessible only to those who should), integrity (data is accurate and not corrupted or not corruptible) and availability (data is available when needed) perspectives
- Processing response and resolution data on security incidents
- Creating trend analyses on security breaches
- Validating success of risk mitigation strategies
- Utilizing the agreed upon reporting format
- Analysing processed data for accuracy.

### 4.1.7.5 Financial management for IT services

Financial management for IT services is responsible for monitoring and collecting data associated with the actual expenditures versus budget and is able to provide input on questions such as whether costing or revenue targets are on track. Financial management for IT services should also monitor the ongoing cost per service etc.

In addition financial management for IT services will provide the necessary templates to assist CSI to create the budget and expenditure reports for the various improvement initiatives as well as providing the means to compute the ROI of the improvements.

## 4.1.8 Role of other processes in analysing the data (Step 5)

### 4.1.8.1 Service level management

SLM supports the CSI data analysis activity by:

- Analysing the service level achievements compared to SLAs and service level targets
- Documenting and reviewing trends over a period of time to identify any consistent patterns
- Identifying improvement opportunities
- Identifying the need to modify existing OLAs or UCs.

### 4.1.8.2 Availability management and capacity management

Availability management and capacity management support the CSI data analysis activity by:

- Analysing and identifying trends on component and service data
- Comparing results with prior months, quarters or annual reports

- Identifying the need for updating the requirement for improvement in gathering and processing data
- Analysing the performance of components against defined technical specifications
- Documenting and reviewing trends over a period of time to identify any consistent patterns
- Identifying improvement opportunities
- Analysing processed data for accuracy.

### 4.1.8.3 Incident management and service desk

Incident management and service desk support the CSI data analysis activity by:

- Documenting and reviewing incident trends on incidents, service requests and telephony statistics over a period of time to identify any consistent patterns
- Comparing results with prior months, quarters or annual reports
- Comparing results with agreed-to levels of service
- Identifying improvement opportunities
- Analysing processed data for accuracy.

### 4.1.8.4 Problem management

Problem management plays a key role in the analysis activity as this process supports other processes in identifying trends and performing root cause analysis. Problem management is usually associated with reducing incidents, but a good problem management process is also involved in helping define process-related problems as well as those associated with services.

Overall, problem management seeks to:

- Perform root cause investigation as to what is leading identified trends
- Recommend improvement opportunities
- Compare results with prior results
- Compare results to agreed service levels.

### 4.1.8.5 Information security management

Information security management relies on the activities of other processes to help determine the cause of security related incidents and problems. Information security management will submit requests for changes to implement corrections or for new updates to, for example, the anti-virus software. Other processes such as availability management (recoverability), capacity management (capacity and performance) and ITSCM (planning on how to handle crisis) will assist in planning longer term. In turn information security management will play a key role in assisting CSI regarding all security aspects of improvement initiatives or for security-related improvements by:

- Documenting and reviewing security incidents for the current time period
- Comparing results with prior results
- Identifying the need for a SIP or improvements
- Analysing processed data for accuracy.

## 4.1.9 Role of other processes in presenting and using the information (Step 6)

### 4.1.9.1 Service level management

SLM presents information to the business and discusses the service achievements for the current time period as well as any longer trends that were identified. These discussions should also include information about what led to the results and any incremental or fine-tuning actions required.

Overall, SLM:

- Conducts consistent service review meetings (internal and external)
- Supports the preparation of reports
- Updates the SLA monitoring (SLAM) chart
- Provides input into prioritizing improvement activities.

### 4.1.9.2 Availability management and capacity management

Availability management and capacity management support the CSI presentation activity by:

- Supporting preparation of the reports
- Providing input into prioritizing SIP or improvements
- Implementing incremental or fine-tuning activities that do not require business approval.

### 4.1.9.3 Incident management and service desk

Incident management and service desk support the CSI presentation activity by:

- Supporting preparation of the reports
- Providing input into prioritizing SIPs or improvements
- Implementing incremental or fine-tuning activities that do not require business approval.

### 4.1.9.4 Problem management

Problem management supports the CSI presentation activity by:

- Providing input into service improvement initiatives and prioritizing improvement initiatives
- Supporting preparation of the reports
- Providing input into prioritizing SIP or improvements
- Implementing incremental or fine-tuning activities that do not require business approval.

## 4.1.10 Role of other processes in implementing improvement (Step 7)

### 4.1.10.1 Change management

When CSI determines that an improvement to a service is warranted, a request for change (RFC) must be submitted. The RFC will be prioritized and categorized according to policies and procedures defined in the change management process. Release and deployment management, as a part of service transition, is responsible for moving this change to the live environment. Once the change is implemented, CSI is part of the PIR to assess the success or failure of the change. All non-standard changes should be assessed by staff involved in CSI.

### 4.1.10.2 Service level management

The SLM process often generates a good starting point for identifying improvement opportunities – and the service review process may drive this. Where an underlying difficulty that is adversely impacting service quality is identified, SLM should, in conjunction with problem management and availability management, log an improvement opportunity in the CSI register. SLM will then be involved in the later review and prioritization

of the CSI register and in building appropriate SIPs to identify and implement whatever actions are necessary to overcome the difficulties and restore service quality. SIP initiatives may also focus on such issues as training, system testing and documentation. In these cases, the relevant people need to be involved and adequate feedback given to make improvements for the future. At any time, a number of separate initiatives that form part of the SIP may be running in parallel to address difficulties with a number of services.

Some organizations have established an annual budget line held by SLM from which SIP initiatives can be funded.

If an organization is outsourcing delivery of service to a third party, the issue of service improvement should be discussed at the outset and covered (and budgeted for) in the contract, otherwise there is no incentive during the lifetime of the contract for the supplier to improve service targets.

## 4.1.11 Information management

As indicated in the activities, the information required to understand what needs to be improved and by how much and when comes from many sources. It is important that to get a full and clear picture we gather and analyse all information. Some important examples are:

- The service catalogue
- SLRs
- Monitored and reported SLA targets
- Service knowledge management system (SKMS) and configuration management system (CMS)
- Process metrics
- Customer satisfactory surveys
- Complaints and compliments
- All data, information, knowledge produced by the process itself.

Much of the data and information will be initially gathered and held in technology-specific repositories but will need to be summarized and held as part of the SKMS for analysis and reporting purposes.

## 4.1.12 Critical success factors and key performance indicators

The following list includes some sample CSFs for the seven-step improvement process. Each organization should identify appropriate CSFs based on its objectives for the process. Each sample CSF is followed by a typical KPI that supports the CSF. These KPIs should not be adopted without careful consideration. Each organization should develop KPIs that are appropriate for its level of maturity, its CSFs and its particular circumstances. Achievement against KPIs should be monitored and used to identify opportunities for improvement, which should be logged in the CSI register for evaluation and possible implementation.

Note that because of the nature of the seven-step improvement process, it has to be applied to appropriate processes, activities, technology, organizational structure, people and partners for the benefits to be realized. This means that the KPIs used to judge the success of the seven-step improvement process are actually the KPIs from the other lifecycle stages and processes to which it has been applied. As a result the examples given here come from other areas.

- **CSF**  All improvement opportunities identified
  - **KPI**  Percentage improvement in defects; for example, 3% reduction in failed changes; 10% reduction in security breaches
- **CSF**  The cost of providing services is reduced
  - **KPI**  Percentage decrease in overall cost of service provision; for example, 2.5% reduction in the average cost of handling an incident; 5% reduction in the cost of processing a particular type of transaction
- **CSF**  The required business outcomes from IT services are achieved
  - **KPI**  A 3% increase in customer satisfaction with the service desk; 2% increase in customer satisfaction with the warranty offered by the payroll service.

## 4.1.13 Challenges and risks

Challenges facing organizations when implementing CSI include getting the required resources to implement and run the process, and gathering the right level of data and having the tools to manipulate it. Another challenge is to get the willingness of the IT organization to approach CSI in a consistent and structured way. The challenge is to make that IT manager realize that there is another way, and get commitment from management to approach it in that better way. Another challenge is obtaining sufficient information from the business regarding improvement requirements and cost reductions. A further challenge is persuading suppliers to include improvement in their contractual agreements; this is especially relevant for outsourced services.

There are several risks that could prevent CSI from achieving the overall desired effect:

- No formalized approach to CSI and initiatives being taken on randomly in an *ad-hoc* manner
- Insufficient monitoring and analysis to identify the areas of greatest need
- Staff attitude such as 'We have always done it this way and it has always been good enough'
- Inability to make the business case for improvement and therefore no funding for improvement initiatives
- Lack of ownership or loss of ownership
- Too much focus on IT improvements without clear understanding of business needs and objectives.

# Continual service improvement methods and techniques

# 5 Continual service improvement methods and techniques

## 5.1 METHODS AND TECHNIQUES

A wide variety of methods and techniques can be used in the continual service improvement (CSI) activities ranging from 'soft and vague' to 'factual and scientific', often providing either both or a mixture of qualitative and quantitative measurement results. To ensure consistency of execution and effective measurement, especially for the activities of gathering and processing data, the techniques and methods that are used should be clearly documented in advance and communicated to the staff who will be responsible for their execution. To increase the trustworthiness of the factual data delivered to these processes it may be required for these processes to be audited for compliance to the agreed and prescribed methods and techniques.

An effective choice of methods and techniques for the analysis, presentation and use of the measurement information is highly dependent on the particular circumstances in which these tasks are performed and can generally not be documented in advance. A goal-oriented attitude and professional expertise and education of the individuals are required.

### 5.1.1 Effort and cost

CSI improvement activities can require a considerable amount of effort and money for larger-scale improvement projects to minimal time and effort for some incremental improvements. If the effort is going to be costly then the organization, both IT and the business, has to ask whether it is worth it. So the business case including an analysis of the return on investment (ROI) will have to be made.

Let's first look at the costs of implementing and operating a measurement framework for IT service provision. Possible major cost topics are:

- **Labour cost** Salaries of the organization's staff who are involved in implementing the measurement framework or who spend effort on performing one of the activities in operating or maintaining the measurement framework,

including costs associated with managing it. If (part of) IT is outsourced, the external provider costs should be included here too.
- **Tooling cost** Purchase, licences, installation and configuration, maintenance costs of hardware, software and other equipment specifically used for the measurement activities. Tools could be a cost on the provider, which they will pass on back to you.
- **Training cost** Cost of training and coaching staff in the use of measurement methods, techniques, tools and procedures.
- **Expertise cost** Payments to hired experts and consulting firms, typically for the planning, implementation and maintenance activities pertaining to the measurement framework. Also includes the out-of-pocket costs of acquiring information used in the measurement framework that is not in the possession of the organization itself such as benchmarking data.

When deciding whether the measurement framework is worth the effort, consider the amounts to spend on:
- **Implementation** Initial costs of the measurement framework, and if it changes. In practice these types of costs can be reliably estimated and controlled by using a project-oriented approach.
- **Operation** The level of costs associated with the operation of the measurement framework is largely fixed as a result of the way it is designed and equipped.
- **Maintenance** The level of these types of cost depends mainly on the expected rate at which the measurement framework will require adaptation to changing circumstances and on the quality of its implementation.

### 5.1.2 Implementation review and evaluation

Implementation review and evaluation is key to determining the effectiveness of a CSI improvement programme. Some common questions for review include:

- Were we correct in our assessment of the current situation and in defining the problem statement?
- When defining the goals for improving IT services did we commit to the right goals?
- When developing our strategy for improving the use and management of IT services, did we make the right choices and take the right decisions?
- When implementing our strategy, did we do it right?
- In the new situation, have we improved the provision of IT services?
- And finally, what are the lessons learned and where are we now?

Review and evaluation of a CSI initiative fall within two broad categories:

- Issues closely tied to the original problem situation for IT service provision to the business and ensuing business aims and strategy for the improvement thereof
- Issues in relation to the planning, implementation and proceedings of the IT improvement programme itself and associated projects such as measurements, problems, actions and changes.

The issues in the first category are closely related to the characteristics of the original problem situation, following which staff instigated the actions for understanding and improvements. These actions will therefore include:

- The ability of IT services to meet business needs
- Business satisfaction with the service provision
- Business benefits in the area of productivity, effectiveness, efficiency and economy
- Financial issues such as understanding the costs of IT service provision, control of IT costs to the business, and accountability of IT costs to the business
- The quality of IT service provision and support of IT use
- Communication between the business and IT service provider and the degree of mutual understanding
- The degree of understanding and control of the management of the IT infrastructure and IT service provision on the part of the business.

For the second category the following issues should be reviewed and evaluated:

- Costs of staff involved in the improvement programme and costs of implementing and maintaining the measurement framework
- Project management such as planning, performance, timeliness of achieving results and milestones, amount of replanning
- Adequacy of methods and techniques used
- Problems, bottlenecks, causes of progress performance problems, improvements and changes
- Communication, information gathering, reporting.

## 5.2 ASSESSMENTS

Assessments are the formal mechanisms for comparing the operational process environment to the performance standards for the purpose of measuring improved process capability and/or to identify potential shortcomings that could be addressed. The advantage of assessments is they provide an approach to sample particular elements of a process or the process organization which impact the efficiency and the effectiveness of the process.

Just by conducting a formal assessment an organization is demonstrating its significant level of commitment to improvement. Assessments involve real costs, staff time and management promotion. Organizations need to be more than just involved in an assessment; they need to be committed to improvement.

Comparison of the operational environment to industry norms is a relatively straightforward process. The metrics associated with industry norms are typically designed into the process control structure. Sampling and comparison then can be considered an operational exercise. Dealing with gaps apparent from such monitoring and reporting are addressed as an element of the check stage of the improvement lifecycle. An assessment based on comparison to a maturity model has been common over the last few years.

A well-designed maturity assessment framework evaluates the viability of all aspects of the process environment including the people, process and technology as well as factors affecting overall process effectiveness within the business – culture of acceptance, process strategy and vision, process organization, process governance, business/IT alignment, process reporting/metrics and decision-making. The balance of this section focuses on this form of assessment. However the principles of maturity assessment can easily be extended to assessments based on industry norms.

The initial step in the assessment process is to choose (or define) the maturity model and in turn the maturity attributes to be measured at each level. A suggested approach is to turn to the best-practice frameworks such as Capability Maturity Model Integration (CMMI), Control OBjectives for Information and related Technology (COBIT), ISO/IEC 20000 or the process maturity framework. These frameworks define maturity models directly or a model can be inferred. The frameworks are also useful in the definition of process maturity attributes.

## 5.2.1 When to assess

Assessments can be conducted at any time. A way to think about assessment timing is in line with the improvement lifecycle:

- **Plan (project initiation)**   Assess the targeted processes to form the basis for a process improvement project. Processes can be of many configurations and design, which increases the complexity of assessment data collection.
- **Plan (project midstream)**   A check during process implementation or improvement activities serves as validation that process project objectives are being met and, most importantly, provides tangible evidence that benefits are being achieved from the investment of time, talent and resources to process initiatives.
- **Do/check (process in place)**   Upon the conclusion of a process project, it is important to validate the maturation of process and the process organization through the efforts of the project team. In addition to serving as a decisive conclusion for a project, scheduling periodic reassessments can support overall organizational integration and quality efforts.

## 5.2.2 What to assess and how

The assessment's scope is one of the key decisions. Scope should be based on the assessment's objective and the expected future use of service and process assessments and assessment reports. Assessments can be targeted broadly at those processes currently implemented or focused specifically where known problems exist within the current process environment. There are three potential scope levels:

- Process only  Assessment only of process attributes based on the general principles and guidelines of the process framework which defines the subject process.
- People, process and technology  Extend the process assessment to include assessment of the organizational structure, skills, roles and talents of the managers and practitioners of the process as well as the ability of the process-enabling technology deployed to support the objectives and transaction state of the process.
- Full assessment  Extend the people, process and technology assessment to include an assessment of the culture of acceptance within the organization, the ability of the organization to articulate a process strategy, the definition of a vision for the process environment as an 'end state', the structure and function of the process organization, the ability of process governance to assure that process objectives and goals are met, the business/IT alignment via a process framework, the effectiveness of process reporting/metrics, and the capability and capacity of decision-making practices to improve processes over time.

All these factors are compared to the maturity attributes of the selected maturity model.

Assessments can be conducted by the sponsoring organization or with the aid of a third party. The pros and cons of these differing approaches are listed in Table 5.1. The advantages of conducting a self-assessment is the reduced cost and the intellectual lift associated with learning how to objectively gauge the relative performance and progress of an organization's processes. Of course the downside is the difficulty associated with remaining objective and impartial during the assessment.

The pitfall of a lack of objectivity can be eliminated by using a third party to conduct the assessment. There are a number of public 'mini-assessments' that are available on various websites, which provide a general perspective of maturity. However a more detailed assessment and resulting report can be contracted through a firm specializing in an assessment practice. Balancing against the obvious increased cost of a third-party assessment is the objectivity and experience of an organization that performs assessments regularly.

Whether conducted internally or externally, the assessment should be reported using the levels of the maturity model. A best-practice reporting

**Table 5.1 Pros and cons of assessment approaches**

| Pro | Con |
|---|---|
| **Using external resources for assessments** | |
| Objectivity | Cost |
| Expert ITIL knowledge | Risk of acceptance |
| Broad exposure to multiple IT organizations | Limited knowledge of existing environments |
| Analytical skills | Improper preparation affects effectiveness |
| Credibility | May not be there to see it through to the end – witness the results, good or not |
| Minimal impact to operations | |
| **Performing self-assessments** | |
| No expensive consultants | Lack of objectivity (internal agendas) |
| Self-assessments available for free | Little acceptance of findings |
| Promotes internal cooperation and communication | Internal politics |
| Good place to get started | Limited knowledge or skills |
| Internal knowledge of environment | Resource intensive |
| Can repeat exercise in future at minimal cost, using newly acquired skills | Inability to see the wood for the trees; assessment often needs a fresh set of eyes |
| | Detracts from the day job; unless back-filled could inadvertently reduce service effectiveness and efficiency during assessment |

method is to communicate assessment results in a graphical fashion. Graphs are an excellent tool as they can fulfil multiple communication objectives. For instance, graphs can reflect changes or trends of process maturity over time or reflect comparison of the current assessment to standards or norms.

### 5.2.3 Advantages and risks of assessments

The advantages include:

- They can provide an objective perspective of the current operational process state compared with a standard maturity model and a process framework. Through a thorough assessment, an accurate determination of any process gaps can be quickly completed, recommendations put forward and action steps planned.
- A well-planned and well-conducted assessment is a repeatable process. Thus the assessment is a useful management process in measuring progress over time and in establishing improvement targets or objectives.

- Using a common or universally accepted maturity framework, applied to a standard process framework, can serve to support comparing company process maturity to industry benchmarks.

The risks include:

- An assessment provides only a snapshot in time of the process environment. Therefore it may not reflect current business or cultural dynamics and process operational issues.

- If the decision is to outsource the assessment process, the assessment and maturity framework can be vendor or framework dependent. The proprietary nature of vendor-generated models may make it difficult to compare to industry standards.

- The assessment can become an end in itself rather than the means to an end. Rather than focusing on improving the efficiency and effectiveness of processes through process improvement, organizations can adopt a mindset of improving process for the sake of achieving maturity targets.

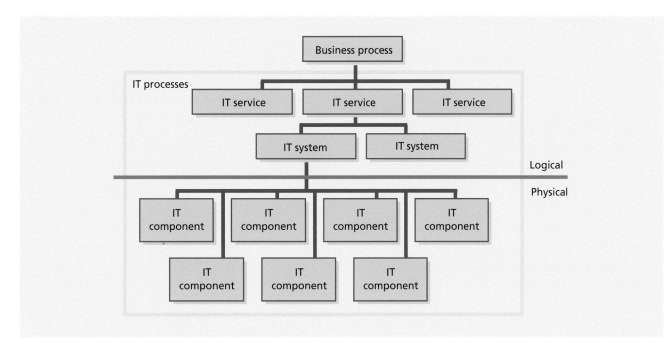

**Figure 5.1 The relationship of services, processes and systems**

- Assessments are labour-intensive efforts. Resources are needed to conduct the assessments in addition to those responding such as process or tool practitioners, management and others. When preparing for an assessment, an honest estimate of time required from all parties is in order.

- Assessments attempt to be as objective as possible in terms of measurements and assessment factors, but ultimately assessment results are still subject to the opinion of assessors. Thus assessments themselves are subjective and the results can have a bias based on the attitudes, experience and approach of the assessors themselves.

Assessments are an effective method of answering the question 'Where are we now?' Understanding how an existing service is performing, or how effective and efficient service management processes are, is important for identifying the gap between where we are and where we want to be. As we begin our discussion of assessments, we need to look at the relationship between business processes, IT services, IT systems and components that make up an IT system. IT service management processes support the IT services, IT systems and components. CSI will need to review the results of each one of these areas for effectiveness and efficiency. This will help identify the areas for improvement. This relationship is shown in Figure 5.1.

In the CSI journey, the decisions on what to improve are critical to the overall results that can be achieved. Any discussion on improvements has to begin with the services being provided to the business. This could lead to improvements on the service itself or to process improvements supporting the business service.

Improvement activities require the investment of human, financial and technological resources in the quest for continual improvement. These resources are allocated from other uses (e.g. customer support initiatives, new product development) to the improvement work. The business rationalizes decisions to allocate resources on the basis of the greatest ROI or value on investment (VOI). An important consideration then becomes understanding and articulating improvement needs and the benefits of improvement.

The goal of service improvement for an organization is two-fold:

- First, the organization seeks to achieve service objectives in a cost-efficient manner. The objectives can (and should) be linked to the overall strategy of the business. The efficiency issue for an organization is determining that the process is achieving its objectives with the most cost-efficient use of resources. There is potential for cost savings through elimination of unnecessary, redundant, overlapping or manual process activities and procedures, which in turn can be a significant benefit driver for justifying a process improvement.

- Second, the organization identifies those elements of process that detract from meeting service objectives effectively. Effectiveness relates to the ability of the process to achieve or exceed its principles and goals. In other words, a process would be considered effective if, through the implementation of the process, the organization meets, sustains and potentially exceeds the strategic goals and tactical objectives of the organization. Thus service improvements focus on addressing perceived or measurable process deficiencies, impacting specific organizational objectives, and can be quantified as delivered improvement benefits.

Service improvements are governed by the improvement lifecycle, which is modelled on the PDCA cycle of Plan, Do, Check, Act (see Figures 3.2 and 3.1 for the CSI approach and Chapter 4 for interfaces with the seven-step improvement process). The model establishes a clear pattern for continual improvement efforts:

- **Plan** Establishes goals for improvement including gap analysis, and defines action steps to close the gap and establish and implement measures to ensure that the gap has been closed and benefits achieved.
- **Do** Development and implementation of a project to close the gap. Implementation or improvement of processes and establishing the smooth operation of the process.
- **Check** Comparison of the implemented environment to the measures of success established in the Plan phase. The comparison determines if a gap still exists between the improvement objectives of the process and the operational process state. Gaps don't necessarily require closure. A gap may be considered tolerable if the actual performance is within allowable limits of performance.
- **Act** The decision process to determine if further work is required to close remaining gaps, and allocation of resources necessary to support another round of improvement. Project decisions at this stage are the input for the next round of the lifecycle, closing the loop as input in the Plan phase.

## 5.2.4 Value of processes versus maturity of processes

Figure 5.2 illustrates the value of a process in comparison to its maturity. For service management process improvement projects, one of the questions asked should be on how mature we need our processes to be. The answer to this is tied directly back to the business. In other words how important is a process to the business.

Let us say that a particular organization has gone through an assessment and found that three key processes, service level management (SLM), availability management and capacity management, shown in Figure 5.2, are not very mature. This particular organization is changing its strategy for selling and delivering products and services to a web-based strategy. Because of the importance of capacity management and availability management to any organization that provides products and services over the web, this company has to implement an improvement programme for increasing the maturity of both processes. Without any improvement initiatives this particular organization is putting itself at risk. We have all read about companies that have experienced larger than planned for usage and how they often create catastrophic results for organizations. The lack of proper capacity planning has in many cases created availability issues that have shut down an organization's ability to sell its products.

Having a low SLM process maturity also will create some issues for CSI activities. How do we know the new business requirements? What is currently being monitored and how well are we doing against targets? Do we have roles identified for reporting and analysing data?

The maturity of a process should ideally fall in the 'safe' areas. If a process is immature but the business heavily depends on it there is a significant danger to the organization. If a process is very mature yet provides very little to the business, then an organization may be over-investing resources and money. When CSI is looking at improving processes in support of IT services, understanding the value of processes to a business is critical.

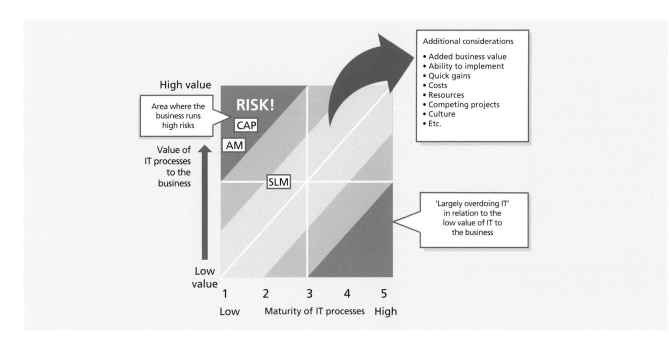

**Figure 5.2 The value of a process versus the maturity of a process**

## 5.2.5 Gap analysis

Gap analysis is a business assessment tool enabling an organization to compare where it is currently and where it wants to go in the future. This provides the organization with insight to areas that have room for improvement. This can be used to determine the gap between 'What do we want?' and 'What do we need?', for example.

The process involves determining, documenting and approving the variance between business requirements and current capabilities. Gap analysis naturally flows from benchmarking or other assessments such as service or process maturity assessments. Once the general expectation of performance is understood, then it is possible to compare that expectation with the level of performance at which the company currently functions. This comparison becomes the gap analysis, which can be performed at the strategic, tactical or operational level of an organization.

Gap analysis can be conducted from different perspectives such as:

■ The organization, including organizational structure and capabilities of the people
■ Business direction
■ Business processes
■ Information technology.

Gap analysis provides a foundation for how much effort in time, money and human resources is

required to achieve a particular goal (e.g. how to bring a service from a maturity level of 2 to 3).

## 5.3 BENCHMARKING

Benchmarking is a specific type of assessment and is a process used in management, particularly strategic management, in which organizations evaluate various aspects of their processes in relation to best practice, usually within their own sector. This then allows organizations to develop plans on how to adopt such best practice, usually with the aim of increasing some aspect of performance. Benchmarking may be a one-time occurrence, but it is often treated as a continuous process in which organizations continually seek to challenge their practices.

Organizations have a growing need to get a clear view on their level of quality and performance compared with that of their competitors and in the eye of their customers. It isn't sufficient any more to have internal self-assessment reports on the status of IT performance; it is equally important to test and compare it with the view the market has on the performance of the organization. A positive result of this test and comparison can give a competitive edge to the organization in the marketplace and generates trust with its customers. The results of benchmarking and self-assessments lead to identification of gaps in terms of people, process and technology. A benchmark can be the catalyst to initiating prioritization of where to begin formal process improvement. The results of benchmarking must clearly display the gaps, identify the risks of not closing the gaps, and facilitate prioritization of development activities and communication of this information.

Benchmarking is actually a logical sequence of stages that an organization goes through to achieve continual improvement in its key processes. It involves cooperation with others as benchmarking partners learn from each other where improvements can be made. It will be necessary to:

- **Ensure senior management support**
- **Take an external view**  Bring together business intelligence and internal performance to draw conclusions about the way internal resources and processes must be improved to achieve and surpass the performance of others.
- **Compare processes, not outputs**  Comparisons with organizations in the same sector are unlikely to identify the significant improvements that have been made elsewhere or overturn the conventions of the sector.
- **Involve process owners**  Their involvement encourages acceptance and buy-in by those who will be affected immediately by the changes which will be required to improve performance.
- **Set up benchmarking teams**  As a benchmarking culture develops, people will apply the method as part of the normal way in which they manage their work.
- **Acquire the skills**  People who undertake benchmarking require a small amount of training and guidance; an experienced in-house facilitator or external consultant will probably be required to provide technical assurance and encouragement in the application of the method.

Organizations should plan their benchmarking process based on their improvement needs, and should understand that this may require measurement of other companies. Some cross-industry figures may be published by the international research organizations, but will not necessarily include the assumptions and measurements a given organization needs. A research organization may, however, be a valuable benchmarking partner, for example, if target companies are competitors.

There is a general expectation that benchmarking is a process of comparing an organization's performance to industry-standard figures. By extension, having such benchmark figures available is often seen as the first hurdle in a benchmarking exercise. However, as this section will show, benchmarks are only relevant when the comparison is of the same performance measures or indicators, and is with organizations of similar size, industry and geography.

### 5.3.1 Benchmarking procedure

Identify your problem areas. Because benchmarking can be applied to any business process or function, a range of research techniques may be required, including:

- Informal conversations with customers, employees, or suppliers
- Focus groups
- In-depth marketing research
- Quantitative research
- Surveys
- Questionnaires
- Re-engineering analysis
- Process mapping
- Quality control variance reports
- Financial ratio analysis.

### 5.3.2 Benchmarking costs

Benchmarking is a moderately expensive process, but most organizations find that it more than pays for itself. The three main types of costs are:

- **Visit costs**  This includes travel- and accommodation-related expenses for team members who need to travel to the site.
- **Time costs**  Members of the benchmarking team will be investing time in researching problems, finding exceptional companies to study, visits and implementation. This will take them away from their regular tasks for part of each day so additional staff might be required.
- **Benchmarking database costs**  Organizations that institutionalize benchmarking into their daily procedures find it is useful to create and maintain a database of best practices and the companies associated with each best practice.

### 5.3.3 Value of benchmarking

Benchmarking is often used as a driver to make changes when the organization is reluctant to change the way of working. This is discussed in section 5.3.4.

To summarize, a benchmark is the basis for:

- Profiling quality in the market
- Boosting self-confidence and pride in employees as well as motivating and tying employees to an organization; this is relevant with today's staff shortages in the IT industry – IT personnel want to work in a highly efficient, cutting-edge environment
- Trust from customers that the organization is a good IT service management provider.

Optimizing service quality is key to all IT organizations to maximize performance and customer satisfaction and provide value for money. Organizations will be required to focus on end results and service quality, rather than simply on their business activities and processes.

### 5.3.4 Benchmarking as a lever

Consider the following 'paradigm blindness': 'The way we do it is the best because this is the way we've always done it.'

Benchmarking is sometimes the only way to open an organization to new methods, ideas and tools to improve their effectiveness. It helps break through resistance to change by demonstrating other methods of solving problems than the one currently employed, and demonstrating that they are irrefutably better, because they are being used successfully by others.

### 5.3.5 Benchmarking as a steering instrument

Benchmarking is a management technique to improve performance. It is used to compare performance between different organizations – or different units within a single organization – undertaking similar processes. Benchmarking is an ongoing method of measuring and improving products, services and practices against the best that can be identified in any industry anywhere. It has been defined as 'the search for industry best practices which lead to superior performance'.

### 5.3.6 Benchmarking categories

Benchmarking is a tool to identify improvement opportunities as well as to verify the outcome of improvement activities. Organizations can conduct internal or external benchmark studies. Improving service management can be as simple as asking: 'Are we better today than we were yesterday?', and looking at incremental improvements.

Here are some benchmarking categories:

- Internal benchmarks – where an organization sets a baseline at a certain point in time for the same system or department and measures how it is doing today compared with the baseline originally set; this type of benchmark is often overlooked by organizations (service targets are a form of benchmark)
- Comparison with industry norms provided by external organizations
- Direct comparisons with similar organizations
- Comparison with other systems or departments within the same company.

### 5.3.7 Benefits

Benchmarking often reveals quick wins – opportunities for improvement that are relatively easy and inexpensive to implement while providing substantial benefits in process effectiveness, cost reduction or staff synergy. The costs are clearly repaid through the improvements realized when organizations use benchmarking successfully. Using benchmark results will help deliver major benefits in achieving:

- Economy in the form of lower prices and higher productivity on the part of the service provider
- Efficiency by comparing the costs of providing IT services and the contribution these services make to the business with what is achieved in other organizations, helping the organization to identify areas for improvement
- Effectiveness of business objectives realized compared with what was planned.

Benchmarking helps the organization to focus on strategic planning by identifying the relative effectiveness of IT support for the business. The economy is the easiest area to investigate although efficiency and effectiveness may deliver the most benefit to the business. To obtain the maximum benefit, it is necessary to look at all of these three areas, rather than focusing on one to the exclusion of the others.

### 5.3.8 Who is involved?

Within an organization there will be three parties involved in benchmarking:

- **The customer**   The business manager responsible for acquiring IT services to meet business objectives. The customer might demonstrate an interest in benchmarking by asking: 'How can I improve my performance in procuring services and managing service providers, and in supporting the business through IT services?'
- **The user or consumer**   Anyone who uses IT services to support his or her work. The user might demonstrate an interest in benchmarking by asking: 'How can I improve my performance by exploiting IT?'
- **The internal service provider**   Providing IT services to users under service level agreements (SLAs) negotiated with and managed by the customer. The provider might demonstrate an interest in benchmarking by asking: 'How can we improve our performance in the delivery of IT services which meet the requirements of our customers and which are cost-effective and timely?'

There will also be participation from external parties:

- **External service providers**   Providing IT services to users under contracts and SLAs negotiated with and managed by the customer
- **Members of the public**   Ordinary people are increasingly becoming direct users of IT services
- **Benchmarking partners**   Other organizations with whom comparisons are made in order to identify the best practices to be adopted for improvements.

### 5.3.9 What to benchmark?

Differences in benchmarks between organizations are normal. All organizations and service-provider infrastructures are unique, and most are continually changing. There are also intangible but influential factors that cannot easily and objectively be measured, such as goodwill, image and culture.

Direct comparison with similar organizations is most effective if there is a sufficiently large group of organizations with similar characteristics. It is important to understand the size and nature of the business area, including the geographical distribution and the extent to which the service is used for business or time-critical activities.

Comparison with other groups in the same organization normally allows a detailed examination of the features being compared, in order to establish whether or not the comparison is of like with like.

**Hints and tips**

When benchmarking one or more services or service management processes, the IT organization has to ascertain which of these the organization should focus on first, if all cannot be implemented simultaneously. Determine which services and supporting processes to compare. Benchmarking of a service management process is used to find out if a process is cost-effective, responsive to the customer's needs and effective in comparison with other organizations. Some organizations use benchmarking to decide whether they should change their service provider.

It is essential in planning for service management to start with an assessment or review of the relevant service management processes. The results of this can provide a baseline for future comparison.

**Example of a poor management decision**

One large company started with the implementation of all service management processes. Senior management never explained why all these processes should be implemented. It sounded like a good thing to do: 'Everybody else is doing service management so why don't we?' After two years the whole project had to be stopped because customers were complaining about poor service. It was decided to restart the service management project. This time senior management decided to implement only a part of service management (the processes where the pain was most felt) and conducted an assessment to provide a baseline of results for future comparison.

Benchmarking techniques can be applied at various levels from relatively straightforward in-house comparisons through to an industry-wide search for best practice. Benchmarking comprises four basic stages: planning, analysis, action and review, or one can apply the seven-step improvement process to benchmarking:

1 Identify the strategy for improvement.
2 Define what you will measure.
   - Select the broad service or service management process or function to benchmark (such as service desk) in relation to stakeholder needs.
   - Draw up a preliminary list of potential benchmarking partners (these may be within the organization or outside).
   - Identify possible sources of information and methods of collection to confirm the suitability of potential partners.
   - Within that process, define the activities to be benchmarked (such as incident lifecycle).
   - Identify the resources required for the study.
   - Confirm the key performance measures or indicators to measure the performance in carrying out the activity.
   - Document the way the activities are currently completed.
   - Agree the plan and its implementation.
3 Gather the data.
   - Collect information to identify the most likely potential benchmarking partner to contact.
4 Process the data.
5 Analyse the information and data.
   - Confirm the best potential benchmarking partner and make a preliminary assessment of the performance gap.
   - Establish contacts and visits, if appropriate, to validate and substantiate the information.
   - Compare the existing process with that of the benchmarking partner to identify differences and innovations.
   - Agree targets for improvement that are expected as a result of adopting the benchmarking partner's ways of doing things.
6 Present and use the information.
   - Communicate the results of the study throughout the relevant parts of the organization and to the benchmarking partner.
   - Plan how to achieve the improvements.
7 Implement improvement.
   - Review performance when the changes have been embedded in the organization.
   - Identify and rectify anything which may have caused the organization to fall short of its target.
   - Communicate the results of the changes implemented to the organization and the benchmarking partner.
   - Consider benchmarking again to continue the improvement process.

Ideally, benchmark reviews should be built into an ongoing service management lifecycle so that regularly scheduled reviews or benchmarks are conducted. The formality and rigour with which they are conducted will vary depending on the environment, rate of business change, complexity of the environment and elapsed time since the last review. Conducting these reviews regularly provides valuable metrics and trend analysis with which to judge improvements (or lack thereof) and take corrective action as early as possible to maximize performance gains.

## 5.3.10 Comparison with industry norms

ITIL is itself an industry-recognized best practice, increasingly providing a framework for service management worldwide. The ITIL core publications provide documented guidance on detailed process assessment and service benchmarking that can be used as checklists and templates for organizations doing their own service reviews and benchmarks. Additionally, many IT service organizations around the world provide consulting and professional expertise in the process of conducting service management benchmarks and assessments to compare the current processes with published best practices and the ITIL recommendations. It may be worthwhile to investigate using these services if the scope of an assessment is very large or complex.

In addition, organizations may wish to compare their own processes against international standards, especially ISO/IEC 20000, ISO/IEC 27001 and ISO/IEC 19770.

### 5.3.10.1 Process maturity comparison

Conducting a process maturity assessment is one way to identify service management improvement opportunities. Often when organizations conduct a maturity assessment they want to know how they compare to the other organizations. Table 5.2 reflects average maturity scores for over 100 separate organizations that went through a maturity assessment using the scoring system detailed in Table 5.3.

As you can, see SLM, which is a key process in support of CSI, is at a fairly low maturity level in the organizations used in the above example. The lack of a mature SLM process that provides for identification of new business requirements, monitoring and reporting of results can make it difficult to identify service improvement opportunities. A prime target for improvements in this example would be first to mature the SLM practice to help achieve measurable targets to improve services going forward.

### 5.3.10.2 Total cost of ownership

The total cost of ownership (TCO), developed by Gartner, has become a key measurement of the effectiveness and the efficiency of services. TCO is defined as all the costs involved in the design, introduction, operation and improvement of services within an organization from its inception until retirement. Often, TCO is measured relating to hardware components. The TCO of an IT service is even more meaningful. CSI needs to take the TCO into perspective when looking at service improvement plans (SIPs).

TCO is often used to benchmark specific services in IT against other organizations – managed service providers.

### 5.3.11 Benchmark approach

Benchmarking will establish the extent of an organization's existing maturity with best practice and help in understanding how that organization compares with industry norms. Deciding what the key performance indicators (KPIs) are going to be and then measuring against them will give solid management information for future improvement and targets.

A benchmark could be either:

■ **An internal conducted benchmark**  Completed internally using resources from within the

**Table 5.2 Average results of over 100 process assessments before improvement**

| | |
|---|---|
| Financial management | 2.67 |
| Incident management/service desk | 2.49 |
| IT service continuity management (ITSCM) | 2.42 |
| Change management | 2.36 |
| Release management | 2.26 |
| Capacity management | 2.02 |
| Availability management | 1.97 |
| SLM | 1.96 |
| Problem management | 1.83 |
| Service asset and configuration management | 1.66 |

**Table 5.3 CMMI maturity model**

| | |
|---|---|
| 0. Non-existent | Nothing present |
| 1. Initial | Concrete evidence of development |
| 2. Repeatable | Some process documentation but some errors likely |
| 3. Defined | Standardized and documented |
| 4. Managed | Monitored for compliance |
| 5. Optimized | Processes are considered best practices through improvement |

organization to assess the maturity of the service management processes against a reference framework

■ **An external conducted benchmark**  Completed by an external third-party company; most have their own proprietary models for the assessment of service management process maturity.

The results and recommendations contained within the benchmarking review can then be used to identify and rectify areas of weakness within the IT service management processes.

Viewed from a business perspective, benchmark measurements can help the organization to assess IT services, performance and spend against peer or competitor organizations and best practice, both across the whole of IT and by appropriate business areas, answering questions such as:

■ How does IT spend compare to other similar organizations – overall, as a percentage of revenue, or per employee?
■ How does IT spend compare for similar functions, e.g. payroll functions either within an organization or with other organizations?

- How does IT spend compare across business units or business processes?
- How does IT spend compare across locations or technologies?
- How effective is IT service delivery (and identify opportunities and measures for improvement)?
- How efficient is IT service delivery (and identify opportunities and measures for improvement)?
- Which is the most appropriate sourcing option?
- Is the value of a long-term sourcing contract being maintained year on year?

Benchmarking activities need to be business-aligned. They can be expensive exercises whether undertaken internally or externally, and therefore they need to be focused on where they can deliver most value. For internal service providers, cost benchmarking can assess the efficiency and effectiveness of the IT organization. For external service providers, especially outsourced services, they can help to ensure the right IT services for the right price. Results of benchmarking not only provide a statement of performance, but can also be used to identify, recommend and plan improvements. They can also demonstrate value to the business and set targets for improvement levels, with subsequent benchmarking to assess achievement.

Comparisons of service performance and workload characteristics between peer organizations, the effectiveness of business process and the IT contribution to IT are also of value as part of a TCO assessment. Third-party specialists are available to conduct benchmarking and assessments, giving the business an external perspective and helping to lend credibility to the results and recommendations for improvements.

There is a variety of IT benchmarking types available separately or in combination, including:

- Cost and performance for internal service providers
- Price and performance for external service providers
- Process performance against industry best practice
- Financial performance of high-level IT costs against industry or peers
- Effectiveness considering satisfaction ratings and business alignment at all levels.

The context for benchmarking requires information about the organization's profile, complexity and relative comparators. An effective and meaningful profile contains four key components:

- **Company information profile**   The company profile defines the landscape of an organization – basic information on the company size, industry type, geographic location and types of user are typical of data gathered to establish this profile.
- **Current assets**   The IT assets mix within the organization may include production IT, desktop and mobile clients, peripherals, network and server assets.
- **Current best practices**   These include policies, procedures and/or tools that improve returns, and their maturity and degree of usage.
- **Complexity**   This includes information about the end-user community, the types and quantities of varied technologies in use and how IT is managed.

## 5.4   SERVICE MEASUREMENT

For all sizes of businesses, private and public organizations, educational institutions, consumers and the individuals working within these organizations, IT services have become an integral means for conducting business. Without IT services many organizations would not be able to deliver the products and services in today's market. As reliance on these IT services increases so do the expectations for availability, reliability and stability. This is why having the business and IT integrated is so important. No longer can they be thought of separately. The same holds true when measuring IT services. It is no longer sufficient to measure and report against the performance of an individual component such as a server or application. IT must now be able to measure and report against an end-to-end service.

The seven-step improvement process described in Chapter 4 discussed the need to define what you will measure after looking at the requirements and the ability to measure.

For services there are three basic measurements that most organizations utilize, which *ITIL Service Design* covers in more detail. They are:

- Availability of the service
- Reliability of the service
- Performance of the service.

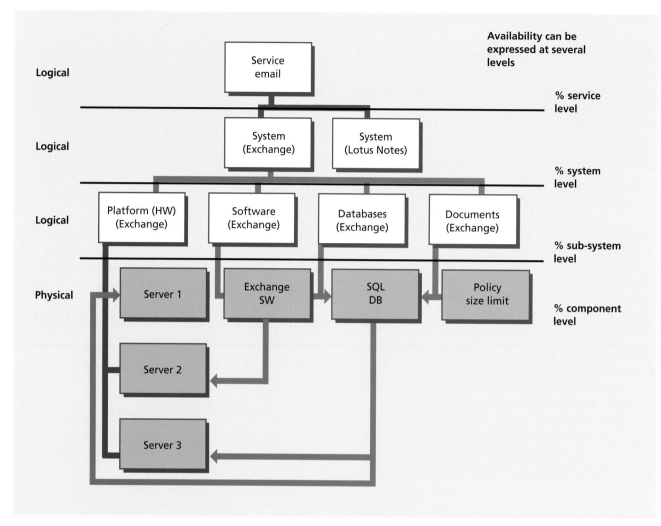

*Figure 5.3 Availability reporting*

In many cases, when an organization is monitoring, measuring and reporting on component levels it is doing so to protect itself and possibly to point the blame elsewhere – 'My server or my application was up 100% of the time.' Service measurement is not about placing blame or protecting oneself but instead provides a meaningful view of the IT service as the customer experiences it. The server may be up, but because the network is down, the customer is not able to connect to the server. Therefore the IT service was not available even though one or more of the components used to provide the service was available the whole time. Being able to measure against a service is directly linked to the components, systems and applications that are being monitored and reported on.

Measuring at the component level is necessary and valuable, but service measurement must go further than the component level. Service measurement will require someone to take the individual measurements and combine them to provide a view of the true customer experience. Too often we provide a report against a component, system or application but don't provide the true service level as experienced by the customer. Figure 5.3 shows how it is possible to measure and report against different levels of systems and components to provide a true service measurement. Even though the figure references availability measuring and reporting, the same can apply for performance measuring and reporting.

## 5.4.1 Design and develop a service measurement framework

A challenge many organizations face is the creation of a service measurement framework that leads to value-added reporting.

One of the activities documented in *ITIL Service Design* is the design of the measurement methods and metrics for the services, the architectures, their constituent components and the processes. These measurements are documented in the service design package and handed over to the service transition stage for the testing and validation of the measurement framework and methods during early life support.

Setting up a framework is as much an art as a science. It may prove difficult at first but the results over time are worth the effort. An organization may go through some trial and error in the beginning so it should not be afraid to admit mistakes on particular measures or targets and make adjustments to the framework.

Keep in mind that service measurement is not an end in itself. The end result should be to improve services and improve accountability.

One of the first steps in developing a service measurement framework is to understand the business processes and identify those that are most critical to the delivery of value to the business. The IT goals and objectives must support the business goals and objectives. There also needs to be a strong link between the operational, tactical and strategic level goals and objectives, otherwise an organization will find itself measuring and reporting on performance that may not add any value.

Service measurement is looking at not only the past but also the future – what do we need to be able to do and how can we do things better? The output of any service measurement framework should allow individuals to make operational, tactical or strategic decisions.

Selecting a combination of measures is important to provide an accurate and balanced perspective. The measurement framework as a whole should be balanced and unbiased, and able to withstand change – the measures are still applicable (or available) after a change has been made.

Whether measuring one or multiple services, the following steps are key to a successful service measurement framework:

- Origins:
  - Defining what success looks like. What are we trying to achieve and how will we know when we've achieved it?

- Building the framework and choosing measures:
  - Ask what we need to measure that will provide us with useful information that allows us to make strategic, tactical and/or operational decisions
  - Ask what measures will provide us with the data and information we need
  - Set targets for all measures by SLAs or service level targets/objectives that have been agreed internally within IT
- Critical elements of a service measurement framework. These should be:
  - Integrated into business planning
  - Focused on business and IT goals and objectives
  - Cost-effective
  - Balanced in their approach on what is measured
  - Able to withstand change
- Performance measures. These should:
  - Be timely
  - Be accurate and reliable
  - Be well-defined, specific and clear
  - Be relevant to meeting the objectives
  - Not create a negative behaviour
  - Lead to improvement opportunities
- Defined roles and responsibilities:
  - Who defines the measures and targets?
  - Who monitors and measures?
  - Who gathers the data?
  - Who processes and analyses the data?
  - Who prepares the reports?
  - Who presents the reports?

## 5.4.2 Different levels of measurement and reporting

Creating a service measurement framework will require the ability to build upon different metrics and measurements. The end result is a view of the way individual component measurements feed the end-to-end service measurement which should support KPIs defined for the service. This will then be the basis for creating a service scorecard and dashboard. The service scorecard will then be used to populate an overall balanced scorecard or IT scorecard. Figure 5.4 shows there are multiple levels that need to be considered when developing a service measurement framework.

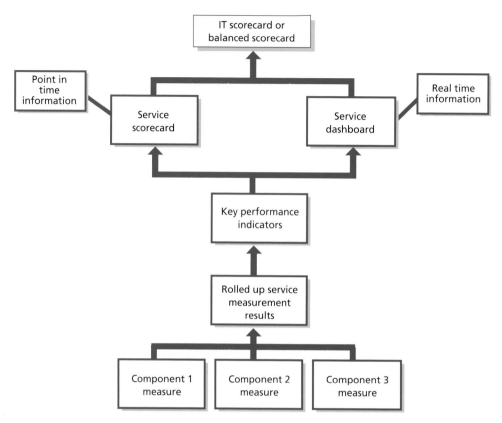

*Figure 5.4 Service measurement model*

What gets reported at each level is dependent on the measures that are selected.

Starting at the bottom, the technology domain areas will be monitoring and reporting on a component basis. This is valuable as each domain area is responsible for ensuring the servers are operating within defined guidelines and objectives. At this level, measurements will be on component availability, reliability and performance. The output of these measurements will feed into the overall end-to-end service measurement as well as the capacity and availability plans. These measurements will also feed into any incremental operations improvements and into a more formal CSI initiative.

A part of service measurement is then taking the individual component measurements and using them to determine the true service measurement for an end-to-end service derived from availability, reliability and performance measurements.

As an example let us use messaging as a service that is provided. Figure 5.5 shows we have four technology domains that often are monitored and reported on:

■ Mainframe availability 99.96%
■ WAN availability 98%
■ LAN availability 97.5%
■ Desktop availability 96%.

The availability numbers are examples provided only for illustrative purposes.

Note the end-to-end service availability in this example is not 96% because it is the lowest availability number. Since all the failures that led to decreased availability did not occur at the same time within each technology domain the availability numbers have to be multiplied together. So the calculation is 99.96% × 98% × 97.5% × 96%. This provides a minimum availability the customer can expect of the email service at 91.69% assuming all components break at different times; 91.69% would therefore be the target that could be agreed although it may end up being higher.

When developing a service management framework it is important to understand which are the most suitable types of report to create, who they are being prepared for, and how they will be used.

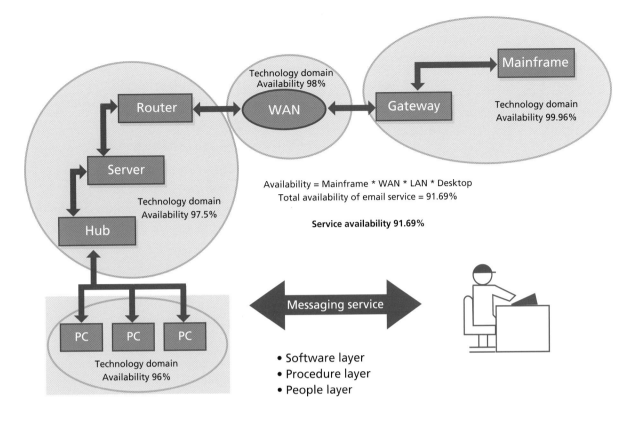

*Figure 5.5 Technology domain versus service management*

### 5.4.3 Service management process measurement

The same principles apply when measuring the efficiency and effectiveness of a service management process. As Figure 5.6 shows, you will need to define what to measure at the process activity level. These activity measures should support the process KPIs. The KPIs need to support higher-level goals. In Figure 5.6, the higher-level goal for change management is to improve the service quality. One of the major reasons for service quality issues is the downtime caused by failed changes. And one of the major reasons for failed changes is often the number of urgent changes an organization implements with no formal process. Therefore it would be advisable to capture the following key activity metrics:

■ The number of urgent changes
■ The number of failed urgent changes
■ Unauthorized changes that failed.

There are four major levels to report on. The bottom level contains the activity metrics for a process and these are often volume type metrics such as number of requests for change (RFCs) submitted, number of RFCs accepted into the process, number of RFCs by type, number approved, number successfully implemented etc. The next level contains the KPIs associated with each process. The activity metrics should feed into and support the KPIs. The KPIs will support the next level, which is the high-level goal such as improving service quality, reducing IT costs or improving customer satisfaction. Finally, this high-level goal will feed into the organization's balanced scorecard or IT scorecard. When first starting out, be careful to not pick too many KPIs to support the high-level goal(s). Additional KPIs can always be added at a later time.

Table 5.4 identifies some KPIs that reflect the value of service management. The KPIs are also linked to the service management process or processes that directly support the KPI. This table is not inclusive of all KPIs but simply an example of how KPIs may be mapped to processes.

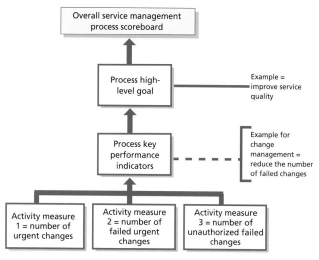

**Figure 5.6 Service management model**

## 5.4.4 Creating a measurement framework grid

It is recommended to create a framework grid that will set out the high-level goals and define which KPIs will support the goal and also which category the KPI addresses (see Table 5.5).

KPI categories can be classified as:

- **Compliance** Are we doing it?
- **Quality** How well are we doing it?
- **Performance** How fast or slow are we doing it?
- **Value** Is what we are doing making a difference?

**Table 5.4 Key performance indicators of the value of service management processes**

| KPI | Service management process | Comment |
|---|---|---|
| Improved availability (by service/systems/ applications) | Availability management | Improved monitoring and reporting on service availability |
| | Capacity management | |
| | Incident management | Expanded incident lifecycle, removing errors from the infrastructure, and reduction of failed changes; improved understanding of business requirements and IT capability – proactive planning. |
| | Problem management | |
| | Change management | |
| | Service level management | |
| Reduction of service level breaches (by service/systems/ applications) | Availability management | Improved monitoring of services |
| | Capacity management | Priority model, incident ownership, monitoring and tracking; removal of errors from the infrastructure |
| | Incident management | |
| | Problem management | |
| | Change management | Reduction of failed changes; explicit SLAs |
| | Service level management | |
| Reduction of mean time to repair (MTTR) (this should be measured by priority level, and not on a cumulative basis) | Incident management | Improved escalations, improved knowledge, improved prioritization |
| | Event management | |
| | Problem management | Priority model and operational level agreements (OLAs) |
| | Availability management | |
| | Change management | |
| Reduce percentage of urgent and emergency changes (by business unit) | Change management | Creating lead time policies |
| | Service level management | Improved planning and scheduling reduces the need for urgent and emergency changes Communicating change lead times to the business |
| Reduction of major incidents | Problem management | Removing errors from the infrastructure, and reduction of failed changes; improved understanding of business requirements and IT capability – proactive planning |
| | Incident management | |
| | Change management | |
| | Service level management | |
| | Capacity management | |
| | Availability management | |
| | Access management | |

**Table 5.5 High-level goals and key performance indicators**

| High-level goal | KPI | KPI category | Measurement | Target | How and who |
|---|---|---|---|---|---|
| Manage availability and reliability of a service | Percentage improvement in overall end-to-end availability of services | Value<br><br>Quality | End-to-end service availability based on the component availability that makes up the service<br><br>AS 400 availability<br><br>Network availability<br><br>Application availability | 99.995% | Technical managers<br><br>Technical analyst<br><br>Service level manager |

## 5.5 METRICS

It is important to remember that there are three types of metrics that an organization will need to collect to support CSI activities as well as other process activities:

- **Technology metrics** These metrics are often associated with component and application-based metrics such as performance, availability etc.
- **Process metrics** These metrics are captured in the form of critical success factors (CSFs), KPIs and activity metrics for the service management processes. They can help determine the overall health of a process. KPIs can help answer four key questions on quality, performance, value and compliance of following the process. CSI would use these metrics as input in identifying improvement opportunities for each process.
- **Service metrics** These metrics are a measure of the end-to-end service performance. Individual technology and process metrics are used when calculating the end-to-end service metrics.

In general, a metric is a scale of measurement defined in terms of a standard, i.e. a well-defined unit. Metrics are a system of parameters or ways of quantitative assessment of a process that is to be measured. Metrics define what is to be measured. Metrics are usually specialized by the subject area, in which case they are valid only within a certain domain and cannot be directly benchmarked or interpreted outside it. Generic metrics, however, can be aggregated across subject areas or business units of an enterprise. Figure 5.7 shows the full

hierarchy from measurement through to the business vision.

Metrics are used in several business models including CMMI, COBIT and Six Sigma. These measurements or metrics can be used to track trends, productivity, resources and much more. Typically, the metrics tracked are KPIs.

### 5.5.1 How many CSFs and KPIs?

Section 4.1.12 details CSFs and KPIs of the seven-step improvement process. It is recommended that no more than two to five KPIs are defined per CSF at any given time and that a service or process has no more that two to five CSFs associated with it at any given time.

It is recommended that in the early stages of a CSI initiative only two to three KPIs for each CSF are defined, monitored and reported on. As the maturity of a service and service management processes increase, additional KPIs can be added. Based on what is important to the business and IT management, the KPIs may change over a period of time. Also keep in mind that as service management processes are implemented, this will often change the KPIs of other processes. As an example, increasing first-contact resolution is a common KPI for incident management. This is a good KPI to begin with, but when you implement problem management this should change. One of problem management's objectives is to reduce the number of recurring incidents. When these types of recurring incidents are reduced it will reduce the number of first-contact resolutions. In this case a reduction in first-contact resolution is a positive trend.

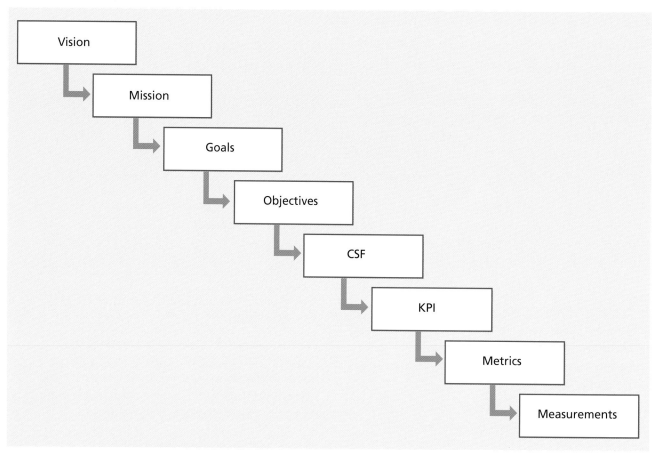

*Figure 5.7 From vision to measurement*

The next step is to identify the metrics and measurements required to compute the KPI. There are two basic kinds of KPI, qualitative and quantitative.

### 5.5.1.1 Qualitative KPIs

Here is a qualitative example:

- CSF: Improving IT service quality
- KPI: 10% increase in customer satisfaction rating for handling incidents over the next six months.

Metrics required:

- Original customer satisfaction score for handling incidents
- Ending customer satisfaction score for handling incidents.

Measurements:

- Incident-handling survey score
- Number of survey scores.

### 5.5.1.2 Quantitative KPIs

Here is a quantitative example:

- CSF: Reducing IT costs
- KPI: 10% reduction in the costs of handling printer incidents.

Metrics required:

- Original cost of handling printer incidents
- Final cost of handling printer incidents
- Cost of the improvement effort.

Measurements:

- Time spent on the incident by first-level operative and their average salary
- Time spent on the incident by second-level operative and their average salary
- Time spent on problem management activities by second-level operative and their average salary
- Time spent on the training first-level operative on the workaround
- Cost of a service call to third-party vendor
- Time and material from third-party vendor.

### 5.5.1.3 Is the KPI fit for use?

An important aspect to consider is whether a KPI is fit for use. Key questions are:

- What does the performance indicator really tell us about goal achievement? If we fail to meet the target set for a performance indicator, does that mean we fail to achieve some of our goals? And if we succeed in meeting certain targets, does this mean we will achieve our goals?
- How easy is it to interpret the performance indicator? Does it help us to decide on a course of action?
- When do we need the information? How often? How rapidly should the information be available?
- To what extent is the performance indicator stable and accurate? Is it sensitive to external, uncontrollable influences? What amount of effort is needed for a change in result that is not marginal?
- How easy is it to change the performance indicator itself? How easy is it to adapt the measurement system to changing circumstances or changes in our goals for IT service provision?
- To what extent can the performance indicator be measured now? Under which conditions can measurement continue? Which conditions impede measurement? Which conditions render the result meaningless?
- Who owns this KPI? Who is responsible for collecting and analysing the data? Who is accountable for improvements based on the information?

## 5.5.2 Tension metrics

The effort from any support team is a balancing act of three elements:

- Resources – people and money
- Functionality – the product or service and its quality
- The schedule.

The delivered product or service therefore represents a balanced trade-off between these three elements. Tension metrics can help create that balance by preventing teams from focusing on just one element – for example, on delivering the product or service on time. If an initiative is being driven primarily towards satisfying a business driver of on-time delivery to the exclusion of other factors, the manager will achieve this aim by flexing the resources and service features in order to meet the delivery schedule. This unbalanced focus will therefore either lead to budget increases or lower product quality. Tension metrics help create a delicate balance between shared goals and delivering a product or service according to business requirements within time and budget. Tension metrics do not, however, conflict with shared goals and values, but rather prevent teams from taking shortcuts and shirking on their assignment. Tension metrics can therefore be seen as a tool to create shared responsibilities between team members with different roles in the service lifecycle.

**Example of tension metrics**

An organization may focus on increasing the number of incidents handled by each member of the service desk but fail to examine the impact on the resolution rate. If the resolution rate reduces because staff are rushing to deal with more incidents, the overall service quality has been damaged. In this case 'the number of incidents handled per service desk analyst' and 'the incident resolution rate' are the tension metrics that need to be examined together to see the true impact.

## 5.5.3 Goals and metrics

Each stage of the service lifecycle requires very specific contributions from the key roles identified in service design, service transition and service operation, each of which has very specific goals to meet. Ultimately, the quality of the service will be determined by how well each role meets its goals, and by how well those sometimes conflicting goals are managed along the way. That makes it crucial that organizations find some way of measuring performance – by applying a set of metrics to each goal.

### 5.5.3.1 Breaking down goals and metrics

It is outside the scope of this publication to dig too deeply into human resources management, and there is no shortage of literature already available on the subject. However, there are some resource specific items that can be said about best practices for goals and metrics as they apply to managing services in their lifecycle.

**Table 5.6 Examples of service quality metrics**

| Measure | Metric | Quality goal | Lower limit | Upper limit |
|---------|--------|--------------|-------------|-------------|
| Schedule | Variation against revised plan (%) | Within 7.5% of estimate | Not to be less than 7.5% of estimate | Not to exceed 7.5% of estimate |
| Effort | Variation against revised plan (%) | Within 10% of estimate | Not to be less than 10% of estimate | Not to exceed 10% of estimate |
| Cost | Variation against revised plan (%) | Within 10% of estimate | Not to be less than 10% of estimate | Not to exceed 10% of estimate |
| Defects | Variation against planned defect (%) | Within 10% of estimate | Not to be less than 10% of estimate | Not to exceed 10% of estimate |
| Productivity | Variation against productivity goal | Within 10% of estimate | Not to be less than 10% of estimate | Not to exceed 10% of estimate |
| Customer satisfaction | Customer satisfaction survey result | Greater than 8.9 on a range of 1 to 10 | Not to be less than 8.9 on a range of 1 to 10 | |

Many IT service organizations measure their IT staff in an abstract and high-level manner. During appraisal and counselling, most managers discuss such things as 'taking part in one or more projects/performing activities of a certain kind', or 'fulfilling certain roles in projects/activities' and 'following certain courses'. Although accomplishing such goals might be important for the professional growth of an individual, it does not facilitate the service lifecycle or any specific process in it. In reality, most IT service organizations do not use more detailed performance measures that are in line with key business drivers, because it is difficult to do, and do correctly.

But there is a way. In the design phase of a service, key business drivers were translated into service level requirements (SLRs) and operations level requirements, the latter consisting of process, skills and technology requirements. This constitutes a translation from a business requirement into requirements for IT services and IT components. There is also the question of the strategic position of IT. In essence, the question is whether IT is viewed as an enabler or a cost centre, the answer to which determines the requirements for IT services and IT components. If IT is viewed as a cost centre, services might be developed to be used centrally in order to reduce TCO. Services will have

those characteristics that will reduce total costs of ownership throughout the lifecycle. On the other hand, if IT is an enabler (which it has to be), services will be designed with the ability to adjust to changing business requirements and meet early time-to-market objectives.

Either way, the important point is that those requirements for IT services and IT components would determine how processes in the lifecycle are measured and managed, and thus how the performance and growth of professionals should be measured.

Metrics can be classified into three categories: financial metrics, learning and growth metrics, and organizational or process effectiveness metrics. An example of financial metrics is the expenses and total percentage of hours spent on projects or maintenance, while an example of learning and growth is the percentage of education pursued in a target skill area, certification in a professional area, and contribution to knowledge management.

Some examples of service quality metrics are shown in Table 5.6. Process quality metrics are the quality metrics related to efficient and effective process management.

*Note:* The figures in Table 5.6 are for illustrative purposes only and are not intended as generic targets. Organizations should consider and set their own targets.

### 5.5.3.2 Using organizational metrics

To be effective, measurements and metrics should be woven through the complete organization, touching the strategic as well as the tactical level. To successfully support the key business drivers, the IT services manager needs to know what and how well each part of the organization contributes to the final success.

It is also important, when defining measurements for goals that support the IT services strategy, to remember that measurements must focus on results and not on efforts. Focus on the organizational output and try to get clear what the contribution is. Each stage in the service lifecycle has its processes and contribution to the service. Each stage of the lifecycle also has its roles, which contribute to the development or management of the service. Based on the process goals and the quality attributes of the service, goals and metrics can be defined for each role in the processes of the lifecycle.

### 5.5.4 Interpreting and using metrics

Results must be examined in the context of the objectives, environment and any external factors. Therefore after collecting the results, organizations will conduct measurement reviews to determine how well the indicators worked and how the results contribute to objectives.

Before starting to interpret the metrics and measures it is important to identify if the results that are being shown even make sense. If they do not, then instead of interpreting the results, take action to identify the reasons the results appear the way they do. The example used earlier in the chapter was of an organization that provided data for the service desk in which the data showed there were more first-contact resolutions at the service desk than there were incidents opened by the service desk. This is impossible and yet this organization was ready to distribute this report. When this kind of thing happens some questions need to be asked, such as:

- How did we collect this data?
- Who collected the data?
- What tools were used to collect the data?
- Who processed the data?

- How was the data processed?
- What could have led to the incorrect information?

When beginning to interpret the results it is important to know the data elements that make up the results, the purpose of producing the results and the expected normal ranges of the results.

Simply looking at some results and declaring a trend is dangerous. Figure 5.8 shows a trend that the service desk is opening fewer incidents over the last few months. One could believe that this is because there are fewer incidents or perhaps it is because the customers are not happy with the service that is being provided, so they go elsewhere for their support needs. Perhaps the organization has implemented a self-help knowledge base and some customers are now using this service instead of contacting the service desk. Some investigation is required to understand what is driving these metrics.

One of the keys to proper interpretation is to understand whether there have been any changes to the service or if there were any issues that could have created the current results.

The chart can be interpreted in many ways so it would not be wise to share it without some discussion of the meaning of the results.

Figure 5.9 is another example of a service desk measurement. Using the same number of incidents we have now also provided the results of first contact resolution. The figure shows that not only are fewer incidents being opened, but the ability to restore service on first contact is also going down. Before coming to hasty conclusions, some questions need to be asked:

- What has happened that could drive down the number of incidents?
- What would impact our ability to restore service on the first contact?
- Did we hire new service desk analysts?
- Did we remove some services?
- Have we provided other means to access our services?
- Have other processes been implemented that could impact incident volume and first contact resolution?

In the case illustrated in Figure 5.9, the organization had implemented problem

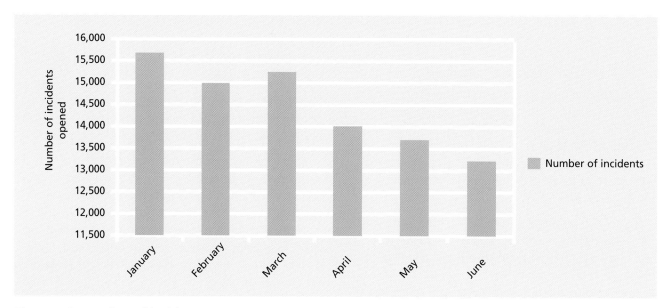

**Figure 5.8  Number of incidents opened by service desk over time**

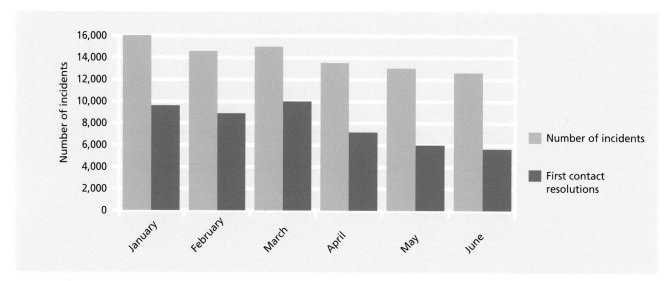

**Figure 5.9  Comparison of incidents opened and resolved on first contact by the service desk**

management. As the process matured and through the use of incident trend analysis, staff were able to use problem management to identify a couple of recurring incidents that created a lot of incident activity each month. Through root cause analysis and submitting a RFC, a permanent fix was implemented, thus stopping the recurring incidents. Through further analysis it was found that these few recurring incidents were able to be resolved on the first contact. By removing these incidents the opportunity to increase first contact resolution was also removed. During this time period the service desk also had some new hires.

Table 5.7 provides a current view and year-to-date (YTD) view for response times for three service desks. It provides a transaction count for each service, the minimum response time measured in seconds, the maximum response time measured in seconds and the average for the month. The table also provided the YTD average for each service. In order to understand if these numbers are good or not it is important to define the target for each service as well as the target for meeting the SLA.

When looking at the results for the three services it may appear that Service 2 is the best, and this might be because it handles fewer transactions each month than the other two services.

**Table 5.7 Response times for three service desks**

| Service measurement response time | | | | | | | |
|---|---|---|---|---|---|---|---|
| Service | Response times (seconds) | | | | YTD | Percentage within SLA (99.5% is the target) | |
| | Current month | | | | | | |
| | Count | Min | Max | Avg | | Monthly | YTD |
| Service 1 Target = 1.5 seconds | 1,003,919 | 1.20 | 66.25 | 3.43 | 1.53 | 99.54% | 98.76% |
| Service 2 Target = 1.25 seconds | 815,339 | 0.85 | 21.23 | 1.03 | 1.07 | 98.44% | 99.23% |
| Service 3 Target = 2.5 seconds | 899,400 | 1.13 | 40.21 | 2.12 | 2.75 | 96.50% | 94.67% |

Interpreting that Service 2 is the best by only looking at the numbers is dangerous, however. Investigations will find that Service 2 is a global service that is accessed 24 × 7 and the other two services have peak time utilization between 8 am and 7 pm. This is no excuse because the services are not hitting targets so further investigation needs to be conducted at the system and component levels to identify any issues that are creating the current response time results. It could be that the usage has picked up, which was not planned for, and some fine tuning on components can improve the response time.

## 5.5.5 Using measurement and metrics

Metrics can be used for multiple purposes such as to:

- Validate – are we supporting the strategy and vision?
- Justify – do we have the right targets and metrics?
- Direct – based on factual data, people can be guided to change behaviour
- Intervene – take corrective actions such as identifying improvement opportunities.

Service measurements and metrics should be used to drive decisions. Depending on what is being measured the decision could be strategic, tactical or operational. This is the case for CSI. There are many improvement opportunities but often only a limited budget to address the improvement opportunities, so decisions must be made. Which improvement opportunities will support the

business strategy and goals, and which will support the IT goals and objectives? What are the ROI and VOI opportunities? ROI is also discussed in Chapters 2 and 4.

Another key use of measurement and metrics is for comparison purposes. Measures by themselves may tell the organization very little unless there is a standard or baseline against which to assess the data. Measuring only one particular characteristic of performance in isolation is meaningless unless it is compared with something else that is relevant. The following comparisons are useful:

- Comparison against the baseline
- Comparison against a target or goal
- Comparison with other organizations – be sure to understand that the strategy, goals and objectives of other organizations may not align with yours so there may be driving factors in the other organization that you don't have or it could be the other way around
- Comparison over time such as day to day, week to week, month to month, quarter to quarter, or year to year
- Comparison between different business units
- Comparison between different services.

Measures of quality allow for measuring trends and the rate of change over a period of time. Examples could be measuring trends against standards that are set up either internally or externally and could include benchmarks, or they could be measuring trends with standards and targets to be established. This is often done when first setting up baselines.

A minor or short-term deviation from targets should not necessarily lead to an improvement initiative. It is important to set the criteria for the deviations before an improvement programme is initiated.

Comparing and analysing trends against service level targets or an actual SLA is important as it allows for early identification of fluctuations in service delivery or quality. This is important not only for internal service providers but also when services have been outsourced. It is important to identify any deviations and discuss them with the external service provider in order to avoid any supplier relationship problems. Speed and efficiency of communication when there are missed targets is essential to the continuation of a strong relationship.

Using measurements and metrics can also help define any external factors that may exist outside the control of the internal or external service provider. The real world needs to be taken into consideration. External factors could include anything from language barriers to governmental decisions.

Individual metrics and measures by themselves may tell an organization very little from a strategic or tactical point of view. Some types of metrics and measures are often more activity based than volume based, but are valuable from an operational perspective. Examples include:

- The services used
- The mapping of customers to services
- Frequency of use of each service
- Times of day each service is used
- The way each service is used (internally or externally through the web)
- The performance of each component used to provide the service
- The availability of each component used to provide the service.

Each of these measures by themselves will provide some information that is important to IT staff including the technical managers who are responsible for availability management and capacity management as well as those who may be responsible for a technology domain such as a server farm, an application or the network, but it is the examination and use of all the measurements and metrics together that delivers

the real value. It is important for someone to own the responsibilities not only to look at these measurements as a whole but also to analyse trends and interpret the meaning of the metrics and measures.

### 5.5.6 Creating scorecards and reports

Service measurement information will be used for three main purposes:

- To report on the service to interested parties
- To compare against targets
- To identify improvement opportunities.

Reports must be appropriate and useful for all those who use them.

There are typically three distinct audiences for reporting purposes.

- **The business**   Is it really focused on delivery to time and budget?
- **IT management**   IT managers will be interested in the tactical and strategic results that support the business.
- **IT operational/technical managers**   These managers will be concerned with the tactical and operational metrics that support better planning, coordination and scheduling of resources. The operational managers will be interested in their technology domain measurements such as component availability and performance.

Many organizations make the mistake of creating and distributing the same report to everyone. This does not provide value for everyone.

#### 5.5.6.1 Creating scorecards that align to strategies

Reports and scorecards should be linked to overall strategy and goals. Using a balanced scorecard approach is one way to manage this alignment.

Figure 5.10 illustrates how the overall goals and objectives can be used to derive the measurements and metrics required to support the overall goals and objectives. The arrows point both ways because the strategy, goals and objectives will drive the identification of required KPIs and measurements, but it is also important to remember that the measures are input in KPIs and the KPIs support the goals in the balanced scorecard.

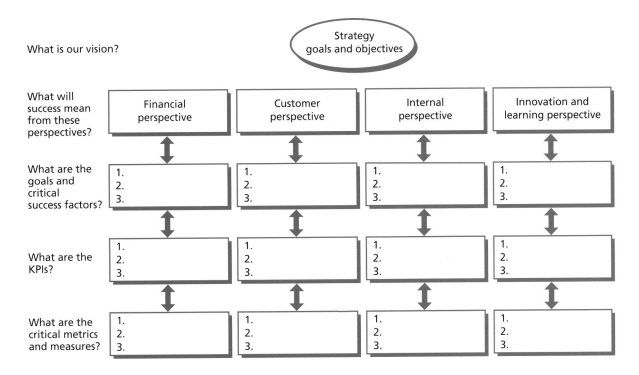

**Figure 5.10 Deriving measurements and metrics from goals and objectives**

It is important to select the right measures and targets to be able to answer the ultimate question of whether the goals are being achieved and the overall strategy supported. The balanced scorecard is discussed in more detail in section 5.5.8.

### 5.5.6.2 Creating reports

When creating reports it is important to know their purpose and the details required. Reports can be used to provide information for a single month, or a comparison of the current month with other months to provide a trend for a certain time period. Reports can show whether service levels are being met or breached.

Before starting the design of any report it is also important to know the following:

- Who is the target audience of the report?
- What will the report be used for?
- Who is responsible for creating the report?
- How will the report be created?
- How frequently is the report to be created?
- What information will be produced, shared or exchanged?

One of the first items to consider is who is the target audience. Most senior managers don't want a report that is 50 pages long. They like to have a short summary report and access to supporting

details if they are interested. Table 5.8 provides an example that will fit the needs of most senior managers. This report should be no longer than two pages but ideally a single page if that is achievable without sacrificing readability.

It is also important to know what report format the audience prefers. Some people like text reports, some like charts and graphs with lots of colour, and some like a combination. Be careful about the type of charts and graphs that are used. They must be understandable and not open to different interpretations.

Many reporting tools today produce canned reports but these may not meet everyone's business requirements for reporting purposes. It is wise to ensure that a selected reporting tool has flexibility for creating different reports, that it will be linked or support the goals and objectives, that its purpose is clearly defined, and that its target audience is identified.

Reports can be set up to show:

- **Results for a service** With supporting reports giving individual measurements on components
- **Health of a service management process** With certain process KPI results
- **Functional reports** Such as telephony reports for the service desk.

**Table 5.8 An example of a summary report format**

| Report for the month of: | |
|---|---|
| Monthly overview | This is a summary of the service measurement for the month and discusses any trends over the past few months. This section can also provide input into [details to be inserted]. |
| Results | This section outlines the key results for the month. |
| What led to the results | Are there any issues or activities that contributed to the results for this month? |
| Actions to take | What action have you taken or would like to take to correct any undesirable results? Major deficiencies may require CSI involvement and the creation of a SIP. |
| Predicting the future | Define what you think the future results will be. |

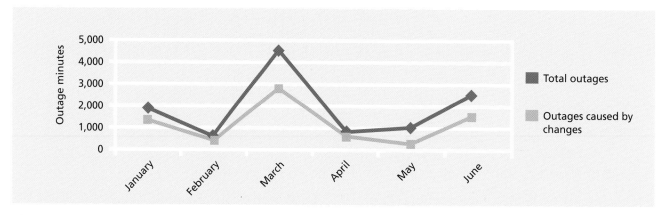

*Figure 5.11 Reported outage minutes for a service*

Figure 5.11 shows the duration of outages (in minutes) for a service. However, through analysis of the results, a direct relationship was discovered between failed changes and the duration of outages. Seeing this information together convinced an organization that it really needed to improve its change management process.

Table 5.9 is another example of a service measurement report. The report clearly states an objective and also provides a YTD status. The report compares this year's outage to last year's outage. The report also addresses the actual customer impact. Depending on needs, this report format can be used for many reporting purposes such as performance, SLAs etc.

Table 5.10 shows incident management data for the number of incidents by priority and the success of meeting the SLA for service restoration.

Table 5.11 provides some sample KPIs for different processes. This is not an all-inclusive list but simply an example. Each organization will need to define what KPIs to report on.

There are many techniques used today to measure the effectiveness and efficiency of IT

and the services it provides. Often organizations use a combination of methods rather than just one individual technique. CSI should assume responsibility for ensuring that the quality of service required by the business is provided within the imposed cost constraints. CSI is also instrumental in determining if IT is still on course with the achievement of planned implementation targets and, if not, plotting course corrections to bring it back into alignment.

However, it must be remembered that although the measurement of progress is vital it is not the end product; rather, it is a means to an end. Often people gather measurements and produce reports as a full-time occupation. It is essential that the production of statistics is not seen as the sole objective of the strategy implementation but rather an indicator of its progress and success.

### 5.5.7 Setting targets

If you have nothing to aim for it is probable that is what you will hit. The CSFs and SLRs will give vital information as to what we are trying to achieve and it is important that we keep the targets in mind when measuring and reporting. Targets

**Table 5.9 Service report of outage minutes compared to goal**

| Actual outage minutes compared to goal | | | | | | |
|---|---|---|---|---|---|---|
| Objective | 20% decrease in outages | | | | | |
| Status | 18% decrease YTD | | | | | |
| Monthly report | Month 1 | Month 2 | Month 3 | Month 4 | Month 5 | Month 6 |
| Previous year's outage minutes | | | | | | |
| This year's outage minutes | | | | | | |
| Running YTD reduction | | | | | | |
| Monthly indicator | Positive | Negative | Positive | Positive | Negative | Positive |
| Reduction in customer impact | | | | | | |
| Objective | Decrease in number of customers impacted (%) | | | | | |
| Status | | | | | | |
| Next steps | | | | | | |

**Table 5.10 Percentage of incidents meeting target time for service restoration**

| | Target | Month 1 | | Month 2 | |
|---|---|---|---|---|---|
| | | Number of Incidents | % | Number of Incidents | % |
| All incidents | | | | | |
| Within target | | 7,540 | 97.15 | 6,647 | 95.34 |
| Missed target | | 221 | 2.85 | 325 | 4.66 |
| Grand total | | 7,761 | | 6,972 | |
| Priority 1 | | | | | |
| Within target | 95% within 1 hour | 24 | 77.42 | 17 | 77.27 |
| Missed target | | 7 | 22.58 | 5 | 22.73 |
| Grand total | | 31 | | 22 | |
| Priority 2 | | | | | |
| Within target | 90% within 4 hours | 127 | 78.40 | 153 | 92.73 |
| Missed target | | 35 | 21.60 | 12 | 7.27 |
| Grand total | | 162 | | 165 | |
| Priority 3 | | | | | |
| Within target | 80% within 1 business day | 2,532 | 89.66 | 2,176 | 90.03 |
| Missed target | | 292 | 10.34 | 241 | 9.97 |
| Grand total | | 2,824 | | 2,417 | |
| Priority 4 | | | | | |
| Within target | 70% within 2 business days | 4,683 | 98.71 | 4,301 | 98.47 |
| Missed target | | 61 | 1.29 | 67 | 1.53 |
| Grand total | | 4,744 | | 4,368 | |

**Table 5.11 Sample key performance indicators**

| Process/function | KPI/description | Type | Progress indicator |
|---|---|---|---|
| Incident management | Incidents resolved within target time | Value | Meets/exceeds target times |
| Incident management | % of incidents closed – first call | Performance | Service desk only – target is 80% |
| Service desk | Abandon rate | | Service desk with automatic call distribution (ACD). 5% or less goal (after 24 seconds) |
| Incident management | Count of incidents submitted by support group | Compliance | Consistency in number of incidents – investigation is warranted for (1) rapid increase, which may indicate infrastructure investigation, and (2) rapid decrease, which may indicate compliance issues |
| Problem management | % of repeated problems over time | Quality | Problems that have been removed from the infrastructure and have re-occurred. Target: less than 1% over a 12-month rolling timeframe |
| Problem management | % root cause with permanent fix | Quality | Calculated from problem start date to permanent fix found. This may not include implementation of permanent fix. Internal target: fix 90% of problems within 40 days. External target: fix 80% of problems within 30 days. External target = third party/vendor |
| Problem management | % and number of incidents raised to problem management | Compliance | Sorted by infrastructure (internal and external) and development (internal and external) |
| Change management | % of RFCs successfully implemented without back out or issues | Quality | Grouped by infrastructure/development |
| Change management | % of RFCs that are emergencies | Performance | Sort by infrastructure or development – and by emergency quick fix (service down) or business requirement |
| Service asset and configuration management | Number of configuration item (CI) additions or updates | Compliance | CI additions or updates broken down by group – configuration management database (CMDB) or change modules |
| Service asset and configuration management | Number of records related to CI | Performance | Number of associations grouped by process |
| Release and deployment management | % of releases using exceptions | Value | Exceptions are criteria deemed mandatory – identify by groups |
| Release and deployment management | % of releases bypassing process | Compliance | Identify groups bypassing release process |
| Capacity management | Action required | Value | Number of services that require action vs. total number of systems |
| Capacity management | Capacity-related problems | Quality | Number of problems caused by capacity issues sorted by group |

set by management are quantified objectives to be attained. They express the aims of the service or process at any level and provide the basis for the identification of problems and early progress towards solutions and improvement opportunities.

Service targets are often defined in response to business requirements or they may result from new policy or regulatory requirements. SLM through SLAs will often drive the target that is required. Unfortunately, many organizations have had targets set with no clear understanding of the IT organization's capability to meet the target. That is why it is important that SLM looks at not only the business requirements but also IT capability to meet business requirements.

When first setting targets against a new service it may be advisable to consider a phased target approach, as the target in the first quarter may be lower than the second quarter. With a new service it would be unwise to enter into a SLA until overall capabilities are clearly identified. Even with the best service design and transition, no one ever knows how a service will perform until it is actually in production.

Setting targets is just as important as selecting the right measures. It is important that targets are realistic but challenging. Good targets will be SMART (specific, measurable, achievable, relevant and time-bound). Targets should be clear, unambiguous and easy to understand by those who will be working toward them.

Remember that the choice of measures and their targets can affect the behaviour of those who are carrying out the work that is being measured. That is why it is always important to have a balanced approach.

Let's look at an example of common measures that are captured for the service desk. It is common for the service desk to measure the average speed of answer, number of calls answered and call duration. These measures are often collected through telephony systems. If a service desk manager emphasizes the above measures more than others such as quality incidents, first contact resolution, customer satisfaction etc., it may be that the service desk analysts are focused on how many calls they can answer in a day and how quickly they can complete one call and start the next. When this happens, with no thought about the quality of service being provided, how well

incidents are being handled or how well the customer is being treated, it will result in negative behaviour that is counter-productive to the goal of providing good service. The focus is only on volume and not quality.

When setting targets it is important to determine the baseline: this is the starting point from which you will measure improvement.

### 5.5.8 Balanced scorecard

This is a technique developed by Kaplan and Norton[4] in the mid-1990s and involves the definition and implementation of a measurement framework covering four different perspectives: customer, internal business, learning and growth, and financial. The four linked perspectives provide a balanced scorecard to support strategic activities and objectives, and can be used to measure overall IT performance.

The balanced scorecard is complementary to ITIL. Some of the links to IT include the following:

- **Client perspective** IT as a service provider, primarily documented in SLAs
- **Internal processes** Operational excellence utilizing incident management, problem management, change management, service asset and configuration management, and release and deployment management, as well as other IT processes; successful delivery of IT projects
- **Learning and growth** Business productivity, flexibility of IT, investments in software, professional learning and development
- **Financial** Align IT with the business objectives, manage costs, manage risks, deliver value; financial management for IT services is the process used to allocate costs and calculate ROI.

Kaplan and Norton first introduced the idea of a balanced scorecard in the early 1992 *Harvard Business Review*. The need for such a method emerged out of a growing recognition that financial measures alone were insufficient to manage the modern organization. Much of the emphasis in today's work environment is preparation to achieve financial goals, achieve process innovations, train workers, and create and maintain new kinds of relationship with customers.

---

[4] Kaplan, R. S. and Norton, D. P. (1992). The balanced scorecard: measures that drive performance. *Harvard Business Review* Jan–Feb, pp. 71–80.

The balanced scorecard is not simply a measurement system but a management system that enables organizations to clarify their vision, mission, goals, objectives and strategies and to translate them into action. When fully deployed, the balanced scorecard transforms strategic planning from an academic exercise into the nerve centre of an enterprise. It provides feedback on both the internal business processes and external outcomes in order to continually improve strategic performance and results.

The balanced scorecard, as an aid to organizational performance management, is a common method of tracking metrics and performing trend analysis. It helps to focus on not only financial targets but also internal processes, customers, and learning and growth issues. The balance should be found between four perspectives, which are focused around the following questions:

- **Customers**   What do customers expect of IT provision?
- **Internal processes**   What must IT excel at?
- **Learning and growth**   How does IT guarantee that the business will keep generating added value in the future?
- **Financial**   What is the cost of IT?

### 5.5.8.1 Cascading the balanced scorecard

Many organizations are structured around strategic business units (SBUs) with each business unit focusing on a specific group of products or services offered by the business. The structure of IT may match the SBU organization or may offer services to the SBU from a common, shared services IT organization or both. This last hybrid approach tends to put the central infrastructure group in the shared services world and the business solutions or application development group in the SBU itself. This often results in non-productive finger-pointing when things go wrong. The business itself is not interested in this blame-storming exercise but rather in the quality of IT service provision. Therefore, the balanced scorecard is best deployed at the SBU level (see Figure 5.12).

Once a balanced scorecard has been defined at the SBU level, it can be cascaded down through the organization. For each strategic business level measure and related target, business units can define additional measures and targets that support the strategic goal and target. In addition,

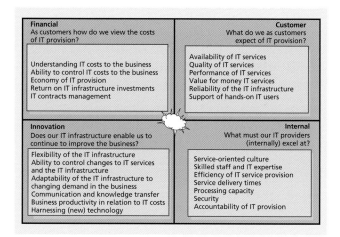

**Figure 5.12  IT balanced scorecard**

action plans and resource allocation decisions can be made with reference to how they contribute to the strategic balanced scorecard. As with any measurement system it is important to link the reward systems to the balanced scorecard objectives. Table 5.12 is an example of a balanced scorecard for a service desk.

The balanced scorecard is not an exclusive IT feature. On the contrary, many organizations use scorecards in other departments – even at the board level.

Start very conservatively when implementing the balanced scorecard. Start with two to three, maybe four, goals and metrics for each perspective. Organizations have to make choices; for many, this will be extremely difficult and time consuming.

Implementation is not the most difficult part of using the balanced scorecard – consolidation is. Usually, consultants are employed to assist in the introduction of the balanced scorecard. The challenge is to keep measuring once they are gone. The danger is in the temptation to fall back on prior measuring techniques or not measuring at all.

### 5.5.8.2 The balanced scorecard and measurement-based management

The balanced scorecard approach focuses on including customer-defined quality, continual improvement, employee empowerment, and measurement-based management and feedback.

The balanced scorecard incorporates feedback around internal business process outputs, as in total quality management (TQM), but also adds a feedback loop around the outcomes of business

**Table 5.12 Service desk balanced scorecard example**

| Financial goal | Performance indicator | Customer goal | Performance indicator |
| --- | --- | --- | --- |
| Ability to control service desk costs | Accuracy of service desk cost forecasts | Quality of service desk services | Availability of service desk (in IT users' perception) |
| Economy of service desk | Competitiveness of service | Reliability of service desk | Compliance to SLAs |
| Value of service desk | Costs of service desk | Performance of service desk | Restoration of service |
| | | Support of hands-on users | On-time service delivery |
| | | | Number of registered user complaints about IT |

| Innovation goal | Performance indicator | Internal goal | Performance indicator |
| --- | --- | --- | --- |
| Business productivity | Minimize mean time to restore service (MTRS) | Incident resolution | Percentage of first-time-right incident resolution |
| Service culture | | Elapsed time for incidents | |
| Flexibility | Improvements in business turnover | Meetings SLAs | Time spent on resolution |
| | Reduction in business costs ascribable to the service desk | Professionalism | Incidents resolved within SLAs |
| | New ways to improve service | | Treating customers with respect |

strategies. This creates a double-loop feedback process in the balanced scorecard.

An old saying goes: 'You can't improve what you can't measure.' Metrics must be developed based on the priorities of the strategic plan, which provides the key business drivers and criteria for metrics that managers most desire to watch. Services and processes are then designed to collect information relevant to these metrics. Strategic management can then examine the outcomes of various measured services, processes and strategies and track the results to guide the company and provide feedback. The value of metrics is in their ability to provide a factual basis for defining:

■ Strategic feedback to show the present status of the organization from many perspectives for decision makers
■ Diagnostic feedback into various services and processes to guide improvements on a continual basis
■ Trends in performance over time as the metrics are tracked
■ Feedback around the measurement methods themselves, and which metrics should be tracked
■ Quantitative inputs to forecasting methods and models for decision-support systems.

## 5.5.9 SWOT analysis

SWOT stands for strengths, weaknesses, opportunities and threats. This section provides guidance on properly conducting and using the result of a SWOT analysis, how to select the scope and range of this common assessment tool, as well as the common mistakes people make when using a SWOT analysis.

This technique involves the review and analysis of four specific areas of an organization: the internal strengths and weaknesses, and the external opportunities and threats. Once analysed, actions should be taken to:

■ Develop, exploit and capitalize on the organization's **strengths**
■ Reduce, minimize or remove **weaknesses**
■ Take maximum advantage of **opportunities**
■ Manage, mitigate and eliminate **threats**.

SWOT analyses can be performed quickly and can be used to target a specific area rather than looking at the entire enterprise.

### 5.5.9.1 Purpose

A SWOT analysis is a strategic planning tool used to evaluate the strengths, weaknesses, opportunities and threats involved in a project, business venture or any other situation requiring a decision. Sizing up a firm's internal strengths and weaknesses and its external opportunities and threats provides a quick overview of a firm's strategic situation.

### 5.5.9.2 How to use

The first step is to define the desired end state or objective. This objective definition must be explicit and approved by all participants in the process.

Once the objective is identified, SWOT are discovered and listed:

- **Strengths** are internal attributes of the organization that are helpful to the achievement of the objective.
- **Weaknesses** are internal attributes of the organization that are harmful to the achievement of the objective.
- **Opportunities** are external conditions that are helpful to the achievement of the objective.
- **Threats** are external conditions that are harmful to the achievement of the objective.

Correct identification of the SWOT is essential because subsequent steps in the process are all derived from the SWOT. To ensure a successful SWOT analysis, it is a good idea to ensure that the objective follows the SMART principle which stands for specific, measurable, achievable, relevant and time-bound.

SWOT analyses are used as inputs to the creative generation of possible strategies, by asking and answering the following four questions many times:

- How can we use each strength?
- How can we stop each weakness?
- How can we exploit each opportunity?
- How can we defend against each threat?

### 5.5.9.3 Scope, reach and range

SWOT analyses can be performed at various levels, from an individual perspective to a departmental, divisional or even corporate perspective. It is important to consolidate the lower hierarchical management levels before proceeding to the next level.

For example, all the members of a functional team perform an individual SWOT analysis. Then a SWOT for the functional team is performed. Each functional team within the department does the

same and a departmental SWOT is conducted and so on until a corporate SWOT is completed.

It is also possible to conduct a SWOT analysis for a service or a process. Table 5.13 provides a list of factors to consider in performing a SWOT analysis, while Table 5.14 gives an example of an analysis performed for CSI.

### 5.5.9.4 Common pitfalls of a SWOT analysis

The failure to correctly identify the end state will result in wasted resources and possibly failure. It is therefore important to align the SWOT analysis with the organization's vision, mission, goals and objectives. The following errors have been observed in published accounts of SWOT analysis. Making these errors can result in serious losses:

- Conducting a SWOT analysis before defining and agreeing on the desired end state
- Confusing opportunities (external to the company) with strengths (internal to the company); keep them separate
- Confusing opportunities with possible strategies; it may also be useful to keep in mind that SWOT is a description of conditions, while possible strategies define actions.

## 5.6 RETURN ON INVESTMENT

### 5.6.1 Creating a return on investment

The ROI challenge needs to take into consideration many factors. On one side is the investment cost. This is the money an organization pays to improve services and service management processes. These costs will be internal resource costs, tool costs, consulting costs etc. It is often easy to come up with these costs.

On the other side is what an organization can gain in a return. These returns are often hard to define or quantify. In order to be able to compute these items it is important to know the following:

- What is the cost of downtime? This includes both lost productivity of the customers and the loss of revenue.
- What is the cost of doing rework? How many failed changes have to be backed out and reworked?
- What is the cost of carrying out redundant work? Many organizations that don't have clear

**Table 5.13 SWOT analysis**

| Strength: things to consider | Weaknesses: things to consider |
|---|---|
| Core competencies | No clear strategic direction |
| Financial resources | Obsolete facilities |
| Reputable buyers | Low profitability |
| Acknowledged as market-leader | Lack of managerial depth and talent |
| Well-conceived functional-area strategies | Missing some key competencies |
| Access to economies of scale | Poor track record for performance |
| Little competitive pressure | Falling behind in R&D |
| Proprietary technology | Too narrow product line |
| Cost advantages | Weak market image |
| Strong campaigns | Weak distribution network |
| Product innovation | Below-average marketing skills |
| Proven management | Unable to finance needed changes |
| Ahead on experience curve | Higher overall unit costs |
| Better development/production capability | |
| Superior technology | |

| Opportunities: things to consider | Threats: things to consider |
|---|---|
| Ability to serve additional customer groups or expand into new market or segments | Entry of lower-cost foreign competitors |
| Ways to expand product line to meet broader range of customer needs | Rising sales of substitute products |
| | Slower market growth |
| Ability to transfer skills or technological know-how to new products or businesses | Adverse shifts in foreign exchange rates and trade policies of foreign governments |
| Integrating forward or backward | Costly regulatory requirements |
| Falling trade barriers in attractive foreign markets | Potentially sudden deregulation |
| Complacency among rival firms | Vulnerability to recession and business cycle |
| Ability to grow rapidly because of strong increases in market demand | Growing bargaining power of customers or suppliers |
| Emerging new technologies | Adverse demographic changes |

**Table 5.14 Sample SWOT analysis for CSI**

| Strengths | Weaknesses |
|---|---|
| People with the right attitude, values and commitment | Reactive organization |
| Management commitment to CSI | Immature processes |
| CSI manager in place | Lack of monitoring and reporting tools |
| | Insufficient data |

| Opportunities | Threats |
|---|---|
| Increased market share of current services | Competition |
| Become a third-party service provider | New regulatory requirements |
| Efficiencies through more integrated operations | New technology |
| Be quicker to market with new products | Lack of trained staff |
| | Lack of knowledge management |

processes in place and good communication often find that redundant work is being done.

■ What is the cost of non-value added projects? Many projects have been fully funded and resourced, but because of changing requirements they no longer add value. Despite this the project moves forward instead of being stopped.

■ What is the cost of late delivery of an application? Does this impact on the ability to deliver a new service or possibly an additional way to deliver an existing service?

■ What is the cost of escalating incidents to second and third level support groups instead of resolving incidents at the first level? There is often a difference in utilization staff in second level and third level support groups. The more we escalate incidents to these groups the less time they have to work on projects that they may also be assigned to.

■ What is the fully allocated hourly cost for different employee levels?

These are only some of the things that have to be considered when creating a ROI statement. The cost of not implementing the improvement also has to be taken into account.

There are different approaches to measuring and reporting on availability. Availability is a good measure to understand the cost of lost productivity, the cost of not being able to complete a business transaction, or the true cost of downtime. Approaches include measuring:

■ Impact by minutes lost – this is a calculation on the duration of downtime multiplied by the number of customers impacted. This can be used to report on lost customer productivity.

■ Impact by business transaction – this calculation is based on the number of business transactions that could not be processed during the downtime. This measurement provides a better indication of business impact.

■ The true cost of downtime that has been agreed on.

Other areas of warranty such as security, recoverability and ensuring there is sufficient capacity also have to be taken into account.

## 5.6.2 Establishing the business case

The business case should articulate the reason for undertaking a service or process improvement initiative. As far as possible, data and evidence should be provided relating to the costs and expected benefits of undertaking process improvement, noting that:

■ Process redesign activities are more complex and therefore more costly than initially expected.

■ Organizational change impact is often underestimated.

■ Changed process usually requires changed competencies and tools, adding further to the expense.

In developing a business case, the focus should not be limited to ROI but also on the business value that service improvement brings to the organization and its customers (VOI), because ROI alone does not capture the real value of service improvement. Should an organization choose to focus solely on ROI, much of the potential benefit achievable will not be disclosed nor reviewed after the fact. This could in turn result in worthwhile initiatives not being approved, or a review of the initiative revealing apparent failure, when it was actually successful.

Not surprisingly, most business and IT executives expect a return on their investment. It is important to recognize that an investment in CSI, and realizing its benefits, can vary depending on the customer base, size of IT and maturity of the ITIL process implemented. Also benefits will cross existing organizational boundaries and true benefits can only be captured in collaboration with the users/customers and ITIL process owners. The focus is therefore to work with the stakeholders to develop business and IT specific indicators that link business value measures with contributions from IT. In other words, how does ITIL process improvement add value to the organization?

Examples of business value measures are:

■ Time to market
■ Customer retention
■ Market share.

IT's contribution can be captured through:

■ Gaining agility
■ Managing knowledge
■ Enhancing knowledge

- Reducing costs
- Reducing risk.

IT should begin by defining the types of business values that each improvement will contribute to.

As an example, the US Sarbanes-Oxley legislation and other international laws require that the business processes be certified to produce financial reports in addition to certifying the reports themselves. Sarbanes-Oxley is about improving transparency and accountability in business processes and corporate accounting to restore confidence in public markets. It regulates processes and business practices. Therefore having a higher level of ITIL maturity will facilitate regulatory compliance.

Without a mature process framework it is natural for organizations to take an ad hoc approach to compliance. They address requirements as they emerge, through a series of one-offs, just-in-time projects. Since compliance affects a lot of ongoing business activity, this is disruptive, increases the required effort and becomes time-consuming and very expensive.

If an investment is well conceived, solid and delivers results, it can lead to cost savings in the long run. Therefore it is important to choose the right investment and make sure they deliver. When presenting a business case for an ITIL process improvement project, it is important to help executives understand the business value of the ITIL process framework. The tendency for most IT executives is to over-emphasize technology and tools. Technology is a means to an end. The benefits are realized from the business changes. It is important to address how people and processes will change, from 'as is' to the 'to be' state.

The 'as is' stage can be defined as a baseline. Capturing the baseline of the performance measurements affected by the proposed implementation is paramount to the business case. The careful preparation of the baseline will facilitate meaningful business information and level setting about relevant business issues, allowing strategic alignment to take place. The focus should be to develop cause-and-effect metrics to link the benefits against the measurements selected along with the impact on other areas of the enterprise. The metrics should be monitored before, during and after the ITIL implementation to determine how the projected values are being delivered.

Another aspect to consider in business case development is situations where value will be lost by not undertaking process improvement activities. There will be situations where failure to take action will severely impact the business and IT – the value of process improvement may, in fact, not be value added, but value retained.

As a final note, care should be taken in developing the business case to ensure that the success criteria are clearly defined, showing how they are to be measured, and when they are going to be measured.

### 5.6.3 Expectations – what's in it for me?

Considerations for business executives include:

- The benefits of ITIL process improvements
- What impact it has on my business
- Revenue increase
- Cost reduction
- VOI.

Considerations for the chief finance officer include:

- The ROI
- Payback time.

Considerations for IT include:

- How ITIL benefits translate to business benefits. Find one or two compelling reasons why the organization should spend the time and money.

Determine the current or anticipated concern of the organization about IT. Estimate the cost if the status quo were to remain and subsequently estimate the savings that could be realized if the IT service management (ITSM) processes were put in place or improved. Examples include new lines of business overseas, poor response time or time taken to handle incidents and problems, and the number of incidents in the organization.

### 5.6.4 Business cases in a data-poor environment

Organizations intending to undertake service improvement activities may find themselves in a situation where the lack of process means that there is no viable body of data or evidence to quantify expected benefits, ROI or VOI. How, then, does such an organization justify process improvement, or recognize how much expenditure is appropriate to achieve cost-effective improvements?

An approach that circumvents this situation is to gain approval to establish basic measurement capabilities, as a means of gathering consistent data. This may be as simple as ensuring that all IT staff record data in a consistent fashion, or start measuring activities or outcomes that are not currently captured. After an agreed period of data capture, some evidence will exist to support (or perhaps not support) a process improvement initiative.

Another approach is to undertake a process maturity assessment of current processes, to

**Example of good management**

XYZ Limited has grown rapidly from a single-site to a multi-site environment and now employs 1,500 people, up from 250 people two years ago. The IT group has struggled to match the business growth with growth in process consistency and service delivery. The business is demanding that the IT group performs better as the shortcomings in IT service are now impacting the business bottom-line.

The IT manager identifies that lack of consistent process and business focus are the roadblock to delivering better service to the business. She realizes that the staff are working very hard, but are often doing re-work or repairing self-inflicted errors. While good technicians, they are averse to documenting activities or outcomes.

Data and measurement are currently inconsistent. While she knows average business and IT staff salary costs, the costs of service outage etc. are not known nor can they be calculated using current data.

Rather than requesting funding to undertake process improvements, the IT manager requests funding for a pilot project to establish a rudimentary measurement framework to start capturing data in a standard fashion, using more or less existing processes. This pilot initiative after three months provides clear evidence that the true failure rate of changes is much higher than previously expected, and a key contributor to business and IT loss of productivity.

Armed with this evidence, the IT manager prepares a business case detailing some of the current deficiencies and expected benefits and returns to be delivered from properly quantifying process gaps and undertaking appropriate process improvement.

identify which processes are most divergent from ITIL practices. It should, however, be noted that this activity will only identify the absence of process and/or data. A process maturity assessment will not in itself provide the data to justify how much to spend on improving process.

Where organizations establish a basic measurement and monitoring capability, some caution should be exercised regarding the quality of this data: be aware of limitations of new data. Even if the data doesn't make any sense, this is reason enough to explore the opportunity for improvements.

It is important that once the decision to start capturing and reporting on data is made, an initial baseline is created so improvements can be measured against it.

### 5.6.5 Measuring benefits achieved

While the initial identification of benefits is an estimate of those likely to be realized by the proposed process improvement initiative, there is also a need subsequently to measure the benefits actually achieved. These measurements attest to whether the improvement activity achieved the intended outcomes and should consider whether:

- The envisaged improvements were realized
- The benefits arising from the improvements were achieved
- The target ROI was achieved
- The intended value-added was actually achieved (VOI)
- The outcomes of the preceding points lead to further process improvement actions being re-evaluated
- Enough time has passed before measuring the benefits. Some benefits will not be immediately apparent, and it is likely that benefits will continue to change over time, as ongoing costs and ongoing benefits continue to move.

A further consideration in the measurement of benefits is that data quality and measurement precision pre- and post-improvement could be different, thus giving rise to the direct comparison not being valid. If this is the case, the data will need to be normalized before validating benefits.

In 2006, the US state of North Carolina implemented some improvements based on the ITIL framework. The improvements took place in a span of less than three months. ITS is the name of the state's IT organization. These are the results of tactical quick-win efforts targeted in tandem with the training programme and the state's awareness campaign. This information is reproduced with permission:

- IT has improved its ability to resolve incidents within its target timeframe by 32%.
- IT has improved its ability to resolve service requests within its target timeframe by 20%.
- Change management process compliance increased more than twofold resulting in fewer incidents and reduced downtime.

The first two processes to be developed and implemented were incident and change management. As with most organizations, the state of North Carolina already had an existing change and incident process. This organization started showing immediate improvement before any formal improvement programme was implemented simply by identifying and communicating the key metrics that were going to be reviewed by senior management. Staff began following their existing process simply because they knew reporting against certain performance measures had started and that these performance measures were discussed among senior managers. Not only were these discussions held but there was clear guidance that the performance measures had to improve. These improvements can easily be translated into overall business improvements.

## 5.7 SERVICE REPORTING

This section will look into the various aspects of reporting such as identifying the purpose, the target audience and what the report will be used for.

As discussed in Chapter 4 a significant amount of data is collated and monitored by IT in the daily delivery of quality service to the business; however, only a small subset is of real interest and importance to the business. Most data and its meaning are more suited to the internal management needs of IT.

The business likes to see a historical representation of the past period's performance that portrays its experience; however, it is more concerned with those historical events that continue to be a threat going forward, and how IT intends to militate against such threats.

Cross-referenced data must still be presented which align precisely to any contracted, chargeable elements of the delivery, which may or may not be technical depending on the business focus and language used within contracts and SLAs.

It is not satisfactory simply to present reports that depict adherence (or otherwise) to SLAs, which in themselves are prone to statistical ambiguity. IT needs to build an actionable approach to reporting: this is what happened, this is what we did, this is how we will ensure it doesn't impact you again, and this is how we are working to improve the delivery of IT services generally.

A reporting ethos that focuses on the future as strongly as it focuses on the past also provides the means for IT to market its wares directly aligned to the positive or negative experiences of the business.

### 5.7.1 Reporting policy and rules

An ideal approach to building a business-focused service-reporting framework is to take the time to define and agree the policy and rules with the business and service design about how reporting will be implemented and managed.

This includes:

- Targeted audience(s) and the related business views on what the service delivered is
- Agreement on what to measure and report
- Agreed definitions of all terms and boundaries
- Basis of all calculations
- Reporting schedules
- Access to reports and medium to be used
- Meetings scheduled to review and discuss reports.

### 5.7.2 Right content for the right audience

Numerous policies and rules can exist as long as it is clear for each report which policies and rules have been applied, e.g. one policy may be applied to manufacturing whereas a variant may be more suited to the sales team. However all policies and rules form part of the single reporting framework.

Once the framework, policies and rules are in place, targeting suitably styled reports becomes simply a task of translating flat historical data into meaningful business views (which can be automated). These need to be annotated around the key questions, threats, mitigations and improvements such data provoke. Reports can then be presented via the medium of choice, e.g. paper-based hard copies, online soft copies, web-enabled dynamic HTML, current snapshot whiteboards, or real-time portal/dashboards.

Simple and effective customizable and automated reporting is crucial to a successful, ongoing reporting system that is seen as adding value to the business. Over time, many of the initial standard reports may become obsolete in favour of the regular production of custom reports which have been shaped to meet changing business needs and become the standard.

The end result is the targeted recipient having clear, unambiguous and relevant information in a language and style that they understand and like, accessible in the medium of their choice, and detailing the delivery of IT into their environment within their boundaries.

## 5.8   CSI AND OTHER SERVICE MANAGEMENT PROCESSES

CSI activities make extensive use of methods and practices found in many ITIL processes throughout the lifecycle of a service. Far from being redundant, the use of the outputs in the form of flows, matrices, statistics or analysis reports provides valuable insight into the service's design and operation. This information, combined with new business requirements, technology specifications, IT capabilities, budgets, trends and possibly legislation, is vital to CSI to determine what needs to be improved – prioritize it and suggest improvements if required.

### 5.8.1   Availability management

Availability management's methods are part of the measuring process explained in Chapter 4. They are part of the measuring process – gathering, processing and analysing activities. When the information is provided to CSI in the form of a report or presentation, it becomes part of CSI's gathering activity. For more details on each method, please consult *ITIL Service Design*.

Availability management provides IT with the business and user perspective about how deficiencies in the infrastructure and underpinning process and procedures impact the business operation. The use of business-driven metrics

can demonstrate this impact in real terms and help quantify the benefits of improvement opportunities.

Availability management plays an important role in helping the IT support organization recognize where it can add value by exploiting technical skills and competencies in an availability context. The continual improvement technique can be used by availability management to harness this technical capability. This can be used with either small groups of technical staff or a wider group within a workshop environment. The information provided by availability management is made available to CSI through the availability management information system (AMIS).

This section provides practical usage and details on how each availability management method mentioned below can be used in various activities of CSI.

### 5.8.1.1 Component failure impact analysis

Component failure impact analysis (CFIA) identifies single points of failure, IT services at risk from failure of various CIs and the alternatives that are available should a CI fail. It should also be used to assess the existence and validity of recovery procedures for the selected CIs. The same approach can be used for a single IT service by mapping the component CIs against the vital business functions and users supported by each component.

When a single point of failure is identified, the information is provided to CSI. This information, combined with business requirements, enables CSI to make recommendations on how to address the failure.

### 5.8.1.2 Fault tree analysis

Fault tree analysis (FTA) is a technique that can be used to determine a chain of events that has caused an incident, or may cause an incident in the future. It offers detailed models of availability, and makes a representation of a chain of events using Boolean algebra and notation. Essentially FTA distinguishes between four events: basic events, resulting events, conditional events and trigger events.

When provided to CSI, FTA information indicates which part of the infrastructure, process or service was responsible in the service disruptions. This information, combined with business requirements, enables CSI to make recommendations about how to address the fault.

### 5.8.1.3 Service failure analysis

Service failure analysis (SFA) is a technique designed to provide a structured approach to identify end-to-end availability improvement opportunities that deliver benefits to the user. Many of the activities involved in SFA are closely aligned with those of problem management. In a number of organizations these activities are performed jointly by problem and availability management. SFA should attempt to identify improvement opportunities that benefit the end user. It is therefore important to take an end-to-end view of the service requirements.

CSI and SFA work hand in hand. SFA identifies the business impact of an outage on a service, system or process. This information, combined with business requirements, enables CSI to make recommendations about how to address improvement opportunities.

### 5.8.1.4 Technical observation

A technical observation (TO) is a prearranged gathering of specialist technical support staff from within IT support. They are brought together to focus on specific aspects of IT availability. The TO's purpose is to monitor events in real time as they occur, with the specific aim of identifying improvement opportunities within the current IT infrastructure. The TO is best suited to delivering proactive business and end-user benefits from within the real-time IT environment. Bringing together specialist technical staff to observe specific activities and events within the IT infrastructure and operational processes creates an environment to identify improvement opportunities.

The TO gathers, processes and analyses information about the situation. Too often the TO is reactive by nature and is assembled hastily to deal with an emergency. Why wait? If the TO is included as part of the launch of a new service, system or process for example, a lot of the issues inherent to any new component would be identified and dealt with more quickly.

One of the best examples of a TO is the mission control room for a space agency. All the specialists from all aspects of the mission are gathered in one

room. Space agencies don't wait for the rocket to be launched and experience a problem before gathering specialists to monitor, observe and provide feedback. They set it up well before the actual launch and practise monitoring, observing and providing feedback.

Certainly, launching a rocket is very costly, but so is launching a new service, system or process. Can the business afford a catastrophic failure of a new enterprise resource planning (ERP) application, for example? Incidentally, rocket launches are often aborted seconds before the launch. Shouldn't organizations (including yours) do the same when someone discovers a major potential flaw in a service or system? CSI starts from the beginning and includes preventing things from failing in the first place. Let's fix the flaw before it goes into production instead of fixing the fixes (what a concept!). This information, combined with business requirements, enables CSI to make recommendations about how to address the TO's findings.

### 5.8.1.5 Expanded incident lifecycle

First, let's define a few items:

- **Availability management** The process responsible for defining, analysing, planning, measuring and improving all aspects of the availability of IT services. Availability management is responsible for ensuring that all IT infrastructure, processes, tools, roles etc. are appropriate for the agreed service level targets for availability.

- **Expanded incident lifecycle** A technique to help with the technical analysis of incidents affecting the availability of components and IT services (see Figure 5.13). The expanded incident lifecycle is further made up of two parts: time to restore service (also known as downtime) and time between failures (also known as uptime). There is a diagnosis part to the incident lifecycle as well as repair, restoration and recovery of the service.

Let's assume that CSI has decided to improve the incident lifecycle by reducing the mean time to restore service (MTRS) and expanding the mean time between failures (MTBF).

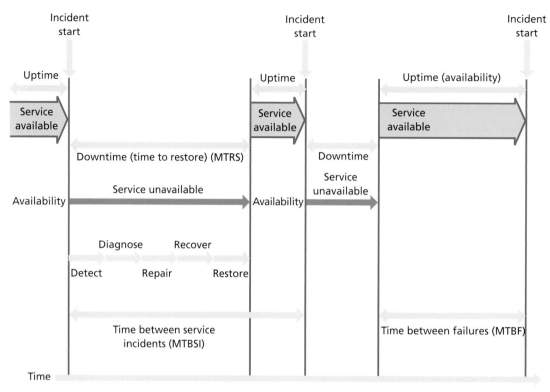

*Figure 5.13 The expanded incident lifecycle*

Here is an example of how availability management can assist in reducing downtime in the expanded incident lifecycle by using many techniques:

- **Monitoring (detection of incident)** By adequately monitoring for availability of vital business functions through automated monitoring tools (set at the right threshold) that record and escalate incidents, the time it takes to detect and record incidents is reduced.
- **Incident recording** Since one of availability management's goals is to 'optimize the … support organization', educating and training first-line staff as well as simplifying and/or automating incident recording helps reduce the time it takes to record incidents.
- **Investigation** Using the FTA method, availability management assists in reducing the time to investigate by creating proper investigation procedures for incident management staff. The same logic applies to the diagnosis of the incident cause, resolution and recovery.

Here is an example of how availability management can assist in increasing up-time in the expanded incident lifecycle by using many techniques:

- Using SFA, availability management can make recommendations to increase the reliability of components, thus reducing the likelihood of an incident occurring in the first place.
- Scheduling and performing adequate and required internal maintenance of components (maintainability), availability management can help to increase the resilience of components, thus reducing the likelihood of an incident causing an outage.
- Ensuring that external maintenance of components (serviceability) is properly scheduled and performed by external vendors, availability management can help to increase the resilience of components, thus reducing the likelihood of an incident causing an outage.
- Conducting a CFIA to predict and evaluate the impact on IT service availability arising from component failures assists in identifying single points of failure. Availability management will either submit recommendations for enhancements to the resilience and reliability of such components or provide better troubleshooting procedures to the support groups.
- Implementing security recommendations coming from information security management

regarding the confidentiality, integrity and availability of associated data helps reduce malicious or unauthorized access to data, ensuring data integrity, and thus reducing the likelihood of an incident occurring or decreasing the time it takes to respond to or resolve an incident.

## 5.8.2 Capacity management

This section provides practical usage and details about how each capacity management method mentioned below can be used in various activities of CSI.

The capacity management process must be responsive to changing requirements for processing capacity. New services are required to underpin the changing business. Existing services will require modification to provide extra functionality. Old services will become obsolete, freeing up capacity. Capacity management must ensure sufficient hardware, software and personnel resources are in place to support existing and future business capacity and performance requirements.

Similarly to availability management, capacity management can play an important role in helping the IT support organization recognize where it can add value by exploiting its technical skills and competencies in a capacity context. The continual improvement technique can be used by capacity management to harness this technical capability. This can be used with either small groups of technical staff or a wider group within a workshop environment.

The information provided by capacity management is made available to CSI through the capacity management information system (CMIS).

## 5.8.3 Business capacity management

A prime objective of the business capacity management sub-process is to ensure that future business requirements for IT services are considered and understood, and that sufficient capacity to support the services is planned and implemented in an appropriate timescale.

As a result, the ability to satisfy the customers' SLRs will be affected. It is the responsibility of capacity management to predict and cater to these changes. These new requirements may come to the attention of capacity management from many different sources and for many different reasons.

They may be generated by the business or may originate from the capacity management process itself. Such examples could be a recommendation to upgrade to take advantage of new technology, or the implementation of a tuning activity to resolve a performance problem.

Information gathered here enables CSI to answer the question 'What do we need?'

## 5.8.4 Service capacity management

A prime objective of the service capacity management sub-process is to identify and understand the IT services, their use of resource, working patterns, peaks and troughs, as well as to ensure that the services can and do meet their SLA targets. In this sub-process, the focus is on managing service performance, as determined by the targets contained in the SLAs or SLRs.

The key to successful service capacity management is to pre-empt difficulties, wherever possible. This is another sub-process that has to be proactive and anticipatory rather than reactive. However, there are times when it has to react to specific performance problems. Based on the knowledge and understanding of the performance requirements for each service, the effects of changes in the use of services can be estimated, and actions taken to ensure that the required service performance can be achieved. Information gathered here enables CSI to answer the question 'What do we need?'

## 5.8.5 Component capacity management

A prime objective of the component capacity management sub-process is to identify and understand the capacity and utilization of each of the components of the IT infrastructure. This ensures the optimum use of the current hardware and software resources in order to achieve and maintain the agreed service levels. All hardware components and many software components in the IT infrastructure have a finite capacity, which, when exceeded, have the potential to cause performance problems.

As in service capacity management, the key to successful component capacity management is to pre-empt difficulties wherever possible. Therefore this sub-process has to be proactive and anticipatory rather than reactive. However, there are times when it has to react to specific problems

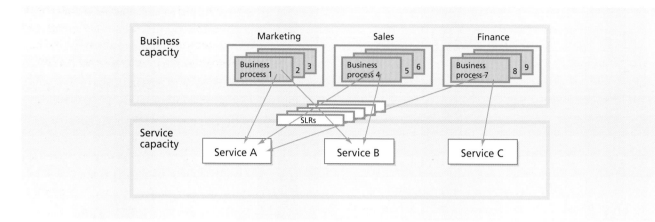

**Figure 5.14  Connecting business and service capacity management**

**Table 5.15  Departmental requirements**

|  | Marketing | Sales | Finance |
|---|---|---|---|
| Employees | 15 | 40 | 5 |
| Number of emails per day | 100 | 200 | 50 |
| Size of attachment | 10 Mb | 5 Mb | 10 Mb |
| Frequency of large attachment | infrequent | very (contracts) | often |
| Requires remote access | No | Yes | Yes |
| Requires hand-held computer | No | Yes | No |

that are caused by a lack or inefficient use of resources.

It is important to understand how the three sub-processes tie together. Let's look at the example in Figure 5.14.

There are three services: A, B and C; and three departments: Marketing, Sales and Finance. Service A is used by all three departments. Service B is used only by Marketing and Sales. Service C is used only by Finance.

The requirements for each service from each department are shown in Table 5.15.

From Table 5.15, the overall size of the email service can be computed. If email was the only service, it would be relatively simple. There are other services offered and each service makes use of four major components: hardware, software, documentation and people. Using the CFIA report from availability management it is possible to identify all the components of each service and which component is used by which service. From there optimizing the capacity of each component

can be reviewed. This, in turn, enables the optimization of the service based on the usage and performance requirements from each customer.

This, however, only focuses on the current utilization. Future business requirements for this service also need to be reviewed. Growth can happen in one of three ways as shown in Figure 5.15. In this figure, curve 1 indicates a steady growth or deployment of the service over time; curve 2 indicates a big-bang approach where everyone starts using the new service at the same time and usage stabilizes over time; and curve 3 indicates a small number of people using the new service before it is eventually deployed to everyone.

You can predict which growth curve is correct as accurately as you can predict the weather a year from now. Looking at curve 2, it is important to ensure sufficient initial capacity for all components – hardware, software, documentation and people. Looking at curve 1 additional capacity is required but can wait if curve 3 is considered. Now what would happen if the business scenario predicts

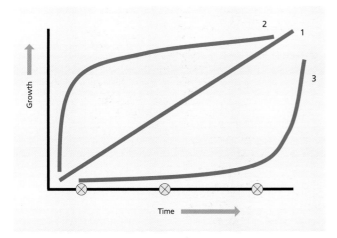

*Figure 5.15 Business capacity growth model*

curve 2 and curve 3 is what actually happens? The result is over-capacity and IT is blamed for poor planning and for overspending. Consider the opposite scenario where the business predicts curve 3 and curve 2 is what actually happens. The result is under-capacity and IT gets blamed for poor planning.

Remember that only one service was reviewed so far. There are three services in the example. You need to understand the service and business along with the component capacity requirements to be able to identify the true capacity requirements. More importantly business capacity can be computed since how much a business unit consumes a service is known. This is when the infrastructure required to deliver and support the services can be properly put in place (see Figures 5.16 and 5.17).

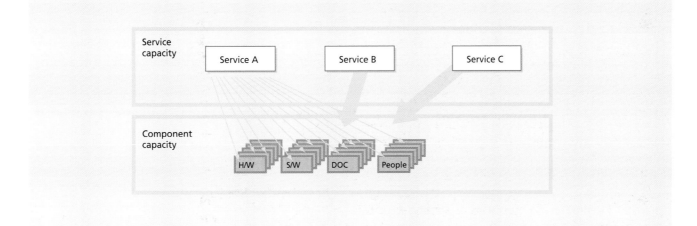

*Figure 5.16 Connecting service and component capacity management*

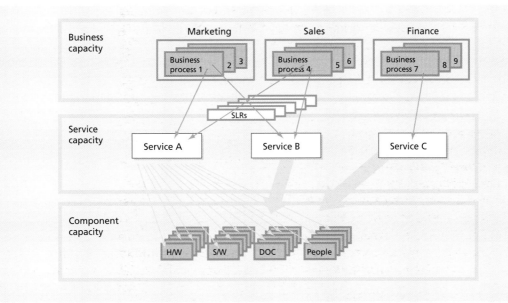

*Figure 5.17 Connecting businesses, service and component capacity management*

From this point, IT is in a better position to improve the service provision. In order to do this IT must start not only to measure but also to influence the business. Influencing the business is part of demand management.

### 5.8.6 Workload management and demand management

Workload management can be defined as understanding which customers use what service, when they use the service, how they use the service, and finally how using the service impacts the performance of a single or multiple systems and/or components that make up a service.

Demand management is often associated with influencing the end users' behaviour. By influencing the end users' behaviour an organization can change the workload thus improving the performance of components that support IT services. Using demand management can be an effective way of improving services without investing a lot of money. A full discussion of demand management can be found in *ITIL Service Strategy* and *ITIL Service Design*.

There are different ways to influence customer behaviour. Charging for services is an obvious way, but it is not always effective. Sometimes people still need to use the service and will use it regardless of the price. Putting in place policies regarding proper usage of the service is another way to influence customer behaviour; communicating expectations for IT and the business, educating people on how to use the service and negotiating maintenance windows are just as effective in influencing customers. Putting in place restrictions such as amount of space allocated for email storage is another way to influence behaviour.

Consider carefully how you try to influence a customer's behaviour and it may become a negative influence rather than a positive influence. As an example, if an organization chooses to charge for every contact to the service desk, this could create a negative behaviour in that end users no longer call or email the service desk, but call second-level support directly, or turn to peer-to-peer support, which ultimately makes the cost of support go up, not down. However if the goal is to move end users to using a new self-service web-based knowledge system, then with a proper communication and education plan on using the new self-service system this could be a positive influencing experience.

CSI needs to review demand management policies to ensure that they are still effective. A policy that was good a couple of years ago may not be workable or useful today. For example, a few years ago, large email attachments were uncommon. It made sense to limit attachments to 2 Mb. Today's reality is different.

### 5.8.7 Iterative activities of capacity management

#### 5.8.7.1 Trend analysis

Trend analysis can be performed on the resource utilization and service performance information that was collected by the service and component capacity management sub-processes. The data can be held in a spreadsheet and the graphical, trend analysis and forecasting facilities used to show the utilization of a particular resource over a previous period of time, and how it can be expected to change in the future. Typically trend analysis only provides estimates of future resource utilization. It is less effective in producing an accurate estimate of response times, in which case either analytical or simulation modelling should be used.

This activity provides insight into resource utilization and is used by both CSI and problem management to identify opportunities for improvements. Trend analysis is rooted in the data analysis activity of the measuring process.

It is important to recognize that trend analysis is also an activity of proactive problem management (see section 4.4 in *ITIL Service Operation*). However, the focus is different. Whereas problem management focuses on trends in errors and faults (the past), capacity management is forward looking. It might be looking for innovation in storage management, or at expected growth versus real growth and recommend adjustments.

#### 5.8.7.2 Modelling

Modelling types range from making estimates based on experience and current resource utilization information, to pilot studies, prototypes and full-scale benchmarks. The former are cheaper and more reasonable for day-to-day small decisions, while the latter are expensive but may be advisable when implementing a large new project.

Since it is impossible to have an exact duplicate of the infrastructure for testing purposes, CSI makes use of the information provided by the capacity management modelling activity to predict the behaviour of service improvements before the improvement is actually carried out. This may prevent costly implementations or problems later. Modelling results can be used by change management to assess the impact of a change on the infrastructure or may be used as part of release testing. Whether it is used by another process before the information makes its way to CSI, modelling is a valuable tool.

Modelling can also be used in conjunction with demand management to predict the possible effects of demand management efforts and initiatives. This allows IT to answer questions such as 'What happens if we fail?' and 'What happens if we are successful?'

### 5.8.7.3 Analytical modelling

Analytical models are representations of computer system's behaviour using mathematical techniques such as multi-class network queuing theory. When the model is run, the queuing theory is used to calculate computer system response times. If the response times predicted by the model are sufficiently close to the response times recorded in real life, the model can be regarded as an accurate representation of the computer system. The technique of analytical modelling requires less time and effort than simulation modelling, but typically gives less accurate results. Also the model must be kept up to date.

### 5.8.7.4 Simulation modelling

Simulation involves the modelling of discrete events, such as transaction arrival rates, against a given hardware configuration. This type of modelling can be very accurate in sizing new applications or predicting the effects of changes on existing applications. It can also be very time-consuming and therefore costly.

When simulating transaction arrival rates, have a number of staff enter a series of transactions from prepared scripts, or use software to input the same scripted transactions with a random arrival rate. Either of these approaches takes time and effort to prepare and run. However it can be cost-justified for organizations with very large systems where

the cost, and associated performance implications, assume great importance.

### 5.8.7.5 Baseline models

Improvements are gradual and incremental by nature. How can one claim to have improved if a baseline is not established before the improvement takes place?

The first stage in modelling is to create a baseline model that accurately reflects the performance that is being achieved. When this baseline model is created, predictive modelling can be undertaken. If the baseline model is accurate, then the accuracy of the result of the predicted changes can be trusted.

Effective service and component capacity management together with modelling techniques enable capacity management to answer the 'What if?' questions: 'What if the throughput of service A doubles?' or 'What if service B is moved from the current processor onto a new processor – how will the response times in the two services be altered?'

Figure 5.18 illustrates how CSI can make use of the intricate relationships between capacity management and other processes and activities. At first glance the diagram seems very busy. However, it illustrates the inputs and outputs from other processes and activities into and out of the various sub-activities of capacity management. CSI will then use this information to assist capacity management in planning for future capacity and performance as well as identifying improvement opportunities.

## 5.8.8 IT service continuity management

This section provides practical usage and details about how each ITSCM method can be used in various activities of CSI.

### 5.8.8.1 Business continuity management, ITSCM and CSI

Any CSI initiative to improve services needs to also have integration with ITSCM as any changes to the service requirements, infrastructure etc. need to be taken into account for any changes that may be required for the continuity plan. That is why it is important for all SIPs to go through change management.

Business continuity management (BCM) is concerned with managing risks to ensure that

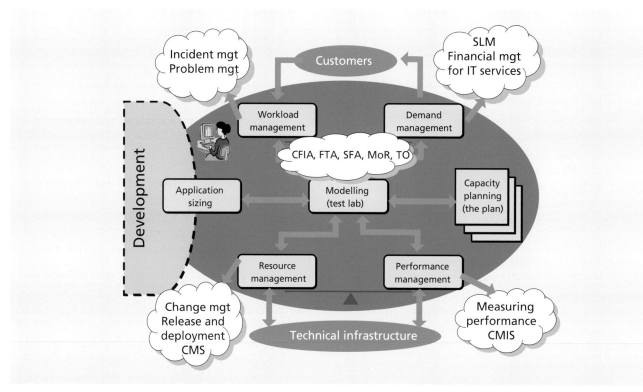

**Figure 5.18 Capacity management activities**

an organization can continue operating to a predetermined minimum level. The BCM process involves reducing the risk to an acceptable level and planning for the recovery of business processes should a risk materialize and a disruption to the business occur.

ITSCM allows an IT organization to identify, assess and take responsibility for managing its risks, thus enabling it to better understand the environment in which it operates, decide which risks it wishes to counteract, and act positively to protect the interests of all stakeholders (including staff, customers, shareholders, third parties and creditors). CSI can complement this activity and help to deliver business benefit.

### 5.8.9 Problem management

CSI and problem management are closely related as one of the goals of problem management is to identify and remove errors permanently that impact services from the infrastructure. This directly supports CSI activities of identifying and implementing service improvements.

Problem management also supports CSI activities through trend analysis and the targeting of preventive action.

Problem management activities are generally conducted within the scope of service operation and CSI must take an active role in the proactive aspects of problem management to identify and recommend changes that will result in service improvements.

Further information on the problem management process can be found in *ITIL Service Operation*.

### 5.8.10 Change management, release and deployment management

It is likely that all CSI improvement activities will fall under the scope of change management and release and deployment management. CSI's goal is to identify and implement improvement activities on IT services that support the business processes as well as to identify and implement improvements to ITSM processes. The improvement activities support the lifecycle approach through service strategy, service design, service transition and service operation.

CSI is an ongoing activity constantly monitoring, analysing and researching improvement opportunities, whereas release and deployment management depends on the change management process for its work.

There are many activities of the release and deployment management process that can be utilized by CSI. Once CSI has come up with a recommendation for improvement, a change request is submitted. The proposed change is then scheduled as part of a release. The release and deployment management process will identify any areas requiring improvement for new or updated services during the early life support phase.

### 5.8.10.1 Post-implementation review

As a part of change management a post-implementation review (PIR) is carried out on certain changes. CSI, working with change management, can require a PIR for all changes that CSI was a part of for improving a service (see *ITIL Service Transition*). CSI needs to participate in any PIR on changes that are implemented to improve a service. As part of a PIR it is important for CSI to identify if the change actually improved the service or if there are still some issues. If a change, once implemented, fails to improve the service as desired, then CSI activities need to continue working with service design, service transition and service operation.

## 5.8.11 Knowledge management

One of the key domains in support of CSI is knowledge management. Capturing, organizing, assessing for quality and using knowledge is great input in CSI activities. An organization has to gather knowledge and analyse what the results are in order to look for trends in service level achievements and/or results and output of service management processes. This knowledge is used to identify improvement opportunities for inclusion in the CSI register, for subsequent review and prioritization of the register, and for building SIPs.

Knowledge management in today's market is vastly different from what it was 10 years ago. Just in that short amount of time there has been:

- An increase in the rate of change in industry and market landscapes, as barriers to entry have decreased and new opportunities opened up
- An increase in employee turnover, as it has become more socially acceptable and often beneficial to change companies during a career to develop and share new experiences and perspectives
- An increase in access to information via the internet and a more open global economy

- Greater market competition forcing company employees to share knowledge between departments and subsidiaries.

### 5.8.11.1 Knowledge management concepts

Effective knowledge management enables a company to optimize the benefits of these changes, while at the same time:

- Enhancing the organization's effectiveness through better decision-making enabled by having the right information at the right time, and facilitating enterprise learning through the exchange and development of ideas and individuals
- Enhancing customer–supplier relationships through sharing information and services to expand capabilities through collaborative efforts
- Improving business processes through sharing lessons learned, results and best practices across the organization.

Knowledge management is key to the overall viability of the enterprise, from capturing the competitive advantage in an industry to decreasing cycle time and cost of an IT implementation. The approach to cultivating knowledge depends heavily on the make-up of the existing knowledge base, and knowledge management norms for cultural interaction.

There are two main components to successful knowledge management:

- An **open culture** where knowledge – best practices and lessons learned – is shared across the organization and individuals are rewarded for it. Many cultures foster an environment where 'knowledge is power' (the more you know that others do not, the more valuable you are to the company). This type of knowledge hoarding is a dangerous behaviour for a company to reward since that knowledge may leave the company at any time. Another tenet of an open culture is a willingness to learn. This is an environment where growing an individual's knowledge base is rewarded and facilitated through open support and opportunities.
- The **infrastructure** – a culture may be open to knowledge sharing, but without the means or infrastructure to support it, even the best intentions can be impaired, and over time this

serves as a demotivator, quelling the behaviour. This infrastructure can be defined in various ways; it may be a technical application or system which allows individuals to conduct online, self-paced training, or it may be processes such as post-mortems or knowledge sharing activities designed to bring people together to discuss best practices or lessons learned.

The identification of knowledge gaps and resulting sharing and development of that knowledge must be built into CSI throughout the IT lifecycle. This also raises the issues of dependencies and priorities. The IT lifecycle itself drives a natural priority of knowledge development and sharing. But regardless of the IT project's lifecycle stage, it is important to identify and develop the necessary knowledge base prior to the moment where the knowledge may be applied. This may seem obvious and yet the majority of organizations fail to recognize the need to train individuals until the process is halted due to a skills shortage. Knowledge sharing is an activity that should be fostered prior to, during and after the application of knowledge to the task.

Knowledge management could be seen at the opposite end of a spectrum from fully automated processes that have all the required knowledge built into the process itself. Service management processes fall somewhere between these two extremes, with the operational processes nearer to the automation of processes than the tactical or strategic processes. This should be taken into account when designing the ITSM processes. Knowledge management may very well enable quick wins on the more knowledge management intensive processes. This is not to imply that there would be a difference of levels of knowledge required for the people participating to the processes – rather that, in order to further develop SLM and vendor-management processes, the tactical knowledge needs to be harvested. It is easier to automate the operational level processes than the tactical or strategic processes, which require a greater breadth and depth of knowledge.

Throughout a CSI initiative, a lot of experience and information is acquired. It is important that this knowledge be gathered, organized and accessible. To ensure the ongoing success of the programme, knowledge management techniques must be applied.

All this knowledge comes from the service knowledge management system (SKMS) (see Figure 5.19). *ITIL Service Transition* explains the principles and structure of the SKMS.

## 5.8.12 Risk management

Although not an ITIL-defined ITSM process, risk management is part of many processes such as change management, ITSCM, availability management, information security management and strategic risk management. Risks to all elements of warranty and utility need to be assessed and mitigated where possible. While risk management is primarily conducted during design and transition stages of the service lifecycle, a good CSI initiative will assess the results of risk management activities to identify service improvements through risk mitigation, elimination and management.

Every organization manages its risk, but not always in a way that is visible, repeatable and consistently applied to support decision-making. The task of risk management is to ensure that the organization makes cost-effective use of a risk process that has a series of well-defined steps. The aim is to support better decision-making through a good understanding of risks and their likely impact.

There are two distinct phases: risk assessment and risk management. Risk assessment is concerned with gathering information about exposure to risk so that the organization can make appropriate decisions and manage risk appropriately. Risk assessment involves the identification and assessment of the level (measure) of the risks calculated from the assessed values of assets and the assessed levels of threats to, and vulnerabilities of, those assets.

Risk management involves having processes in place to monitor risks, access to reliable and up-to-date information about risks, the right balance of control in place to deal with those risks, and decision-making processes supported by a framework of risk assessment and evaluation. Risk management also involves the identification, selection and adoption of countermeasures justified by the identified risks to assets when considering their potential impact on services if failure occurs, and the reduction of those risks to an acceptable level.

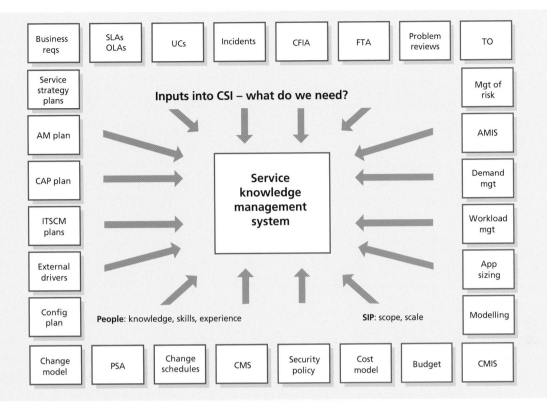

*Figure 5.19  Sources of knowledge*

Risk management covers a wide range of topics, including BCM, security, programme/ project risk management and operational service management. These topics need to be placed in the context of an organizational framework for the management of risk. Some risk-related topics, such as security, are highly specialized and this guidance provides only an overview of such aspects.

A certain amount of risk taking is inevitable if an organization is to achieve its objectives. Effective management of risk helps to improve performance by contributing to:

- Increased certainty and fewer surprises
- Better service delivery
- More effective management of change
- More efficient use of resources
- Better management at all levels through improved decision-making
- Reduced waste and fraud, and better value for money
- Innovation
- Management of contingent and maintenance activities.

### 5.8.12.1 Relating management of risk to safety, security and business continuity

Management of risk should be carried out in the wider context of safety concerns, security and business continuity:

- **Health and safety** policy and practice is concerned with ensuring that the workplace is a safe environment.
- **Security** is concerned with protecting the organization's assets, including information, buildings and so on.
- **Business continuity** is concerned with ensuring that the organization could continue to operate in the event of a disaster, such as loss of a service, flood or fire damage.

Figure 5.20 illustrates the reasons for having a risk management process.

### 5.8.12.2 Business perspective on risk management

Risk management from the business perspective, in the context of working with suppliers, centres on assessing vulnerabilities in supplier arrangements that pose threats to any aspect of the business including:

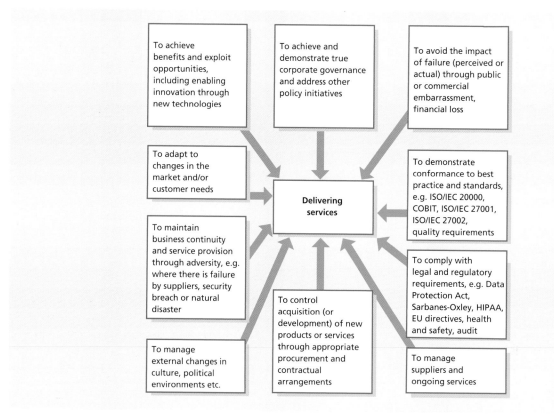

*Figure 5.20 Reasons for a risk management process*

- Customer satisfaction
- Brand image
- Market share
- Share price
- Profitability
- Regulatory impacts or penalties (in some industries).

The nature of the relationship affects the degree of risk to the business.

Risks associated with an outsourced supplier are likely to be greater in number, and more complex to manage, than those associated with an internal supplier. It is rarely possible to outsource risk. Blaming a supplier does not impress customers or internal users affected by a security incident or a lengthy system failure. New risks arising from the relationship need to be identified and managed, with communication and escalation as appropriate.

A substantial risk assessment should have been undertaken pre-contract, but this needs to be maintained in the light of changing business needs, changes to the contract scope or changes in the operational environment.

### 5.8.12.3 Risk profiles and responsibilities

The organization and the supplier must consider the threats posed by the relationship to their own assets, and have their own risk profile. Each must identify their respective risk owners. In a well-functioning relationship it is possible for much or all of the assessment to be openly shared with the other party. By involving supplier experts in risk assessments, the organization may gain valuable insights into how best to mitigate risks, as well as improving the coverage of the assessment.

Risk assessments typically consider threats which may exploit vulnerabilities to impact the confidentiality, integrity or availability of one or more assets.

The scope of risk assessments includes:

- Identification of risks (threats and vulnerabilities)
- Target – the assets under threat
- Impact of risks, qualitative and quantitative
- Probability of occurrence
- Possible mitigating actions or controls

**Table 5.16  Risk register**

| Reference | Description | Weighted priority | | | Proposed actions or controls and costs | Owner |
|---|---|---|---|---|---|---|
| | | Prob. HML | Impact HML | Prob. × impact = Exposure | | |
| R1 | | H | H | 9 | | |
| R2 | | H | M | 6 | | |
| R3 | | M | L | 3 | | |
| R4 | | L | L | 1 | | |

- Identification of stakeholders who are accountable for the risk, and responsible for selecting an appropriate action (including possibly accepting the risk with no control)
- Responsibility for implementing selected actions or controls
- Choice of actions or controls, based on an evaluation of impact versus the cost of action or control.

For outsourced operations, particular care needs to be taken when considering the ownership of the assets at risk. These will be different for each party.

Risk management processes need to be considered as cyclical, reviewing the suitability of previous actions, and reassessing risks in the light of changing circumstances. Risks are likely to be managed through a risk register such as the example provided in Table 5.16.

For further information on risk management, consult Appendix C.

## 5.9  SUMMARY

Many methods and techniques are used to support CSI activities. Each organization can choose what works best for them. However, you should never adopt only one as it takes a blend of different methods to have an effective CSI initiative.

CSI relies on the activities of all other service management processes. Don't overlook the value incident management, problem management, availability management and capacity management can provide to CSI. Of course SLM plays a key role and most organizations will be hard pressed to have an effective CSI initiative without some form of SLM in place.

# Organizing for continual service improvement

# 6 Organizing for continual service improvement

This chapter describes organizing for service management in relation to continual service improvement (CSI) and the related practices. It includes generic roles, responsibilities and competencies that apply across the service lifecycle and specific aspects for the processes described in this publication.

Section 2.2.3 describes the basic concepts of organization, function, group, team, department, division and role that are used in this chapter.

All stages of the lifecycle will be looking for opportunities to improve and most roles could be involved in CSI. It is a responsibility of all elements and processes within the lifecycle to look for opportunities to improve quality, to be more cost-effective and to enable the business overall to be more successful by better alignment. Therefore organizing for improvement is not restricted to one lifecycle stage or process but is the responsibility of everyone and to some extent all roles.

## 6.1 ORGANIZATIONAL DEVELOPMENT

There is no single best way to organize, and best practices described in ITIL need to be tailored to suit individual organizations and situations. Any changes made will need to take into account resource constraints and the size, nature and needs of the business and customers. The starting point for organizational design is strategy. Organization development for service management is described in more detail in Chapter 6 of *ITIL Service Strategy*.

## 6.2 FUNCTIONS

A function is a team or group of people and the tools or other resources they use to carry out one or more processes or activities. In larger organizations, a function may be broken out and performed by several departments, teams and groups, or it may be embodied within a single organizational unit (e.g. service desk). In smaller organizations, one person or group can perform multiple functions – e.g. a technical management department could also incorporate the service desk function.

For CSI to be successful, an organization will need to define clearly the roles and responsibilities required to undertake the processes and activities identified in Chapters 4 and 5. These roles will need to be assigned to individuals, and an appropriate organization structure of teams, groups or functions established and managed.

*ITIL Continual Service Improvement* does not define any functions of its own, but it does rely on the technical and application management functions described in *ITIL Service Operation*. Technical and application management provide the technical resources and expertise to manage the whole service lifecycle, and practitioner roles within CSI may be performed by members of these functions.

## 6.3 ROLES

A number of roles need to be performed in support of CSI. Please note that this section provides guidelines and examples of role descriptions. These are not exhaustive or prescriptive, and in many cases roles will need to be combined or separated. Organizations should take care to apply this guidance in a way that suits their own structures and objectives.

A role is a set of responsibilities, activities and authorities granted to a person or team. A role is defined in a process or function. One person or team may have multiple roles; for example, the roles of configuration manager and change manager may be carried out by a single person.

Roles are often confused with job titles, but it is important to realize that they are not the same. Each organization will define appropriate job titles and job descriptions that suit its needs, and individuals holding these job titles can perform one or more of the required roles.

It should also be recognized that a person may, as part of their job assignment, perform a single task that represents participation in more than one process. For example, a technical analyst who submits a request for change (RFC) to add memory to a server to resolve a performance problem is participating in activities of the change management process at the same time as taking part in activities of the capacity management and problem management processes.

Roles fall into two main categories – generic roles such as process manager and process owner, and specific roles that are involved within a particular lifecycle stage or process such as a change administrator or service desk staff. Roles can be combined in a number of different ways, depending on the organizational context. For example, in many organizations there will be someone with the job title of change manager who combines the roles of the change management process owner, change management process manager, change administrator and chair of a change advisory board (CAB). In a small organization the change manager role may be combined with roles from service asset and configuration management or release and deployment management. In larger organizations there may be many different people carrying out each of these roles, split by geography, technology or other criteria. The exceptions to this are that there must be only one process owner for each process and one service owner for each service.

Roles are accountable or responsible for an activity. They may also be consulted or informed about something: for example a service owner may be consulted about a change during an impact assessment activity. The RACI model, described in section 6.5, provides a useful way of defining and communicating roles and responsibilities.

**What is a service manager?**

Service manager is a generic term for any manager within the service provider. The term is commonly used to refer to a business relationship manager, a process manager or a senior manager with responsibility for IT services overall. A service manager is often assigned several roles such as business relationship management, service level management (SLM) and CSI.

## 6.3.1 Generic service owner role

To ensure that a service is managed with a business focus, the definition of a single point of accountability is absolutely essential to provide the level of attention and focus required for its delivery.

The service owner is accountable for the delivery of a specific IT service. The service owner is responsible to the customer for the initiation, transition and ongoing maintenance and support of a particular service and accountable to the IT director or service management director for the delivery of the service. The service owner's accountability for a specific service within an organization is independent of where the underpinning technology components, processes or professional capabilities reside.

Service ownership is as critical to service management as establishing ownership for processes which cross multiple vertical silos or departments. It is possible that a single person may fulfil the service owner role for more than one service.

The service owner has the following responsibilities:

- Ensuring that the ongoing service delivery and support meet agreed customer requirements
- Working with business relationship management to understand and translate customer requirements into activities, measures or service components that will ensure that the service provider can meet those requirements
- Ensuring consistent and appropriate communication with customer(s) for service-related enquiries and issues
- Assisting in defining service models and in assessing the impact of new services or changes to existing services through the service portfolio management process
- Identifying opportunities for service improvements, discussing these with the customer and raising RFCs as appropriate
- Liaising with the appropriate process owners throughout the service lifecycle
- Soliciting required data, statistics and reports for analysis and to facilitate effective service monitoring and performance
- Providing input in service attributes such as performance, availability etc.
- Representing the service across the organization
- Understanding the service (components etc.)
- Serving as the point of escalation (notification) for major incidents relating to the service
- Representing the service in change advisory board (CAB) meetings

- Participating in internal service review meetings (within IT)
- Participating in external service review meetings (with the business)
- Ensuring that the service entry in the service catalogue is accurate and is maintained
- Participating in negotiating service level agreements (SLAs) and operational level agreements (OLAs) relating to the service
- Identifying improvement opportunities for inclusion in the CSI register
- Working with the CSI manager to review and prioritize improvements in the CSI register
- Making improvements to the service.

The service owner is responsible for continual improvement and the management of change affecting the service under their care. The service owner is a primary stakeholder in all of the underlying IT processes which enable or support the service they own. For example:

- **Incident management** Is involved in (or perhaps chairs) the crisis management team for high-priority incidents impacting the service owned
- **Problem management** Plays a major role in establishing the root cause and proposed permanent fix for the service being evaluated
- **Release and deployment management** Is a key stakeholder in determining whether a new release affecting a service in production is ready for promotion
- **Change management** Participates in CAB decisions, authorizing changes to the services they own
- **Service asset and configuration management** Ensures that all groups which maintain the data and relationships for the service architecture they are responsible for have done so with the level of integrity required
- **Service level management** Acts as the single point of contact for a specific service and ensures that the service portfolio and service catalogue are accurate in relation to their service
- **Availability management and capacity management** Reviews technical monitoring data from a domain perspective to ensure that the needs of the overall service are being met
- **IT service continuity management** (ITSCM) Understands and is responsible for ensuring that

all elements required to restore their service are known and in place in the event of a crisis
- **Information security management** Ensures that the service conforms to information security management policies
- **Financial management for IT services** Assists in defining and tracking the cost models in relation to how their service is costed and recovered.

### 6.3.2 Generic process owner role

The process owner role is accountable for ensuring that a process is fit for purpose. This role is often assigned to the same person who carries out the process manager role, but the two roles may be separate in larger organizations. The process owner role is accountable for ensuring that their process is performed according to the agreed and documented standard and meets the aims of the process definition.

The process owner's accountabilities include:

- Sponsoring, designing and change managing the process and its metrics
- Defining the process strategy
- Assisting with process design
- Ensuring that appropriate process documentation is available and current
- Defining appropriate policies and standards to be employed throughout the process
- Periodically auditing the process to ensure compliance to policy and standards
- Periodically reviewing the process strategy to ensure that it is still appropriate and change as required
- Communicating process information or changes as appropriate to ensure awareness
- Providing process resources to support activities required throughout the service lifecycle
- Ensuring that process technicians have the required knowledge and the required technical and business understanding to deliver the process, and understand their role in the process
- Reviewing opportunities for process enhancements and for improving the efficiency and effectiveness of the process
- Addressing issues with the running of the process
- Identifying improvement opportunities for inclusion in the CSI register

- Working with the CSI manager and process manager to review and prioritize improvements in the CSI register
- Making improvements to the process.

Further detail on the role and responsibilities of the process owner can be found in *ITIL Service Strategy* and *ITIL Service Design*.

### 6.3.3 Generic process manager role

The process manager role is accountable for operational management of a process. There may be several process managers for one process, for example regional change managers or IT service continuity managers for each data centre. The process manager role is often assigned to the person who carries out the process owner role, but the two roles may be separate in larger organizations.

The process manager's accountabilities include:

- Working with the process owner to plan and coordinate all process activities
- Ensuring all activities are carried out as required throughout the service lifecycle
- Appointing people to the required roles
- Managing resources assigned to the process
- Working with service owners and other process managers to ensure the smooth running of services
- Monitoring and reporting on process performance
- Identifying improvement opportunities for inclusion in the CSI register
- Working with the CSI manager and process owner to review and prioritize improvements in the CSI register
- Making improvements to the process implementation.

### 6.3.4 Generic process practitioner role

A process practitioner is responsible for carrying out one or more process activities.

In some organizations, and for some processes, the process practitioner role may be combined with the process manager role, in others there may be large numbers of practitioners carrying out different parts of the process.

The process practitioner's responsibilities typically include:

- Carrying out one or more activities of a process

- Understanding how their role contributes to the overall delivery of service and creation of value for the business
- Working with other stakeholders, such as their manager, co-workers, users and customers, to ensure that their contributions are effective
- Ensuring that inputs, outputs and interfaces for their activities are correct
- Creating or updating records to show that activities have been carried out correctly.

### 6.3.5 CSI manager

The role of CSI manager is essential for a successful improvement programme. The CSI manager is ultimately responsible for the success of all improvement activities. This single point of accountability coupled with competence and authority improves the chances of a successful improvement programme. The role of CSI manager can also fulfil the role of the seven-step improvement process owner/manager.

The CSI manager's responsibilities typically include:

- Developing the CSI domain
- Communicating the vision of CSI across the IT organization
- Ensuring that CSI roles have been filled
- Designing the CSI register and associated activities
- Working with service owners, service level managers, the seven-step improvement manager, other process managers and functions to identify and manage improvement opportunities:
  - Identifying improvement opportunities for inclusion in the CSI register
  - Reviewing and prioritizing improvements in the CSI register
  - Building improvement plans and making improvements
- Working with service level managers to ensure that monitoring requirements are defined
- Ensuring that monitoring tools are in place to gather data
- Ensuring that baseline data is captured to measure improvement against it
- Defining and creating reports on CSI critical success factors (CSFs), key performance indicators (KPIs) and CSI activity metrics

- Identifying other frameworks, models and standards that will support CSI activities
- Ensuring that knowledge management is an integral part of routine operations
- Ensuring that CSI activities are coordinated throughout the service lifecycle
- Reviewing analysed data
- Presenting recommendations to senior management for improvement
- Helping prioritize improvement opportunities
- Leading, managing and delivering cross-functional and cross-divisional improvement projects
- Building effective relationships with the business and IT senior managers
- Identifying and delivering process improvements in critical business areas across manufacturing and relevant divisions
- Setting direction and providing a framework through which improvement objectives can be delivered
- Coaching, mentoring and supporting fellow service improvement professionals.

The CSI manager should possess the ability to influence positively all levels of management to ensure that service improvement activities are receiving the necessary support and are resourced sufficiently to implement solutions.

## 6.3.6 Seven-step improvement roles

This section describes a number of roles that need to be performed in support of the seven-step improvement process. These roles are not job titles, and each organization will have to define appropriate job titles and job descriptions for their needs.

### 6.3.6.1 Seven-step improvement process owner

The seven-step improvement process owner's responsibilities typically include:

- Carrying out the generic process owner role for the seven-step improvement process (see section 6.3.2 for more detail)
- Working with the CSI manager, service owners, process owners and functions to include appropriate elements of the seven-step improvement process throughout the service lifecycle.

### 6.3.6.2 Seven-step improvement process manager

The seven-step improvement process manager's responsibilities typically include:

- Carrying out the generic process manager role for the seven-step improvement process (see section 6.3.3 for more detail)
- Planning and managing support for improvement tools and processes
- Working with the CSI manager, service owners, process owners and functions to maintain the CSI register
- Coordinating interfaces between the seven-step improvement process, other processes, service managers and functions.

### 6.3.6.3 Reporting analyst

The reporting analyst is a key role for CSI and will often work in concert with SLM. The reporting analyst reviews and analyses data from components, systems and sub-systems in order to obtain a true end-to-end service achievement. The reporting analyst will also identify trends and establish if they are positive or negative. This information is then used to present the data. The reporting analyst's responsibilities typically include:

- Participating in CSI meetings and SLM meetings to ensure the validity of the reporting metrics, notification thresholds and overall solution
- Responsibility for consolidating data from multiple sources
- Responsibility for producing trends and providing feedback on the trends such as whether the trends are positive or negative, what their impact is likely to be, and if they are predictable for the future
- Responsibility for producing reports on service or system performance based on the negotiated OLAs and SLAs and improvement initiatives.

The reporting analyst's key skills and competencies typically include:

- Good understanding of statistical and analytical principles and processes
- Strong technical foundation in the reporting tool(s)
- Good communication skills
- Good technical understanding and an ability to translate technical requirements and specifications into easily understood reporting requirements.

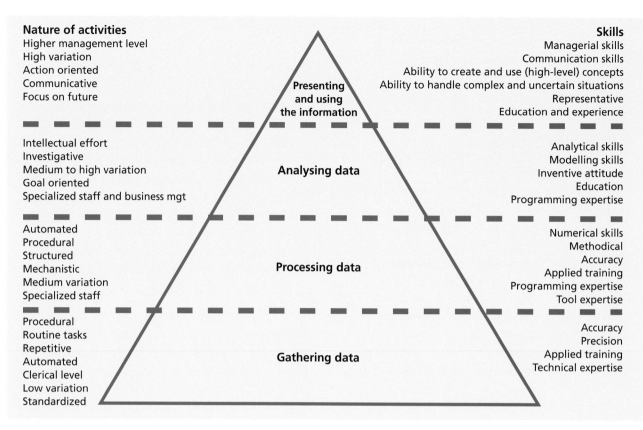

**Figure 6.1 Activities and skill levels needed for continual service improvement**

### 6.3.6.4 Other roles involved in the seven-step improvement process

In addition to the specific roles and activities described above, many activities of the seven-step improvement process take place in other processes and functions throughout the service lifecycle. CSI will only be successful if the required activities are clearly identified and assigned to appropriate roles.

Figure 6.1 lists the nature of many of these activities and the skills required to perform them.

*Note:* Figure 6.1 covers steps 3 to 6 of the seven-step improvement process covered in full in Chapter 4. The following section expands on this by detailing each step in the seven-step improvement process and highlighting related activities.

*Step 1 – Identify the strategy for improvement*

Roles: individuals involved with strategic decision-making on the vision for the business and how IT enables that vision to succeed; individuals who will be looking at strategic, technical and operational goals.

Examples: strategy manager, service owner, service level manager, CSI manager, customers, senior business managers, business/IT analysts and senior IT managers (see Table 6.1).

*Step 2 – Define what you will measure*

Roles: individuals involved with decision-making from IT and the business who understand the internal and external factors that influence the necessary elements that should be measured to support the business, governance and, possibly, regulatory legislation; individuals involved with providing the service (internal and external providers) who understand the capabilities of the measuring processes, procedures, tools and staff.

Examples: service owner, service level manager, CSI manager, process owner, process managers, customers, business/IT analysts, senior IT managers, and internal and external providers (see Table 6.2)

*Step 3 – Gather the data*

Roles: individuals involved in day-to-day process activities within the lifecycle stages, in particular in the operational aspects of the processes where the results of many of the processes can be collected.

Examples: service desk staff, technical management staff, application management staff, IT security staff and many more (see Table 6.3).

**Table 6.1 Skills involved in Step 1 – Identify the strategy for improvement**

| Nature of activities | Skills |
| --- | --- |
| Senior management | Ability to create a high level vision and strategy |
| High variation | Communication |
| Action-oriented | Ability to create, use high-level concepts |
| Communicative | Ability to handle complex/uncertain situations |
| Focused on future | Ability to set longer-term goals |

**Table 6.2 Skills involved in Step 2 – Define what you will measure**

| Nature of activities | Skills |
| --- | --- |
| Senior management | Managerial |
| High variation | Communication |
| Action-oriented | Ability to create, use (high-level) concepts |
| Communicative | Ability to handle complex/uncertain situations |
| Intellectual effort | Analytical |
| Investigative | Modelling |
| Medium to high variation | Inventive attitude |

**Table 6.3 Skills involved in Step 3 – Gather the data**

| Nature of activities | Skills |
| --- | --- |
| Procedural | Accuracy |
| Routine | Precision |
| Repetitive | Meticulous nature |
| Automated | Technical ability |
| Clerical | Ability to document |

**Table 6.4 Skills involved in Step 4 – Process the data**

| Nature of activities | Skills |
| --- | --- |
| Automated | Numerical |
| Procedural | Methodical |
| Structural | Accuracy |
| Mechanistic | Meticulous nature |
| Medium variation | Programming skills |
| Specialized | Tool and technical skills and experience |

*Step 4 – Process the data*

Roles: individuals involved in day-to-day process activities within the lifecycle stages.

Examples: service desk staff, technical management staff, application management staff and IT security staff (see Table 6.4).

*Step 5 – Analyse the information and data*

Roles: individuals involved with providing the service (internal and external providers) who understand the capabilities of the measuring services, processes, procedures, tools and staff.

Examples: service owner, process owner, process managers, business/IT analysts, senior IT analysts, supervisors and team leaders (see Table 6.5).

**Table 6.5 Skills involved in Step 5 – Analyse the information and data**

| Nature of activities | Skills |
|---|---|
| Intellectual | Analytical |
| Investigative | Modelling |
| Medium to high variation | Inventive attitude |
| Goal-oriented | Ambitious |
| Specialized and business management | Programming skills |

**Table 6.6 Skills involved in Step 6 – Present and use the information**

| Nature of activities | Skills |
|---|---|
| Higher management | Managerial |
| High variation | Communication |
| Action-oriented | Ability to create, use (high-level) concepts |
| Communicative | Ability to handle complex/uncertain situations |
| Focused on future | Ambitious |

**Table 6.7 Skills involved in Step 7 – Implement improvement**

| Nature of activities | Skills |
|---|---|
| Intellectual effort | Analytical |
| Investigative | Modelling |
| Medium to high variation | Inventive attitude |
| Goal-oriented | Ambitious |
| Specialized staff and business management | Programming skills |

*Step 6 – Present and use the information*

Roles: individuals involved with providing the service (internal and external providers) who understand the capabilities of the service and the underpinning processes, and possess good communication skills; key personnel involved with decision-making from IT and the business.

Examples: CSI manager, service owner, service level manager, process owner, process managers, customers, business/IT analysts, senior IT managers, internal and external providers (see Table 6.6).

*Step 7 – Implement improvement*

Roles: individuals involved with providing the service (internal and external providers).

Examples: CSI manager, service owner, service level manager, process owner, process managers, customers, business/IT analysts, senior IT managers, and internal and external providers (see Table 6.7).

### 6.3.7 Business relationship manager

The objective of business relationship management is to establish and maintain a good relationship between the service provider and the customer based on understanding the customer and their business drivers. The customer's business drivers could require changes in SLAs and thus become input into service improvement opportunities. Service strategy provides more detail on business relationship management and the role of business relationship managers.

Business relationship managers work closely with service level managers, service owners and the CSI manager to deliver high quality services. Their roles are compared in Table 6.8.

**Table 6.8 Comparison of CSI manager, service level manager, service owner and business relationship manager roles**

| | CSI manager | Service level manager | Service owner | Business relationship manager |
|---|---|---|---|---|
| **Focus** | | | | |
| IT services | S | P | P | P |
| IT systems | S | | P | |
| Processes | P | S | S | S |
| Customers | S | P | S | P |
| Technology | P | S | P | |
| **Responsibilities** | | | | |
| Developing and maintaining the catalogue of existing services | | P | S | P |
| Developing and maintaining OLAs | | P | S | |
| Gathering service level requirements (SLRs) from the customer | S | P | S | P |
| Negotiating and maintaining SLAs with the customer | S | P | S | S |
| Understanding underpinning contracts (UCs) as they relate to OLAs and SLAs | S | P | S | S |
| Ensuring appropriate service level monitoring is in place | P | P | S | |
| Producing, reviewing and evaluating reports on service performance and achievements regularly | P | P | P | P |
| Conducting regular meetings with the customer to discuss service level performance and improvement | S | P | S | S |
| Conducting yearly SLA review meetings with the customer | S | P | S | S |
| Ensuring customer satisfaction with the use of a customer satisfaction survey | S | P | S | P |
| Initiating appropriate actions to improve service levels through service improvement plans (SIPs) | P | P | P | P |
| Negotiating and agreeing OLAs and SLAs | S | P | S | S |
| Ensuring the management of UCs as they relate to OLAs and SLAs | S | S | S | |
| Working with the service level manager to provide services to meet the customer's requirements | P | | P | P |
| Appropriate monitoring of services or systems | P | P | S | |
| Producing, reviewing and evaluating reports on service or system performance and achievement to the service level manager and the service level process manager | P | P | P | S |
| Assisting in appropriate actions to improve service levels (SIP) | P | P | P | P |

*Table continues*

**Table 6.8** *continued*

| | CSI manager | Service level manager | Service owner | Business relationship manager |
|---|---|---|---|---|
| **Skills, knowledge and competencies** | | | | |
| Relationship management skills | P | P | P | P |
| A good understanding of IT services and qualifying factors in order to understand how customer requirements will affect delivery | P | P | P | P |
| An understanding of the customer's business and how IT contributes to the delivery of that product or service | P | P | P | P |
| Good communication skills | P | P | P | P |
| Good negotiation skills | P | P | P | P |
| Knowledge and experience of contract and/or supplier management roles | S | P | S | S |
| Good people management and meeting facilitating skills | P | P | P | P |
| Good understanding of statistical and analytical principles and processes | P | S | S | S |
| Good presentation skills | P | P | P | P |
| Good technical understanding and an ability to translate technical requirements and specifications into easily understood business concepts and vice versa | S | P | S | S |
| Innovative in respect of service quality and ways in which it can be improved within the bounds of the organization's limits (resource, budgetary, legal etc.) | P | P | P | P |
| Good organizational and planning skills | P | P | P | P |
| Good vendor management skills | S | S | S | S |

P = primary responsibility; S = secondary responsibility; Blank = no specific responsibility

## 6.4 CUSTOMER ENGAGEMENT

A number of roles have been discussed in this chapter and they embody the concepts of a service-oriented organization. When running a more traditional IT organization focusing on technical excellence, these roles may seem extraneous, but to run a forward-thinking, service-oriented IT partner to the business, these roles are crucial. Improvement will not happen by itself. It requires a structured programme and mature processes. Those in the key roles shown in Figure 6.2 are responsible for that programme.

## 6.5 RESPONSIBILITY MODEL – RACI

Clear definitions of accountability and responsibility are essential for effective service management. To help with this task the RACI model or 'authority matrix' is often used within organizations to define the roles and responsibilities in relation to processes and activities. The RACI matrix provides a compact, concise, easy method of tracking who does what in each process and it enables decisions to be made with pace and confidence.

RACI is an acronym for the four main roles of being:

- **Responsible** The person or people responsible for correct execution – for getting the job done
- **Accountable** The person who has ownership of quality and the end result. Only one person can be accountable for each task
- **Consulted** The people who are consulted and whose opinions are sought. They have

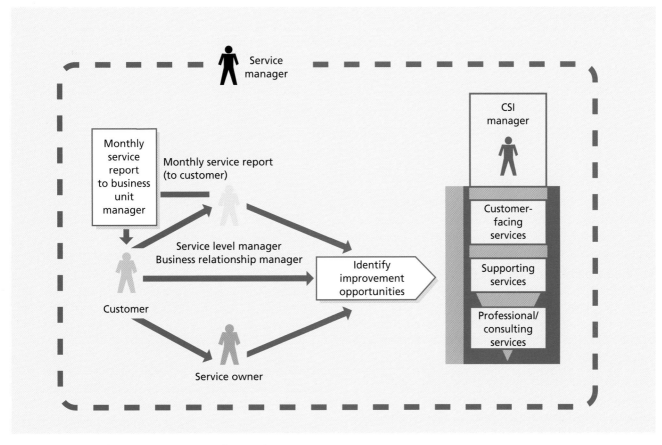

*Figure 6.2 Service management roles and customer engagement*

involvement through input of knowledge and information

■ **Informed** The people who are kept up to date on progress. They receive information about process execution and quality.

When using RACI, there is only one person accountable for an activity for a defined scope of applicability. Several people may be responsible for executing parts of the activity. In this model, accountable means end-to-end accountability for the process. Accountability should remain with the same person for all activities of a process.

The RACI chart in Table 6.9 shows the structure and power of RACI modelling. The rows represent a number of required activities and the columns identify the people who make the decisions, carry out the activities or provide input.

Whether RACI or some other tool or model is used, the important thing is to not just leave the assignment of responsibilities to chance or leave it to the last minute to decide. For example, if there is a transfer of a service from one service provider to another, RACI models should be designed in

the service design lifecycle stage, and tested and deployed in service transition. In service operation, people assigned to specific roles will perform the activities in the RACI matrix.

Further details on the RACI matrix are described in Chapter 3 of *ITIL Service Design*.

## 6.6 COMPETENCE AND TRAINING

### 6.6.1 Competence and skills for service management

Delivering service successfully depends on personnel involved in service management having the appropriate education, training, skills and experience. People need to understand their role and how they contribute to the overall organization, services and processes to be effective and motivated. As changes are made, job requirements, roles, responsibilities and competencies should be updated if necessary.

Each service lifecycle stage depends on appropriate skills and experience of people and their knowledge to make key decisions. In

**Table 6.9 An example of a simple RACI matrix**

|  | Director service management | Service level manager | Problem manager | Security manager | Procurement manager |
|---|---|---|---|---|---|
| Activity 1 | AR | C | I | I | C |
| Activity 2 | A | R | C | C | C |
| Activity 3 | I | A | R | I | C |
| Activity 4 | I | A | R | I |  |
| Activity 5 | I | R | A | C | I |

many organizations, personnel will deliver tasks appropriate to more than one lifecycle stage. They may well find themselves allocated (fully or partially) from operational tasks to support a design exercise and then follow that service through service transition. They may then, via early life support activities, move into support of the new or changed services that they have been involved in designing and implementing into the live environment.

The specific roles within ITIL service management all require specific skills, attributes and competences from the people involved to enable them to work effectively and efficiently. However, whatever the role, it is imperative that the person carrying out that role has the following attributes:

- Awareness of the business priorities, objectives and business drivers
- Awareness of the role IT plays in enabling the business objectives to be met
- Customer service skills
- Awareness of what IT can deliver to the business, including latest capabilities
- The competence, knowledge and information necessary to complete their role
- The ability to use, understand and interpret the best practice, policies and procedures to ensure adherence.

The following are examples of attributes required in many of the roles, dependent on the organization and the specific roles assigned:

- Management skills – both from a person management perspective and from the overall control of process
- Ability to handle meetings – organizing, chairing and documenting meetings and ensuring that actions are followed up
- Communication skills – an important element of all roles is raising awareness of the processes

in place to ensure buy-in and conformance. An ability to communicate at all levels within the organization will be imperative
- Articulateness – both written (e.g. for reports) and verbal
- Negotiation skills – required for several aspects, such as procurement and contracts
- An analytical mind – to analyse metrics produced from the activity.

Many people working in service management are involved with continual service improvement. *ITIL Continual Service Improvement* provides specific guidance on the skill levels needed for CSI activities.

### 6.6.2 Competence and skills framework

Standardizing job titles, functions, roles and responsibilities can simplify service management and human resource management. Many service providers use a common framework of reference for competence and skills to support activities such as skill audits, planning future skill requirements, organizational development programmes and resource allocation. For example, resource and cost models are simpler and easier to use if jobs and roles are standard.

The Skills Framework for the Information Age (SFIA) is an example of a common reference model for the identification of the skills needed to develop effective IT services, information systems and technology. SFIA defines seven generic levels at which tasks can be performed with the associated professional skills required for each level. A second dimension defines core competencies that can be combined with the professional skills. SFIA is used by many IT service providers to identify career development opportunities.

More information on SFIA can be found at www.sfia.org.uk

### 6.6.3 Training

Training in service management helps service providers to build and maintain their service management capability. Training needs must be matched to the requirements for competence and professional development.

The official ITIL qualification scheme enables organizations to develop the competence of their personnel through approved training courses. The courses help students to gain knowledge of ITIL best practices, develop their competencies and gain a recognized qualification. The scheme has four levels:

- Foundation level
- Intermediate level
- ITIL Expert
- ITIL Master.

More information on ITIL qualifications can be found at www.itil-officialsite.com

# Technology considerations

**7**

# 7 Technology considerations

Continual service improvement (CSI) activities require software tools to support the monitoring and reporting on IT services and to underpin the IT service management (ITSM) processes. These tools are used for data gathering, monitoring and analysis reporting for services, and also assist in determining the efficiency and effectiveness of IT service management processes. The longer-term benefits to be gained are cost savings and increased productivity, which in turn can lead to an increase in the quality of the IT service provision.

From a service perspective the use of tools enables an organization to gain the ability to understand the health of its services from an end-to-end perspective. Even if an organization is not able to monitor end-to-end services it should be able to monitor, identify trends and perform analyses on the key components that make up an IT service.

From a process perspective the use of tools enables centralization of key processes and automation and integration of core service management processes. The raw data collected in the databases can be analysed resulting in the identification of trends. Preventive measures can then be implemented thereby increasing the stability, reliability and availability of the IT infrastructure.

The ITSM software tools of today have expanded their scope from mere 'point' solutions focusing on the service desk or change management to complete, fully integrated solution suites. Current tools represent a paradigm shift into the new era of enterprise resource planning (ERP) systems for IT. For decades, IT has provided systems to run the business; now there are systems to run IT.

Many of these service management product suites are now offered in a Software as a Service (SaaS) format via cloud computing (see *ITIL Service Strategy*, section C.2), giving the advantage of full functionality without the management overheads.

## 7.1 TOOLS TO SUPPORT CSI ACTIVITIES

As part of the assessment of 'Where do we want to be?' the requirements for enhancing tools need to be addressed and documented. These requirements vary depending on the process and technology maturity. Technology specifically means systems and service management toolsets used for monitoring and controlling the systems and infrastructure components, and for managing process-based workflows, such as incident management.

Without question, service management tools are indispensable. However, good people, good process descriptions, and good procedures and working instructions are the basis for successful service management. The need for and the sophistication of the tools required depend on the business need for IT services and, to some extent, the size of the organization.

In a very small organization a simple in-house developed database system may be sufficient for logging and controlling incidents. However, in large organizations, very sophisticated distributed and integrated service management tools may be required, linking all the processes with systems management toolsets. While tools can be important assets, in today's IT-dependent organizations, they are a means, not an end in themselves. When implementing service management processes, look at the way current processes work. Each organization's unique need for management information should always be its starting point. This will help define the specifications for the tools best suited to that organization.

There are many tools that support the core ITSM processes and others that support IT governance as a whole, which will require integration with the ITSM tools. Information from both of these toolsets typically needs to be combined, collated and analysed collectively to provide the overall business intelligence required to improve effectively on the overall IT service provision.

These tools can be defined into broad categories that support and annotate different aspects of the systems and service management domains.

### 7.1.1 IT service management suites

The success of ITIL within the industry has encouraged software vendors to provide tools and suites of tools that are very compatible with the ITIL process framework, providing significant levels of integration between the processes and their associated record types. As mentioned earlier, many of these tools and suites of tools are offered via cloud computing. There are tools for just about every process documented in ITIL and many are beneficial to achieving the objectives of CSI. Examples include capacity and availability monitoring and automated event identification. The functionality of all these types of tool creates a rich source of data and provides many of the inputs to CSI. Additional examples include:

- **Incidents**   Incidents that capture the service or the configuration item (CI) affected are a prime input to CSI enabling an understanding of the issues affecting the overall service provision and related support activities. Incident matching functionality allows the service desk to quickly relate like issues and create master records that highlight common situations affecting the users with associated resolution data to enhance problem identification and reduce the mean time to restore service (MTRS).

- **Problems**   These are defined with integrated links to the associated incidents that confirmed their existence. Using the configuration data from the configuration management system (CMS) to understand the relationships, problem management now has a source of related data to enable the root cause analysis process including change and release history of the affected CI or service.

- **Changes**   These are often the first area of investigation following a service failure, again using the integration capabilities of the ITSM tool suite; it can be easier to trace the changes that have been made to a service or a CI. The change schedule and projected service outage (PSO) can be automated using calendaring capabilities to ensure visibility of changes and calculated impacts to the service level agreements (SLAs). Recent improvements in the ITSM tools now allow for automated risk assessment and prioritization of changes, highlighting potential conflicts and reducing the administrative overhead for the change advisory board.

*Note:* The integration of incidents, problems and changes within a single solution also provides a platform for these toolsets to introduce web-style enterprise search functionality, which will search across this semi-structured data looking for specific error codes, phrases and issues.

#### 7.1.1.1 Configuration data

Tool functionality in support of service asset and configuration management and the CMS has never been more advanced, with extensive discovery and service dependency mapping capabilities. Figure 7.1 shows the layers in a CMS, starting with multiple data sources (including one or more configuration management databases) to the information integration layer to knowledge processing and finally the presentation layer. The CMS is the foundation for the integration of all ITSM tool functionality and is a critical data source for the CSI mission. While the service provider must still define the overall service asset and configuration management process and create the data model associated with their specific environment, the tools to establish and manage the CMS and the overall service delivery architecture have become very powerful. Key functionality includes: discovery and reconciliation capabilities to capture CIs within the environment; visualization of the hierarchy and CI relationships for ease of understanding and support; audit tools to streamline the verification activities; and the ability to federate data sources where appropriate.

#### 7.1.1.2 Releases

The ability to coordinate releases and manage the contents of these releases is also more mature, with native support for the definitive libraries and key integration points to the CMS and to specialized version control software packages. Functionality typically includes support for release records that consolidate and contain release contents, enabling the attachment of related objects and documents pertaining to the release. Integration is normally provided to enable hyperlinking to the associated change records that are part of a release and the related incident, problem or service request records that were the catalyst for the original request for change (RFC). Release versions are also supported with predefined naming and numbering standards that enhance the understanding of the overall process. Overall reporting of release status and associated

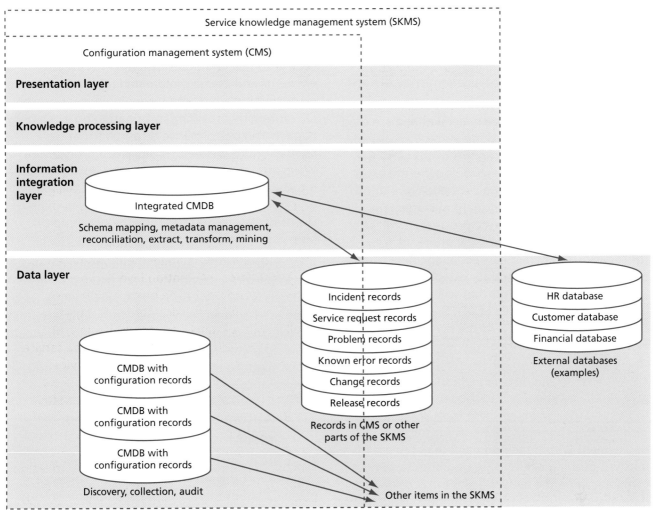

*Figure 7.1 The application of the architectural layers of the CMS*

performance metrics are required as inputs to CSI ensuring that the deployment of new services are of the highest possible quality.

### 7.1.1.3 Service level management

Service level management (SLM) functionality is also well supported within the ITSM tool suites of today, enabling the linkage of incidents, problems, changes and releases to associated SLM records such as SLAs, operational level agreements (OLAs) and underpinning contracts (UCs). Most tool suites support automated SLA monitoring (SLAM) charts highlighting which agreements are within tolerance, are threatened or have been broken. This automation is driven by the ability to define key SLA criteria and use related operational support records to trigger thresholds (e.g. a priority one incident is about to break the one-hour resolution target time or a change has caused a longer downtime than was agreed).

CMS functionality can also support the concept of prioritized CIs that underpin specific service levels, highlighting a greater impact if a failed component supports a critical service or business process. Some suites also provide the ability to trigger availability impacts to SLAs by capturing incident data related to service outages. Many of the suites also facilitate the definition of the service portfolio and the service catalogue while managing the workflow associated with the fulfilment of service requests. Some standalone point solutions support specialized functionality in this area (see below).

Reporting is one of the key benefits of an integrated ITSM suite with the ability to provide management information in a common format utilizing the combined data from all operational areas of the service lifecycle. This is of significant benefit, enabling analysis of the relationships between service management events (e.g. incidents that result in problems, changes that cause incidents, and releases that encapsulate certain changes) and all of the associated performance metric data that will feed the overall CSI initiatives.

### 7.1.2 Systems and network management

These tools are typically specific to the technology platforms that are under management and are used to administer the various domains but can provide a wide variety of data in support of the service management mission. These tools generate error messages for event management and correlation that ultimately feed the incident management and availability management processes. Utilization data from these platforms is the prime source for capacity and performance management and the most accurate method for establishing true availability of components that will support improvements in the area of MTRS and mean time between failures (MTBF). As the dynamic, real-time view of the current state of the service delivery chain, this information can be integrated with the known service dependencies within the CMS to give enhanced visibility into the service provision to the end user. Many of these tools also support technology proprietary methods for software deployment within their domains (e.g. release of patches, pushing of firmware upgrades to remote components on the network) and can provide metric data in support of CSI for the change management and release and deployment management processes, along with dynamic updates to the CMS.

### 7.1.3 Event management

An event can be defined as any detectable or discernible occurrence that has significance for the management of the IT infrastructure or the delivery of IT services. There should be an evaluation of the impact any deviation might cause to the services. Events are typically created by an IT service, CI or monitoring tool. Events can be programmed to communicate operational information as well as warnings and exceptions. Warning and exception events are created when a tool senses a threshold has been met or an error condition is discovered. The major issue with this capability can be the significant volume of messages that are created from both the actual event and the up- and down-stream impact, which can make it difficult to determine the real issue.

Specialized event management software can perform event correlation, impact analysis and root cause analysis to separate out these false-positive messages. Events are captured and assessed by rules-based, model-based and policy-based correlation technologies that can interpret a series of events and derive, isolate and report on the true cause and impact. These technologies support the CSI mission by providing information on availability impacts and performance thresholds that have been exceeded related to capacity or utilization. Well-correlated event management data provides a cost-effective method to improve the reliability, efficiency and effectiveness of the cross-domain IT infrastructure that supports the provision of business services.

A by-product of the extensive and often complex checks performed by these event management products is the collection of raw performance data to be used by many processes – for example, within capacity management analysis activities. This would allow simulated log-ons at any time during the day or night to check database availability and performance.

### 7.1.4 Automated incident/problem resolution

There are many products in the marketplace that support the automation of the traditional manual, labour-intensive and error-prone process of incident and problem discovery and resolution. Utilizing data from proactive detection monitors, any component or service outage generates an alert that automatically triggers diagnosis and repair procedures. These procedures then identify the root cause and resolve the issue using preprogrammed and scripted self-healing techniques, reducing the MTRS of many common causes of incidents, and in some cases preventing service outages completely. These tools also document audit-related information within the incident or problem record for future analysis and identification of other potential proactive CSI opportunities.

### 7.1.5 Knowledge management

There are specialist tools available that support and streamline the discipline of knowledge management. Providing efficient and accurate access to previous cases with proven resolution data, these tools address the symptoms associated with the current incident or problem. Capturing data throughout the incident and problem management lifecycles enables a knowledge management engine to assign related keywords and service relationships that will enhance the search process providing a high percentage of hits, thus speeding up the overall resolution process. Knowledge management tools also generate significant metrics aimed at measuring the improvement process itself. Key CSI data adds transparency to incident recurrence and frequency, utilization rates, the effectiveness of the stored resolutions and the impact knowledge management has on the efficacy of the overall support function.

### 7.1.6 Requesting services (service catalogue and workflow)

As mentioned in section 7.1.1, there are specialized tools that deal with service catalogue definition, requests for services and the workflow associated with their fulfilment. Some of these tools provide the workflow engines and some rely heavily on the capabilities of the companion ITSM suite. These tools provide the technology required to define the services within a catalogue structure in conjunction with business customers and create a service portal (normally web-based) that allows users to request services. The request is then managed through the workflow engine assigning resources according to a defined process of tasks and related activities for each request type. These tools typically also capture related cost information to be fed to the financial systems for later charging activities. This functionality does much to support IT's integration with the business, defining services that underpin their mission and streamlining the delivery of commodity services that so often become a source of customer frustration. As in other tools, the true CSI benefit is that the data that is collected and reported relates to the quality of the services delivered, any bottlenecks encountered, and the ability to track the achievement of related service levels.

### 7.1.7 Performance management

Performance management tools allow for the collection of availability, capacity and performance data from a multitude of domains and platforms within the IT infrastructure environment. This data is used to populate the availability management information system (AMIS) and capacity management information system (CMIS), giving IT organizations a historical, current and future view of performance, resource and service

usage for offline analysis and modelling activities. Capabilities of these tools generally include:

- Analysis of responsiveness, transaction and traffic throughput and utilization levels, supporting the balancing of resources to optimize performance of the IT services
- Workload assessment with predictive trend analysis of future growth and required capacity for each of the IT services being provided
- The construction of performance, resource and data usage profiles, enabling the comparison of actual utilization with planned models
- Predictive performance technology enabling the evaluation of tuning alternatives for systems, networks, databases and applications that support modelling of the expected outcomes
- Generation of the data required to report on SLAs, identify opportunities for improvement to include in the CSI register, and for building service improvement plans (SIPs).

There are many tools in the marketplace that support the overall CSI initiative across many aspects of performance management including business, service and resource capacity planning, feasibility analysis, modelling, solution development, implementation, management and ongoing monitoring of the IT service provision.

### 7.1.8 Application and service performance monitoring

There has always been a challenge related to understanding the true user experience related to service provision. Recognizing this need, many vendors provide tools that monitor the end-to-end delivery of services, using either active or passive technologies, to fully instrument and probe the many components of the service delivery chain. The software provides key metrics such as availability, transaction throughput, transaction response time, network latency, server efficiency, database input and output, and Structured Query Language (SQL) effectiveness. This data provides system managers, application managers, availability management managers, capacity managers and service owners with the ability to analyse the delivery of services at all key points in the chain and look for potential improvements to streamline the overall delivery mechanisms. Usage trend data is vital for the availability management and capacity management processes, providing the information required to assess current performance and plan for future growth. This capability also enhances SLM's ability to track conformance to SLAs accurately and identify candidates for the service improvement process.

### 7.1.9 Statistical analysis tools

Most of the tools that are available to support the service management and systems management environments provide reporting capabilities but this is typically not enough to support robust availability management and capacity management capabilities. Raw data from many of the above tools needs to be captured into a single repository for collective analysis. This data provides input to the availability management and capacity management processes and supports the analysis of MTRS, MTBF, service failure, demand management, workload analysis, service modelling, application sizing and their related opportunities for improvement. This type of software provides the functionality to group data logically, model current services and enable predictive models to support future service growth, utilizing a wide array of analysis techniques.

### 7.1.10 Software version control/software configuration management

These tools support the control of all mainframe, open systems, network and applications software, providing a definitive media library type repository for the development environment. Version information must seamlessly integrate with the CMS and with release and deployment management.

### 7.1.11 Software test management

These tools support the testing and deployment activities of release and deployment management, providing development, regression testing, user acceptance testing and pre-production QA testing environments. Typically, there is additional functionality to support testing of specific functional requirements that were captured early in the development lifecycle. These tools should integrate with incident management to capture testing-related incidents that may affect the production version of the same software.

### 7.1.12 Information security management

These tools support and protect the integrity of the network, systems and applications, guarding against intrusion and inappropriate access and usage. As in the systems and network management area, all security-related hardware and software solutions should generate alerts that trigger the auto-generation of incidents for management through the normal processes.

### 7.1.13 Project and portfolio management

These tools support the registration, decision support, costing, resource management, portfolio visibility and project management of new business functionality and the services and systems that underpin them. These tools are typically used to manage the business-related aspects of IT. Integration points generally include: task assignments for development activities, change and release build information based on the agreed portfolio, capture of resource data from ITSM, total cost of ownership (TCO) of the service portfolio, and resource utilization data to financial management for IT services etc. These tools are typically utilized to underpin the management board approval process related to strategic or major change projects.

### 7.1.14 Financial management for IT services

Financial management is a critical component of the IT services mission to ensure there are enough financial resources to maintain and develop the IT infrastructure and professional capabilities in support of the current and future needs of the business. A balanced budget in IT through the recovery of IT costs, with a solid understanding of the fiscal aspects of their operations, enables IT executives to justify their expenses on business services being supported.

In an increasing number of IT organizations this requires keeping track of resource and service utilization for the purpose of billing and chargeback of the shared IT resources. The costing and resource consumption measurement becomes critical to charge business customers effectively and accurately in an equitable, visible and auditable way.

Financial management for IT services tools collect raw metering data from a variety of sources including operating systems, databases, middleware and applications, associating this usage with users of services from specific departments. Data collectors gather critical usage metrics for each of the technologies being measured, link in the costing information from accounting software, and then report, analyse and allocate costs, enabling customers to evaluate the information in many dimensions.

Most tools interface with the CMS to manage costs for each CI and resource to generate data related to billing, reporting, charging and cost analysis. These tools typically federate with the organization's enterprise financial management applications and ERP system to acquire and share aggregate costs. Interfaces are also normally supported with project and portfolio management tools to facilitate the overall portfolio of investments.

Effective cost management is a basic requirement for the IT organizations of today; financial management for IT services tools is required to ensure that customers can not only understand the IT costs of their business operations, but also more accurately budget and enable IT to evaluate the overall effectiveness of the services provision. Successful implementation and usage of these tools supports the continual improvement of cost management and drive ever-increasing IT value to the business.

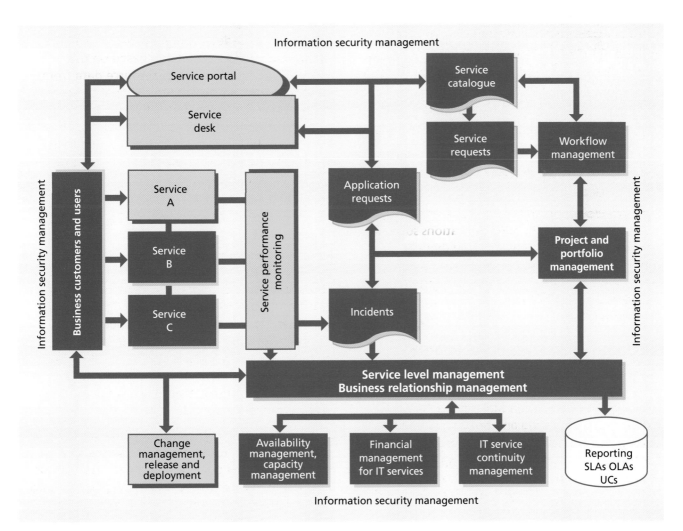

**Figure 7.2 Service-centric view of the IT enterprise**

### 7.1.15 Business intelligence/reporting

In addition to the statistical analysis environment that requires a toolset to support technical data, there is also a need for a common repository of all service information and business-related data. Often these tools are provided by the same vendors who support the statistical analysis software but the focus in this instance is on providing business-related data from all of the above toolsets, representing a guide to direct the activities of IT as a whole in support of the business customer.

As the technology used to deliver IT services becomes increasingly complex, the distribution of services expands and the amount of centralized control we can apply is diminished, there will be a growing reliance on tools and software functionality to administer, manage, improve and ensure overall governance of IT service provision. As stated earlier, best-practice processes should determine what support functionality is required but we can be assured that the software industry will continue to develop a wide and varied set of tools that can reduce the administrative overhead of managing processes and improve the overall quality of IT service provision.

### 7.2 SUMMARY

For effective CSI it is important for organizations to view their tool requirements from an enterprise perspective. Figure 7.2 shows how an integrated toolset is required to underpin all the ITIL processes and provide a diverse range of data required for effective and efficient CSI. Tools for CSI should support the key operational activities of the seven-step improvement process: data gathering, data processing, data analysis and data presentation. Tools must provide for monitoring of each level of the service hierarchy: services, systems and components, as well as support the reporting activities for SLAs, OLAs and UCs.

# Implementing continual service improvement

**8**

# 8 Implementing continual service improvement

This publication has discussed implementing continual service improvement (CSI) from two perspectives: the implementation of CSI activities around services, and the implementation of CSI around service management processes. However, if your organization does not have very mature service management processes then it is usually difficult to execute the seven-step improvement process for services.

Immature processes usually have poor data quality if any at all. This is often because there are no processes or very ad hoc processes. Other organizations have multiple processes working with multiple tools being used to support the processes. If any monitoring is going on it may be at a component or application level but not from an end-to-end service perspective. There is no central gathering point for data, no resources allocated to process and analyse the data, and reporting consists of too much data broken into too many segments for anyone to analyse. Some organizations don't have any evidence of reporting at all.

## 8.1 CRITICAL CONSIDERATIONS FOR IMPLEMENTING CSI

Before implementing CSI it is important to have identified and filled the critical roles that have been identified in Chapter 6. These include a CSI manager, service owner and reporting analyst. A service level manager facilitates the liaison between the customers and IT.

Monitoring and reporting on technology metrics, process metrics and service metrics need to be in place.

Internal service review meetings need to be scheduled in order to review from an internal IT perspective the results achieved each month. These internal review meetings should take place before any external review meeting with the business.

## 8.2 WHERE DO I START?

### 8.2.1 Where do I start – the service approach

An organization can choose to implement CSI activities in many different ways. One way is to identify a certain service pain point such as a service that is not consistently achieving the desired results. Work with the service owner to validate the desired results and the trend results over the past few months. Review any monitoring that has been done. If there hasn't been any end-to-end monitoring in place but some component monitoring, then review what has been monitored and see if there are any consistent issues that are leading to the lower than expected service results. Even if there hasn't been any component monitoring conducted, review your incidents and see if you can find some trends and CIs that are consistently failing more than others and which impact the service. Also review the change records for the different CIs that together underpin the service.

The bottom line is that you have to start somewhere. If you don't feel you have adequate data from monitoring or from another process then the first step is to identify what to monitor, define the monitoring requirements, and put in place or begin using the technology required for monitoring.

Be sure to analyse the data to see if the trends make sense and whether there are any consistent failures or deviation from expected results. Report findings and identify improvement opportunities.

### 8.2.2 Where do I start – the lifecycle approach

Another approach is to start looking at the output from the different lifecycle stages. For example, service design personnel need to monitor and report on their activities and, through trend evaluation and analysis, identify improvement opportunities to implement. This needs to be done by every part of the lifecycle and CSI is engaged in this activity. Until the service is implemented we may not know if the right strategy was identified, so we may not have input until later for service strategy improvement.

As service transition personnel begin working with the designed service they may identify improvement opportunities for service design. CSI can be effective well before a service is implemented into the live environment.

### 8.2.3 Where do I start – the functional group approach

Perhaps your organization is experiencing a lot of failures or issues with servers. If this is the case, it may be a good opportunity to focus CSI activities within the functional group responsible for the servers, as server failures have a direct impact on service availability.

This should be a short-term solution only, as CSI activities should be reviewing services from an end-to-end perspective; however, it is often easier to have a small group focused on CSI activities. Perhaps this could be a pilot of CSI activities before a full deployment across the organization.

## 8.3 GOVERNANCE

No matter if you are implementing CSI around service management or services, it is critical that governance is addressed from a strategic view. Organizations are facing the need to expand their IT service management strategies from an operational level to tactical and strategic levels to address business process automation, market globalization and the increasing dependency on IT for the efficient and reliable management and delivery of core business services. To address this requirement, formalized service management processes and specialized service and work management tools are being introduced to manage today's complex and distributed IT environments. Introducing service management processes into internal IT organizations requires a transformation to the IT culture.

Some internal IT organizations are still system/technology-management-based organizations, which are reactive in nature. Transforming to a service-management-based organization, which is more proactive in nature, is a step to aligning IT with business. It is also fundamental to achieving the goal of providing efficient and reliable management and delivery of core business services.

Implementing an IT service management (ITSM) process governance organization will support the development of, and transformation to, a process- and service-based organization and provide the organizational infrastructure to manage process improvement initiatives.

A comprehensive and integrated approach to the design, implementation and ongoing compliance to accepted ITSM standards includes:

■ Organizational structures, roles and responsibilities
■ IT processes, policies and controls.

### 8.3.1 Business drivers

The implementation of a standard ITSM process and governance is deemed as imperative to support current and future business plans:

■ Support the organization's vision
■ Provide standard IT processes and a stable and reliable IT environment to enable timely and efficient integration of new services and systems
■ Provide process policies, standards and controls to comply with internal audit and external regulatory and legislation requirements
■ Foster a climate of commitment to best practices
■ Provide a standard ITSM process across the IT organization to support the organizational transformation to an enterprise IT services model while maintaining operational stability and reliability to the business.

### 8.3.2 Process changes

Implementing CSI will have an impact on many parts of the IT organization. Processes, people, technology and management will undergo change. CSI needs to become a way of life within the organization. This may require new management structure, new technology and changes to processes to support CSI, and people will need to be trained and understand the importance of CSI within the organization.

If you only focus on changing a single process or technology CSI may not be effective. Figure 8.1 identifies how CSI should instead take a holistic view to improvements.

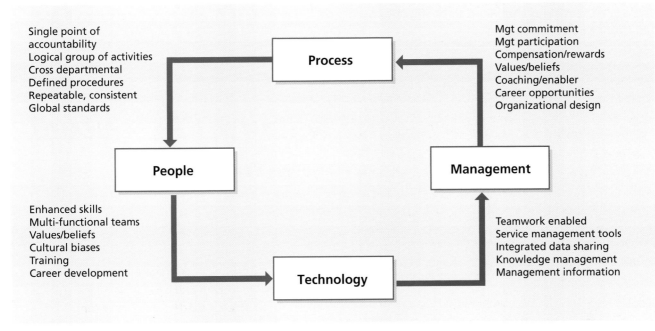

*Figure 8.1 Process re-engineering changes everything*

## 8.4 CSI AND ORGANIZATIONAL CHANGE

Project management structures and frameworks fail to take into account the softer aspects involved in organizational change such as overcoming resistance to change, gaining commitment, empowering, motivating, involving and communicating. Experience reveals that it is precisely these aspects that prevent many CSI initiatives from realizing their intended aims. The success of a CSI initiative depends on the buy-in of all stakeholders. Gaining their support from the outset, and keeping it, will ensure their participation in the development process and acceptance of the solution. The first five steps in Table 8.1 identify the basic leadership actions required.

Those responsible for managing and steering the CSI initiative should consciously address these softer issues. Using an approach such as John P. Kotter's 'eight steps to transform your organization', coupled with formalized project management skills and practices, will significantly increase the chance of success.

Kotter, Professor of Leadership at Harvard Business School, investigated more than 100 companies involved in, or having attempted, a complex change programme and identified eight main steps that need to be implemented in order to successfully change. The eight steps, which are shown in Table 8.1, apply equally to ITSM implementation programmes.

### 8.4.1 Create a sense of urgency

Half of all transformations fail to realize their goals because they lack adequate attention to this step. Not enough people accept that change is essential. To create a sense of urgency, ask the question 'What if we do nothing?' Answering this question at all organizational levels will help gain commitment and provide input to a business justification for investing in CSI.

Examples of the consequences of doing nothing are:

■ The business will lose money because of outages of crucial IT services, systems and applications.
■ The business will find IT costs unacceptable and may insist on staffing reductions as an easy option for reducing costs.

The question 'What if we do nothing?' should be answered from the perspective of different stakeholders. This step could be taken in the form of one-on-one dialogues with stakeholders, workshops and team meetings. The aim is to create a real awareness and commitment that the status quo is no longer acceptable.

**Table 8.1 Eight steps that need to be implemented, and the main reasons why transformation efforts fail (from Kotter, 1996)**

| Step | | Reasons for failure (quotes) |
|---|---|---|
| 1 | Create a sense of urgency | '50% of transformations fail in this phase' |
| | | 'Without motivation, people won't help and the effort goes nowhere' |
| | | '76% of a company's management should be convinced of the need' |
| 2 | Form a guiding coalition | 'Underestimating the difficulties in producing change' |
| | | 'Lack of effective, strong leadership' |
| | | 'Not a powerful enough guiding coalition … opposition eventually stops the change initiative' |
| 3 | Create a vision | 'Without a sensible vision, a transformation effort can easily dissolve into a list of confusing, incompatible projects that can take the organization in the wrong direction, or nowhere at all' |
| | | 'An explanation of 5 minutes should obtain a reaction of "understanding" and "interest"' |
| 4 | Communicate the vision | 'Without credible communication, and a lot of it, the hearts and minds of the troops are never captured' |
| | | 'Make use of all communications channels' |
| | | 'Let the managers lead by example … "walk the talk"' |
| 5 | Empower others to act on the vision | 'Structures to underpin the vision … and removal of barriers to change' |
| | | 'The more people involved, the better the outcome' |
| | | 'Reward initiatives' |
| 6 | Plan for and create quick wins | 'Real transformation takes time … without quick wins, too many people give up or join the ranks of those opposing change' |
| | | 'Actively look for performance improvements and establish clear goals' |
| | | 'Communicate successes' |
| 7 | Consolidate improvements and produce more change | 'Until changes sink deeply into the culture, new approaches are fragile and subject to regression' |
| | | 'In many cases, workers revert to old practice' |
| | | 'Use credibility of quick wins to tackle even bigger problems' |
| 8 | Institutionalize the change | 'Show how new approaches, behaviour and attitude have helped improve performance' |
| | | 'Ensure selection and promotion criteria underpin the new approach' |

## 8.4.2 Form a guiding coalition

Experience shows a need for assembling a group with sufficient power to lead the change effort and work together as a team. Power means more than simply formal authority but also experience, respect, trust and credibility. This team is the guiding coalition for the CSI.

It is important that the team leading the CSI has a shared understanding of the urgency and what it wants to achieve. A guiding coalition team does not have to comprise solely of senior managers. A guiding coalition should ensure that the organization is motivated and inspired to participate. A single champion cannot achieve success alone. Those initiating a CSI should try to gain full support from the stakeholders, including the business managers, IT staff and the user community. The team must be prepared to spend time and effort convincing and motivating others to participate.

In the beginning this team will be small and should include an influential business or IT sponsor. As the programme buy-in grows, and throughout the programme itself when more and more successes are achieved and benefits realized, this team should be increased to involve a wider range of people and functions. Conscious attention should be given to managing a formal and informal network that forms the basis of a guiding coalition, asking the questions 'Do we have the right people on board?' and, if not, 'Who should we have on board?'

## 8.4.3 Create a vision

The guiding coalition should be responsible for ensuring that a vision is produced describing the aim and purpose of CSI. A good vision statement can serve four important purposes. It can:

- Clarify the direction of the programme
- Motivate people to take action in the right direction
- Coordinate the actions of many different people
- Outline the aims of senior management.

Without a sensible and easily understood vision, a CSI implementation can easily dissolve into a list of confusing, incompatible projects that can take the organization in the wrong direction, or even nowhere at all. A vision that is easy to understand is also easy to explain. As a rule of thumb, if one

cannot explain the vision in five minutes, the vision itself is not clear and focused enough.

A sound vision statement is important when forming a business justification for CSI; if one is already under way then having clear aims will help set more specific goals. The goals of CSI should be SMART (specific, measurable, achievable, relevant and time-bound) and addressed in terms relating to the business itself.

## 8.4.4 Communicate the vision

Although the vision is a powerful tool in helping guide and coordinate change, the real power is unleashed when the vision is effectively communicated to the stakeholders. Every stakeholder should understand the vision.

The sense of urgency ('What if we do nothing?') and the vision ('What's in it for me?') should form the basis of all communication to the stakeholders involved in or impacted by the CSI initiative. These messages should be aimed at motivating, inspiring and creating the necessary energy and commitment to buy in to the change programme. An important aspect of the communication is demonstrating by example.

It is important to make use of all communications channels to get the messages across. Use the organization's newsletters, intranet site, posters, theme and team meetings, and seminars. Aim the communication at the specific needs and wants of each target group. For example, a presentation to computer operators, stressing the benefits of lower management costs and increased business availability, may be less likely to inspire them than the idea that they will have the chance to gain new skills and opportunities, or that they will be supported by the latest advanced management technology so they spend less time fire-fighting.

## 8.4.5 Empower others to act on the vision

Establishing the urgency, creating a guiding coalition, and creating and communicating a vision are all aimed at creating energy, enthusiasm, buy-in and commitment to enable successful change. In the empowering phase, two important aspects need to be stressed: enabling and removing barriers.

It is crucial to understand what is meant by empowerment. It is a combination of enabling people and removing barriers. Empowerment means giving people the tools, training, direction and assurance that they will be given clear and unambiguous fixed goals. Once people are empowered, they are accountable. That is why confirming their confidence before going ahead is important.

### 8.4.6 Plan for and create short-term wins

Implementing service management improvements can be a lengthy programme of change. It is important that, during the programme, short-term wins are realized and communicated. Short-term wins help to keep a change effort on track and to keep the energy and commitment levels high. Real transformation takes time. Without short-term wins, too many people give up or join the ranks of those opposing the change. Short-term wins can also be used to help:

- Convince sceptics of the benefits
- Retain support of influential stakeholders
- Expand the guiding coalition and get more people on board and committed to the programme
- Build confidence to tackle even more complex implementation issues and process integration.

Try to identify some short-term wins for each service and/or process and plan these into the CSI. It is also important that short-term wins are made visible and are communicated to all stakeholders. When planning to communicate the short-term wins, obtain answers to the questions 'For whom is it a short-term win?' and 'To what degree does it support the overall aims and goals?' and work these answers into the communication.

### 8.4.7 Consolidate improvements and produce more change

The success of short-term wins keeps the momentum going and creates more change. In CSI it is important to recognize short-, medium- and long-term wins. Changes should sink deeply into the new culture or the new approaches will be fragile and subject to regression:

- **Short-term wins** have the characteristics of convincing, motivating and showing immediate benefits and gains.

- **Medium-term wins** have the characteristics of confidence and capability, and having a set of working processes in place.
- **Long-term wins** have the characteristics of self-learning and expertise, and fully integrated processes that have self-learning and improvement built into them; reaching this stage requires a baseline of confident, capable delivery and real understanding. Trying to reach this level before having gone through the other levels is like trying to win an Olympic medal before commencing training.

### 8.4.8 Institutionalize the change

Change needs to be institutionalized within the organization. Many changes fail because they are not consolidated into everyday practice. This is akin to buying a membership to a gym but not going to the gym. To institutionalize a change means showing how new working practices have produced real gain and benefits, and ensuring that the improvements are embedded in all organizational practices.

Often the CSI team is disbanded before the working practices are institutionalized; there is a danger that people may revert to old working practices. This has to stop. CSI must be a way of life not a knee-jerk reaction to a failure of some sort.

These are some ways of institutionalizing changes:

- Hire people with ITIL experience or proven customer- or service-focused experience.
- When inducting new employees (in business and IT), include service management familiarization: 'This is the way we do things.'
- Include ITIL or service-management-focused training in employee training plans and offerings.
- Match service goals and management reporting to changing requirements, showing that they are used and requests are made for new sets of steering information.
- Identify clear action items in meeting minutes and act on them in a timely manner.
- Integrate new IT solutions and development projects into existing processes.

Signs that the changes have been institutionalized include:

- People defend the procedures and declare 'This is the way we work', rather than 'This is the way I've been told to do it'.

- People make suggestions for improving procedures and work instructions to make them more effective or efficient.
- Service and process owners are proud of their achievements and offer to give presentations and write articles.

### 8.4.9 Organization culture

Organizational culture is the whole of the ideas, corporate values, beliefs, practices and expectations about behaviour and daily customs that are shared by the employees in an organization – the normal way of doing things. Component parts of the culture include:

- The way authority is exercised and people rewarded
- Methods of communication
- The degrees of formality required in working hours and dress, and the extent to which procedures and regulations are enforced.

One could say culture is the heart of the matter or a key issue in implementing CSI. Culture could support an implementation or it could be the bearer of resistance.

Culture is continually named as one of the barriers in realizing any type of organizational change. When an organization has embraced CSI, the new organizational structure and technology receives overwhelming attention and almost no attention is paid to the effect on the culture. Culture isn't good or bad – it's just there.

An organization's culture can be immediately recognized by an outsider from the staff's attitudes and morale, their vocabulary – the phrases and buzzwords they use, and the stories and legends they tell of the organization's heroes. Continual improvement is about moving away from the hero mentality and focusing more on proactive planning and improving, instead of always reacting to fix something when it breaks.

#### 8.4.9.1 Key concept

One of the keys to changing the culture of an organization is to understand that you do not start out to change the culture. You start out to change the employee's behaviour. In other words, when implementing CSI around services and service management processes you are asking the staff members to change how they do things. You

want them to follow the new CSI activities and procedures, and use the tools appropriately.

As you change employees' behaviour then over time this changed behaviour becomes the organization's new culture. Senior management plays an important part in changing behaviour. Senior managers have to be the proper role models: if they don't follow a process they are giving permission to others to follow their lead. Senior managers have to ensure that people are rewarded for following the new process, and for CSI it means ongoing monitoring, analysing, reviewing, trend evaluation, reporting, identification of improvement opportunities and, of course, implementing those opportunities.

This will also require the help of your organization's human resource department, as changing employees' behaviour is directly tied to ensuring the job descriptions are up to date, employees' goals and objectives take into consideration service management responsibilities, and expectations include CSI activities. Also employee performance plans should be directly related to fulfilling these responsibilities and expectations. Whether an employee is performing an activity for service improvement or a change management activity, this should be recognized and employees rewarded based on the performance.

The following two statements are important when thinking about changing an employee's behaviour.

- **What gets rewarded gets done** This is why it is important to set up performance plans, performance appraisal systems and compensation plans to tie into CSI activities as well as other service management activities. If you are rewarding an employee for simply doing the daily activities of their job, and not for understanding the full end-to-end service management processes, there will be no incentive for them to gain a broader understanding. It will be hard to change an employee's behaviour when they get rewarded for doing what they do today.
- **You get what you inspect not what you expect** Organizations always expect employees to do certain things, but unless they are actually monitoring and checking to see if the tasks and activities are being done, there is little reason for an employee to do them. Remember the

state of North Carolina example in section 5.6.5. The state achieved results through training, creating an awareness campaign and letting people know they were tracking results and would be discussing the results with the managers each month.

## 8.5 COMMUNICATION STRATEGY AND PLAN

Timely and effective communication forms an important part of any service improvement project. In an effort to transform an organization from performing CSI activities ad hoc to undertaking more formal and ongoing CSI activities, it is critical that participants and stakeholders are informed of all changes to the processes, activities, roles and responsibilities.

The goal of the communications plan is to build and maintain awareness, understanding, enthusiasm and support among key influential stakeholders for the CSI initiative.

When developing a communication plan, it is important to realize that effective communication is not based solely on a one-way flow of information, and it is more than just meetings. A communications plan must incorporate the ability to deal with responses and feedback from the targeted audiences.

The plan should include a role to:

■ Design and deliver communications to the different CSI roles, stakeholders such as other ITSM process roles and identified target audiences
■ Identify forums for customer and user feedback
■ Receive and deliver responses and feedback to the project manager and/or process team members.

Key activities for the communications plan include:
■ Identifying stakeholders and target audiences
■ Developing communications strategies and tactics
■ Identifying communication methods and techniques
■ Developing the communications plan (a matrix of who, what, why, when, where and how)
■ Identifying the project milestones and related communications requirements
■ The tools and techniques to use to gain a perspective on the level of audience understanding, e.g. surveys, website hits, event participation etc.

In order to change behaviours and ultimately an organization's culture will require a well-thought-out communication strategy and plan. An effective communication strategy and plan will focus on creating awareness of why the organization is implementing service management, why we want to formalize a CSI process, and why ITIL was chosen as the best-practice framework. The plan will also need to address how to provide service management education through formal training programmes or internal meetings, how to provide formal training on the new processes and tools that sets new expectations, and how to provide updates on progress and achievements.

When developing your communication strategy and plan it is important to take into consideration how corporate communication works today. In some organizations, if you want the chief information officer (CIO) to communicate something on behalf of CSI or any service management project, it may take a long time. This needs to be planned for.

Also keep in mind the culture around communicating with the business. In some organizations there are strict guidelines on who can communicate with the business. Often this is through the service level management (SLM) and business relationship management processes. No matter what the method is, always have communicating with the business as one of your key communication activities.

### 8.5.1 Defining a communication plan

Defining your plan needs to take into consideration the following topics:

■ **Who is the messenger?** This is often overlooked when assessing the importance of aligning the messenger with the message. There are times when it is appropriate for the CIO to deliver a communication. Another time it may be a service owner or process owner who should be doing the communicating.
■ **What is the message?** Define the purpose and objective of the message. This needs to be tailored to the target audience. Keep in mind the importance of communicating the benefits of the CSI initiative. The what's-in-it-for-me approach is still valid and needs to be addressed.

**Table 8.2 Table for sample communication plan**

| Messenger | Target audience | Message | Method of communication | Date and frequency | Status |
|-----------|-----------------|---------|-------------------------|--------------------|--------|
| CIO | All of IT | CSI initiative is kicking off | Town hall meeting | Month/day | Planned |

- **Who is the target audience?** The target audience for CSI could be senior management, mid-level managers or the staff who will be tasked with performing CSI activities. The target audience will often dictate who will deliver the message based on what the message is.

- **Timing and frequency of communication** Be sure to plan and execute your communication in a timely manner. The one constant about managing change is that for communication to be effective, it will take more than a one-time communication. If reporting is what is being communicated you will want to define your reporting timelines and frequency.

- **Method of communication** The old standby of sending emails and putting something on the web can work for some forms of communication, but in order to manage change effectively it is important to have a number of face-to-face meetings where there is an opportunity for two-way communications to take place. Attending staff meetings, holding information meetings open to all IT personnel and conducting town hall meetings are all effective methods that need to be considered.

- **Provide a feedback mechanism** Be sure to provide some method for employees to ask questions and provide feedback on the change initiative. Someone should have ownership of checking and ensuring that responses are provided to questions or comments.

Be sure to keep a record of all your communications as they illustrate how the communication plan has been executed.

You can develop a simple table for your communication plan as shown in Table 8.2. Keep in mind that you will be communicating to various groups within IT. Be sure to include senior management, mid-level managers and line contributors, as well as those working or supporting CSI activities.

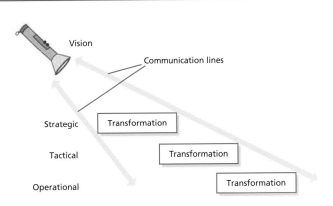

**Figure 8.2 Vision becomes blurred**

### 8.5.2 Communication transformation

The strategic management level usually initiates the communication about new initiatives and this should be true for implementing CSI within your organization. The CSI initiative is handed down from the strategic level to the tactical level and then to the operational level. It is more the rule than the exception that each level goes through its own transformation process. It is important that the same message is being sent and received as the vision is communicated down the organization. The outcome of this process is the cause and often the demand for the next level in an organization to transform. Information about this process and how people are dealing with it are seldom handed down. Unfortunately the higher level gives little feedback about this process to the next level.

What also happens is that the content of the vision and reasons for the organizational change becomes less understood as it moves down through the organization. Only parts of the rationale behind the organizational change come through to the operational level. Figure 8.2 shows how only part of the original content of the vision is handed down ('the shadow of the upper level') to the operational level. As the message is passed through the organizational levels, the clarity and content of the vision is blurred even further.

Because each management level has its own separate transformation processes they fail to

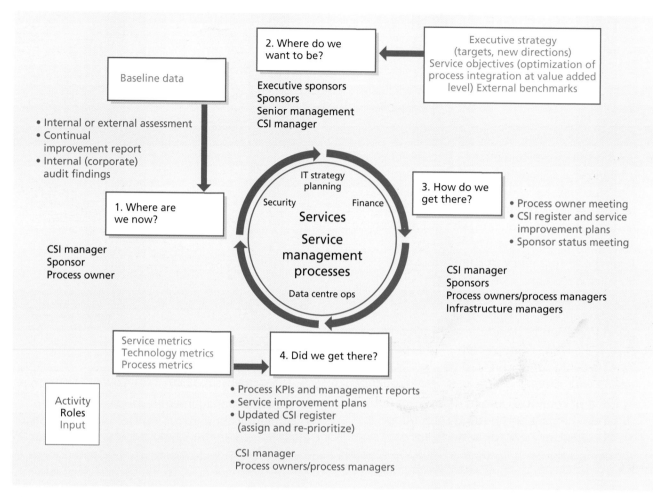

*Figure 8.3 CSI roles and inputs*

appreciate the feelings of the other levels. This is most evident for operational level staff, who feel particularly vulnerable if they have not been involved in the discussions. Yet the commitment and energy of operational level staff are essential to the success of any organizational change.

## 8.6 SUMMARY

Developing a governance structure is important for formalizing CSI in your organization. CSI will require that key roles are filled for trend evaluation, analysis reporting and decision-making. Process compliance is critical for ensuring the proper output for process metrics to be used for identifying process improvement initiatives. Technology will need to be in place for monitoring and reporting. Communication is critical to help change employees' behaviour. Communication will be necessary to identify the target audience, who the messenger is, what message is being communicated and what is the best way to communicate the message.

Figure 8.3 shows the roles and key inputs that are involved in the different phases of continual improvement.

# Challenges, risks and critical success factors

# 9 Challenges, risks and critical success factors

## 9.1 CHALLENGES

Every organization has its unique set of challenges. As with implementing any type of change within an organization, one of the major challenges is managing the behavioural changes required.

Another issue is that continual service improvement (CSI) often requires adequate tools for monitoring and gathering the data, analysing the data for trends and reporting on the data. CSI does not happen only through automation but also requires resources to be allocated to CSI activities. Those allocating resources need to understand their roles and responsibilities and have the correct skill sets to execute the CSI activities.

These are some of the common challenges you may encounter when implementing CSI:

- Lack of management commitment
- Inadequate resources, budget and time
- Lack of mature service management processes
- Lack of information, monitoring and measurements
- Lack of knowledge management
- A resistance to planning and a reluctance to be proved wrong
- Lack of corporate objectives, strategies, policies and business direction
- Lack of IT objectives, strategies and policies
- Lack of knowledge and appreciation of business impacts and priorities
- Diverse and disparate technologies and applications
- Resistance to change and cultural change
- Poor relationships and communication, and lack of cooperation between IT and the business
- Lack of tools, standards and skills
- Tools too complex and costly to implement and maintain
- Over-commitment of resources with an associated inability to deliver (e.g. projects always late or over budget)
- Poor supplier management and/or poor supplier performance.

## 9.2 CRITICAL SUCCESS FACTORS

These are some critical success factors (CSFs):

- Appointing a CSI manager
- Adopting CSI within the organization
- Management commitment – ongoing, visible participation in CSI activities such as creating vision for CSI, communicating vision, direction setting and decision-making, when appropriate
- Defining clear criteria for prioritizing improvement projects
- Adopting the service lifecycle approach
- Having sufficient and ongoing funding for CSI activities
- Resource allocation – people dedicated to the improvement effort not as just another add-on to their already long list of tasks to perform
- Technology supporting the CSI activities
- Adopting processes – embracing service management processes instead of adapting it to suit their own personal needs and agenda.

## 9.3 RISKS

These are some risks:

- Being over-ambitious – don't try to improve everything at once; be realistic with timelines and expectations
- Not discussing improvement opportunities with the business – the business has to be involved in improvement decisions that will impact it
- Not focusing on improving both services and service management processes
- Not prioritizing improvement projects
- Implementing CSI with little or no technology
- Implementing a CSI initiative with no resources – this means that people must be allocated and dedicated to this
- Implementing CSI without knowledge transfer and training – this means educating first (acquire knowledge), then training (practise using the newly acquired knowledge); training should be undertaken as close to the launch of improvement as possible

■ Not performing all steps of the seven-step improvement process – it is important that all steps of the improvement process are followed; missing any one step can lead to a poor decision on what and how to improve

■ Lack of making strategic, tactical or operational decisions based on knowledge gained – reports are actually used; people see that the reports are being used

■ Lack of management taking action on recommended service improvement opportunities

■ Lack of meeting personnel in the business to understand new business requirements

■ Lack of communication/awareness campaign for any improvement, or it is late or missing altogether

■ Not involving the right people at all levels to plan, build, test and implement the improvement

■ Removing testing before implementation or only partially testing so all aspects of the improvement (people, process and technology) must be tested, including the documentation.

## 9.4 SUMMARY

Implementing CSI is not an easy task: it requires a change in management and staff attitudes and values that continual improvement is something that needs to be carried out proactively and not reactively.

Identifying the risks and challenges before implementing CSI is a critical first step. A SWOT analysis (examining strengths, weaknesses, opportunities and threats) can help identify these items. It is important to define mitigation strategies for the risks and identify how to best overcome challenges that an organization may encounter.

Knowing the CSFs before undertaking CSI implementation will help manage the risks and challenges. Don't try to change everything at once.

Afterword

# Afterword

For centuries people have been sailing across the oceans in ships. While a very few have been intrepid explorers intent on charting new territory and new routes to far-off lands, most have simply set off on a journey from their home port to a distant destination. They plotted a course which would get them there safely in a reasonable time and then set sail. The risks were high, but the rewards were even higher. If the final destination was too far they plotted a series of smaller journeys with stops at points along the way allowing them to get to their destination in steps. The course would often take them far from the sight of land, so each day they would need to check if they were still on course. In the beginning they used the stars, then the compass, the sextant, radio beacons and now global positioning satellites. The technology has changed radically but the goal is still the same: determine where you are right now and if the winds or the currents have moved you off course you must make adjustments in order to reach your destination. Continual service improvement is your journey. Your destination is your vision of a near-perfect future state. The vision may be far off, requiring you to set smaller goals along the way. You set the course for near perfection and continually check to see whether you are still on course. Continually making the necessary adjustments on your journey will enable you to reach your destination. Good sailing!

# Appendix A:
# Related guidance

# Appendix A: Related guidance

This is a common appendix across the ITIL core publications. It includes frameworks, best practices, standards, models and quality systems that complement and have synergy with the ITIL service lifecycle.

Section 2.1.7 describes the role of best practices in the public domain and references some of the publications in this appendix. Each core publication references this appendix where relevant.

Related guidance may also be referenced within a single ITIL core publication where the topic is specific to that publication.

## A.1 ITIL GUIDANCE AND WEB SERVICES

ITIL is part of the Best Management Practice (BMP) portfolio of best-practice guidance (see section 1.3). BMP products present flexible, practical and effective guidance, drawn from a range of the most successful global business experiences. Distilled to its essential elements, the guidance can then be applied to every type of business and organization.

The BMP website (www.best-management-practice.com) includes news, reviews, case studies and white papers on ITIL and all other BMP best-practice guidance.

The ITIL official website (www.itil-officialsite.com) contains reliable, up-to-date information on ITIL – including information on accreditation and the ITIL software scheme for the endorsement of ITIL-based tools.

Details of the core publications are as follows:

- Cabinet Office (2011). *ITIL Service Strategy*. TSO, London.
- Cabinet Office (2011). *ITIL Service Design*. TSO, London.
- Cabinet Office (2011). *ITIL Service Transition*. TSO, London.
- Cabinet Office (2011). *ITIL Service Operation*. TSO, London.
- Cabinet Office (2011). ITIL *Continual Service Improvement*. TSO, London.

The full ITIL glossary, in English and other languages, can be accessed through the ITIL official site at:

www.itil-officialsite.com/InternationalActivities/ITILGlossaries.aspx

The range of translated glossaries is always growing, so check this website for the most up-to-date list.

Details of derived and complementary publications can be found in the publications library of the Best Management Practice website at:

www.best-management-practice.com/Publications-Library/IT-Service-Management-ITIL/

## A.2 QUALITY MANAGEMENT SYSTEM

Quality management focuses on product/service quality as well as the quality assurance and control of processes to achieve consistent quality. Total Quality Management (TQM) is a methodology for managing continual improvement by using a quality management system. TQM establishes a culture involving all people in the organization in a process of continual monitoring and improvement.

ISO 9000:2005 describes the fundamentals of quality management systems that are applicable to all organizations which need to demonstrate their ability to consistently provide products that meet customer and applicable statutory and regulatory requirements. ISO 9001:2008 specifies generic requirements for a quality management system.

Many process-based quality management systems use the methodology known as 'Plan-Do-Check-Act' (PDCA), often referred to as the Deming Cycle, or Shewhart Cycle, that can be applied to all processes. PDCA can be summarized as:

- **Plan** Establish the objectives and processes necessary to deliver results in accordance with customer requirements and the organization's policies.
- **Do** Implement the processes.
- **Check** Monitor and measure processes and product against policies, objectives and

requirements for the product and report the results.

- **Act** Take actions to continually improve process performance.

There are distinct advantages of tying an organization's ITSM processes, and service operation processes in particular, to its quality management system. If an organization has a formal quality management system that complies with ISO 9001, then this can be used to assess progress regularly and drive forward agreed service improvement initiatives through regular reviews and reporting.

Visit www.iso.org for information on ISO standards.

See www.deming.org for more information on the W. Edwards Deming Institute and the Deming Cycle for process improvement.

## A.3 RISK MANAGEMENT

A number of different methodologies, standards and frameworks have been developed for the assessment and management of risk. Some focus more on generic techniques widely applicable to different levels and needs, while others are specifically concerned with risk management relating to important assets used by the organization in the pursuit of its objectives. Each organization should determine the approach to risk management that is best suited to its needs and circumstances. It is possible that the approach adopted will leverage the ideas reflected in more than one of the recognized standards and/or frameworks.

Appendix C gives more information on risk management. See also:

- Office of Government Commerce (2010). *Management of Risk: Guidance for Practitioners.* TSO, London.
- ISO 31000:2009 Risk management – principles and guidelines.
- ISO/IEC 27001: 2005 Information technology – security techniques – information security management systems – requirements.
- ISACA (2009). *The Risk IT Framework* (based on COBIT, see section A.5).

## A.4 GOVERNANCE OF IT

Corporate governance refers to the rules, policies, processes (and in some cases, laws) by which businesses are operated, regulated and controlled. These are often defined by the board or shareholders, or the constitution of the organization; but they can also be defined by legislation, regulation or consumer groups.

ISO 9004 (Managing for the sustained success of an organization – a quality management approach) provides guidance on governance for the board and executive of an organization.

The standard for corporate governance of IT is ISO/IEC 38500. The purpose of this standard is to promote effective, efficient and acceptable use of IT in all organizations by:

- Assuring stakeholders (including consumers, shareholders and employees) that, if the standard is followed, they can have confidence in the organization's corporate governance of IT
- Informing and guiding directors in governing the use of IT in their organization
- Providing a basis for objective evaluation of the corporate governance of IT.

Typical examples of regulations that impact IT include: financial, safety, data protection, privacy, software asset management, environment management and carbon emission targets.

Further details are available at www.iso.org

*ITIL Service Strategy* references the concepts of ISO/IEC 38500 and how the concepts can be applied.

## A.5 COBIT

The Control OBjectives for Information and related Technology (COBIT) is a governance and control framework for IT management created by ISACA and the IT Governance Institute (ITGI).

COBIT is based on the analysis and harmonization of existing IT standards and good practices and conforms to generally accepted governance principles. It covers five key governance focus areas: strategic alignment, value delivery, resource management, risk management and performance management. COBIT is primarily aimed at internal and external stakeholders within an enterprise who wish to generate value from IT investments; those who provide IT services; and those who have a control/risk responsibility.

COBIT and ITIL are not 'competitive', nor are they mutually exclusive – on the contrary, they can be used in conjunction as part of an organization's overall governance and management framework. COBIT is positioned at a high level, is driven by business requirements, covers the full range of IT activities, and concentrates on *what* should be achieved rather than *how* to achieve effective governance, management and control. ITIL provides an organization with best-practice guidance on *how* to manage and improve its processes to deliver high-quality, cost-effective IT services. The following COBIT guidance supports strategy management and continual service improvement (CSI):

■ COBIT maturity models can be used to benchmark and drive improvement.
■ Goals and metrics can be aligned to the business goals for IT and used to create an IT management dashboard.
■ The COBIT 'monitor and evaluate' (ME) process domain defines the processes needed to assess current IT performance, IT controls and regulatory compliance.

Further details are available at www.isaca.org and www.itgi.org

## A.6 ISO/IEC 20000 SERVICE MANAGEMENT SERIES

ISO/IEC 20000 is an internationally recognized standard for ITSM covering service providers who manage and deliver IT-enabled services to internal or external customers. ISO/IEC 20000-1 is aligned with other ISO management systems standards such as ISO 9001 and ISO/IEC 27001.

One of the most common routes for an organization to achieve the requirements of ISO/IEC 20000 is by adopting ITIL best practices. ISO/IEC 20000-1 is based on a service management system (SMS). The SMS is defined as a management system to direct and control the service management activities of the service provider. ISO/IEC 20000 includes:

■ ISO/IEC 20000-1:2005 – Information technology – Service management – Part 1: Specification
■ ISO/IEC 20000-1:2011 – Information technology – Service management – Part 1: Requirements for a service management system (the most recent edition of the ISO/IEC 20000 standard)

■ ISO/IEC 20000-2:2005 – Information technology – Service management – Part 2: Code of practice (being updated to include guidance on the application of service management systems and to support ISO/IEC 20000-1:2011)
■ ISO/IEC 20000-3:2005 – Information technology – Service management – Part 3: Scope and applicability
■ ISO/IEC TR 20000-4 – Information technology – Service management – Part 4: Process reference model
■ ISO/IEC TR 20000-5:2010 – Information technology – Service management – Part 5: Exemplar implementation plan for ISO/IEC 20000-1.

A closely related publication that is under development is ISO/IEC TR 15504-8 – Process assessment model for IT service management.

Further details can be found at www.iso.org or www.isoiec20000certification.com

Organizations using ISO/IEC 20000-1: 2005 for certification audits will transfer to the new edition, ISO/IEC 20000-1: 2011.

ITIL guidance supports organizations that are implementing service management practices to achieve the requirements of ISO/IEC 20000-1: 2005 and the new edition ISO/IEC 20000-1: 2011.

Other references include:

■ Dugmore, J. and Lacy, S. (2011). *Introduction to ISO/IEC 20000 Series: IT Service Management*. British Standards Institution, London.
■ Dugmore, J. and Lacy, S. (2011). *BIP 0005: A Manager's Guide to Service Management* (6th edition). British Standards Institution, London.

## A.7 ENVIRONMENTAL MANAGEMENT AND GREEN/SUSTAINABLE IT

The transition to a low-carbon economy is a global challenge. Many governments have set targets to reduce carbon emissions or achieve carbon neutrality. IT is an enabler for environmental and cultural change that will help governments to achieve their targets – for example, through enabling tele- and video-conferencing, and remote and home working. However, IT is also a major user of energy and natural resources. Green IT refers to environmentally sustainable computing where the use and disposal of computers and printers are carried out in sustainable ways that do not have a negative impact on the environment.

Appendix E in *ITIL Service Design* includes further information on environmental architectures and standards. Appendix E in *ITIL Service Operation* also provides useful considerations for facilities management, including environmental aspects.

The ISO 14001 series of standards for an environment management system is designed to assure internal and external stakeholders that the organization is an environmentally responsible organization. It enables an organization of any size or type to:

■ Identify and control the environmental impact of its activities, products or services

■ Improve its environmental performance continually

■ Implement a systematic approach to setting and achieving environmental objectives and targets, and then demonstrating that they have been achieved.

Further details are available at www.iso.org

## A.8 ISO STANDARDS AND PUBLICATIONS FOR IT

ISO 9241 is a series of standards and guidance on the ergonomics of human system interaction that cover people working with computers. It covers aspects that impact the utility of a service (whether it is fit for purpose) such as:

■ ISO 9241-11:1999 Guidance on usability

■ ISO 9241-210:2010 Human-centred design for interactive systems

■ ISO 9241-151:2008 Guidance on world wide web user interfaces.

ISO/IEC JTC1 is Joint Technical Committee 1 of ISO and the International Electrotechnical Commission (IEC). It deals with information technology standards and other publications.

SC27 is a subcommittee under ISO/IEC JTC1 that develops ISO/IEC 27000, the information security management system (ISMS) family of standards. For further details, Appendix C includes information on ISO/IEC 27001. SC7 is a subcommittee under ISO/IEC JTC1 that covers the standardization of processes, supporting tools and supporting technologies for

the engineering of systems, services and software. SC7 publications include:

■ ISO/IEC 20000 Information technology – service management (see section A.6)

■ ISO/IEC 19770-1 Information technology – software asset management processes. ISO/IEC 19770-2:2009 establishes specifications for tagging software to optimize its identification and management

■ ISO/IEC 15288 Systems and software engineering – systems life cycle processes. The processes can be used as a basis for establishing business environments – e.g. methods, procedures, techniques, tools and trained personnel

■ ISO/IEC 12207 Systems and software engineering – software life cycle processes

■ ISO/IEC 15504 Process assessment series. Also known as SPICE (software process improvement and capability determination), it aims to ensure consistency and repeatability of the assessment ratings with evidence to substantiate the ratings. The series includes exemplar process assessment models (PAM), related to one or more conformant or compliant process reference model (PRM). ISO/IEC 15504-8 is an exemplar process assessment model for IT service management that is under development

■ ISO/IEC 25000 series – provides guidance for the use of standards named Software product Quality Requirements and Evaluation (SQuaRE)

■ ISO/IEC 42010 Systems and software engineering — recommended practice for architectural description of software-intensive systems.

SC7 is working on the harmonization of standards in the service management, software and IT systems domains. Further details are available at www.iso.org

## A.9 ITIL AND THE OSI FRAMEWORK

At around the time that ITIL V1 was being written, the International Standards Organization launched an initiative that resulted in the Open Systems Interconnection (OSI) framework. Since this initiative covered many of the same areas as ITIL V1, it is not surprising that there was considerable overlap.

However, it is also not surprising that they classified their processes differently, used different terminology, or used the same terminology in different ways. To confuse matters even more, it is common for different groups in an organization to use terminology from both ITIL and the OSI framework.

The OSI framework made significant contributions to the definition and execution of ITSM programmes and projects around the world. It has also caused a great deal of debate between teams that do not realize the origins of the terminology that they are using. For example, some organizations have two change management departments – one following the ITIL change management process and the other using the OSI installation, moves, additions and changes (IMAC) model. Each department is convinced that it is completely different from the other, and that it is performing a different role. Closer examination will reveal that there are several areas of commonality.

In service operation, the management of known errors may be mapped to fault management. There is also a section related to operational capacity management, which can be related to the OSI concept of performance management.

Information on the set of ISO standards for the OSI framework is available at: www.iso.org

## A.10 PROGRAMME AND PROJECT MANAGEMENT

Large, complex deliveries are often broken down into manageable, interrelated projects. For those managing this overall delivery, the principles of programme management are key to delivering on time and within budget. Best management practice in this area is found in *Managing Successful Programmes* (MSP).

Guidance on effective portfolio, programme and project management is brought together in *Portfolio, Programme and Project Offices* (P3O), which is aimed at helping organizations to establish and maintain appropriate business support structures with proven roles and responsibilities.

Structured project management methods, such as PRINCE2 (PRojects IN Controlled Environments) or the Project Management Body of Knowledge (PMBOK) developed by the Project Management Institute (PMI), can be used when improving IT services. Not all improvements will require a

structured project approach, but many will, due to the sheer scope and scale of the improvement. Project management is discussed in more detail in *ITIL Service Transition*.

Visit www.msp-officialsite.com for more information on MSP.

Visit www.p3o-officialsite.com for more information on P3O.

Visit www.prince-officialsite.com for more information on PRINCE2.

Visit www.pmi.org for more information on PMI and PMBOK.

See also the following publications:

- Cleland, David I. and Ireland, Lewis R. (2006). *Project Management: Strategic Design and Implementation* (5th edition). McGraw-Hill Professional.
- Haugan, Gregory T. (2006). *Project Management Fundamentals*. Management Concepts.
- Office of Government Commerce (2009). *Managing Successful Projects with PRINCE2*. TSO, London.
- Cabinet Office (2011). *Managing Successful Programmes*. TSO, London.
- Office of Government Commerce (2008). Portfolio, *Programme and Project Offices*. TSO, London.
- The Project Management Institute (2008). *A Guide to the Project Management Body of Knowledge* (PMBOK Guide) (4th edition). Project Management Institute.

## A.11 ORGANIZATIONAL CHANGE

There is a wide range of publications that cover organizational change including the related guidance for programme and project management referred to in the previous section.

Chapter 5 in *ITIL Service Transition* covers aspects of organizational change elements that are an essential part of, or a strong contributor towards, service transition. *ITIL Service Transition* and *ITIL Continual Service Improvement* (this volume) refer to Kotter's 'eight steps for organizational change'.

Visit www.johnkotter.com for more information. See also the following publications:

- Kotter, John P. (1996). *Leading Change*. Harvard Business School Press.

- Kotter, John P. (1999) *What Leaders Really Do.* Harvard Business School Press.
- Kotter, J. P. (2000). Leading change: why transformation efforts fail. *Harvard Business Review* January–February.
- Kotter, John P. and Cohen, Dan S. (2002) *The Heart of Change: Real-Life Stories of How People Change their Organizations.* Harvard Business School Press.
- Kotter, J. P. and Schlesinger, L. C. (1979). Choosing strategies for change. *Harvard Business Review* Vol. 57, No. 2, p.106.
- Kotter, John P., Rathgeber, Holger, Mueller, Peter and Johnson, Spenser (2006). *Our Iceberg Is Melting: Changing and Succeeding Under Any Conditions.* St. Martin's Press.

## A.12 SKILLS FRAMEWORK FOR THE INFORMATION AGE

The Skills Framework for the Information Age (SFIA) enables employers of IT professionals to carry out a range of human resource activities against a common framework including a skills audit, planning future skill requirements, development programmes, standardization of job titles and functions, and resource allocation.

SFIA provides a standardized view of the wide range of professional skills needed by people working in IT. SFIA is constructed as a simple two-dimensional matrix consisting of areas of work on one axis and levels of responsibility on the other. It uses a common language and a sensible, logical structure that can be adapted to the training and development needs of a very wide range of businesses.

Visit www.sfia.org.uk for further details.

## A.13 CARNEGIE MELLON: CMMI AND ESCM FRAMEWORK

The Capability Maturity Model Integration (CMMI) is a process improvement approach developed by the Software Engineering Institute (SEI) of Carnegie Mellon University. CMMI provides organizations with the essential elements of effective processes. It can be used to guide process improvement across a project, a division or an entire organization. CMMI helps integrate traditionally separate organizational functions, sets process improvement goals and priorities, provides guidance for quality processes, and suggests a point of reference for appraising current processes. There are several CMMI models covering different domains of application.

The eSourcing Capability Model for Service Providers (eSCM-SP) is a framework developed by ITSqc at Carnegie Mellon to improve the relationship between IT service providers and their customers.

Organizations can be assessed against CMMI models using SCAMPI (Standard CMMI Appraisal Method for Process Improvement).

For more information, see www.sei.cmu.edu/cmmi/

## A.14 BALANCED SCORECARD

A new approach to strategic management was developed in the early 1990s by Drs Robert Kaplan (Harvard Business School) and David Norton. They named this system the 'balanced scorecard'. Recognizing some of the weaknesses and vagueness of previous management approaches, the balanced scorecard approach provides a clear prescription as to what companies should measure in order to 'balance' the financial perspective. The balanced scorecard suggests that the organization be viewed from four perspectives, and it is valuable to develop metrics, collect data and analyse the organization relative to each of these perspectives:

- The learning and growth perspective
- The business process perspective
- The customer perspective
- The financial perspective.

Some organizations may choose to use the balanced scorecard method as a way of assessing and reporting their IT quality performance in general and their service operation performance in particular.

Further details are available through the balanced scorecard user community at www.scorecardsupport.com

## A.15 SIX SIGMA

Six Sigma is a data-driven process improvement approach that supports continual improvement. It is business-output-driven in relation to customer specification. The objective is to implement a measurement-oriented strategy focused on process improvement and defects reduction. A Six Sigma defect is defined as anything outside customer specifications.

Six Sigma focuses on dramatically reducing process variation using statistical process control (SPC) measures. The fundamental objective is to reduce errors to fewer than 3.4 defects per million executions (regardless of the process). Service providers must determine whether it is reasonable to expect delivery at a Six Sigma level given the wide variation in IT deliverables, roles and tasks within IT operational environments.

There are two primary sub-methodologies within Six Sigma: DMAIC (Define, Measure, Analyse, Improve, Control) and DMADV (Define, Measure, Analyse, Design, Verify). DMAIC is an improvement method for existing processes for which performance does not meet expectations, or for which incremental improvements are desired. DMADV focuses on the creation of new processes. For more information, see:

- George, Michael L. (2003). *Lean Six Sigma for Service: How to Use Lean Speed and Six Sigma Quality to Improve Services and Transactions. McGraw-Hill.*
- Pande, Pete and Holpp, Larry (2001) *What Is Six Sigma?* McGraw-Hill.
- Pande, Peter S., Neuman, Robert P. and Cavanagh, Roland R. (2000). *The Six Sigma Way: How GE, Motorola, and Other Top Companies are Honing their Performance*. McGraw-Hill.

# Appendix B: Example of a continual service improvement register

| Opportunity no. | Date raised | Size (small, medium, large) | Timescale (short, medium, long) | Description | Priority (urgent, 1, 2, 3) | KPI metric | Justification | Raised by | To be actioned by | Date required by |
|---|---|---|---|---|---|---|---|---|---|---|
| 1 | 01/04/2011 | Small | Short | A number of failures have occurred when implementing updated or new applications. This has been caused by the testing procedure in release and deployment using out-of-date test data. The requirement is to update the test data in repository test 4371 | Urgent | n% reduction in failures | Significant reduction in failures after transition and resulting business impact | A. Other | J. Doe | 14/4/2011 |
| 2 | 01/05/2011 | Medium | Long | Event management: the number of alerts from the ABC 479 module of the payroll suite is still excessive causing unnecessary analysis time. Additional filtering required | 2 | n% reduction in spurious events | Will help reduce the amount of analysis time and avoid potential oversight of significant events | N. More | J. Smith | 01/07/2011 |
| 3 | 01/06/2011 | Medium | Long | Training issue: Service desk staff would benefit from additional training in the use of the human resources (HR) joiners and leavers application | 3 | n% improvement in relevant staff trained in the HR joiners and leavers application | All queries to the service desk on this application currently have to be escalated to the application management team. With some basic training a number of these could be dealt with by first line support | B. Floor | F. Less | 01/09/2011 |
| 4 | 01/07/2011 | Large | Medium | Change management process: having multiple authorization channels has caused issues with some users because of uncoordinated changes | 3 | Alignment to single channel | Redesign of the change management process will reduce confusion and impact to stakeholders | J. Jones | B. Car | 10/10/2011 |

# Appendix C:
# Risk assessment and management

# Appendix C: Risk assessment and management

This appendix contains basic information about several broadly known and used approaches to the assessment and management of risk. It is not intended to be a comprehensive study of the subject, but rather to provide an awareness of some of the methods in use.

## C.1 DEFINITION OF RISK AND RISK MANAGEMENT

Risk may be defined as uncertainty of outcome, whether a positive opportunity or negative threat. It is the fact that there is uncertainty that creates the need for attention and formal management of risk. After all, if an organization were absolutely certain that a negative threat would materialize, there would be little difficulty in determining an appropriate course of action. Likewise, if an organization could be guaranteed that the positive opportunity would be realized, then its path would be clear. Managing risks requires the identification and control of the exposure to those risks which may have an impact on the achievement of an organization's business objectives.

Every organization manages its risk, but not always in a way that is visible, repeatable and consistently applied to support decision-making. The purpose of formal risk management is to enable better decision-making based on a sound understanding of risks and their likely impact on the achievement of objectives. An organization can gain this understanding by ensuring that it makes cost-effective use of a risk framework that has a series of well-defined steps. Decision-making should include determining any appropriate actions to take to manage the risks to a level deemed to be acceptable by the organization.

A number of different methodologies, standards and frameworks have been developed for risk management. Some focus more on generic techniques widely applicable to different levels and needs, while others are specifically concerned with risk management relating to important assets used by the organization in the pursuit of its objectives. Each organization should determine the approach

to risk management that is best suited to its needs and circumstances, and it is possible that the approach adopted will leverage the ideas reflected in more than one of the recognized standards and/or frameworks.

In this appendix the following approaches to managing risks are briefly explained:

- Management of Risk (M_o_R)
- ISO 31000
- ISO/IEC 27001
- Risk IT.

## C.2 MANAGEMENT OF RISK (M_o_R)

Management of Risk (M_o_R) is intended to help organizations put in place an effective framework for risk management. This will help them take informed decisions about the risks that affect their strategic, programme, project and operational objectives.

M_o_R provides a route map of risk management, bringing together principles, an approach, a process with a set of interrelated steps and pointers to more detailed sources of advice on risk management techniques and specialisms. It also provides advice on how these principles, approach and process should be embedded, reviewed and applied differently depending on the nature of the objectives at risk.

The M_o_R framework is illustrated in Figure C.1.

The M_o_R framework is based on four core concepts:

- **M_o_R principles** Principles are essential for the development and maintenance of good risk management practice. They are informed by corporate governance principles and the international standard for risk management, ISO 31000: 2009. They are high-level and universally applicable statements that provide guidance to organizations as they design an appropriate approach to risk management as part of their internal controls.

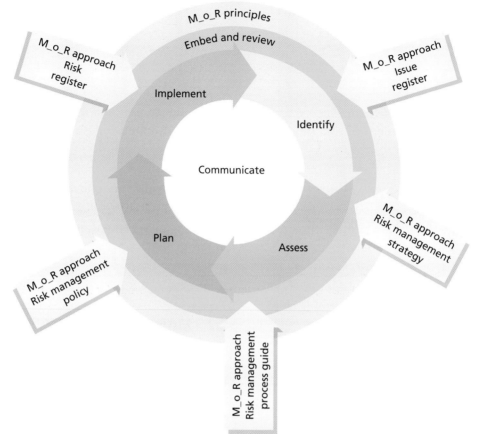

*Figure C.1 The M_o_R framework*

- **M_o_R approach**   Principles need to be adapted and adopted to suit each individual organization. An organization's approach to the principles needs to be agreed and defined within a risk management policy, process guide and strategies.
- **M_o_R process**   The process is divided into four main steps: identify, assess, plan and implement. Each step describes the inputs, outputs, tasks and techniques involved to ensure that the overall process is effective.
- **Embedding and reviewing M_o_R**   Having put in place an approach and process that satisfy the principles, an organization should ensure that they are consistently applied across the organization and that their application undergoes continual improvement in order for them to be effective.

There are several common techniques which support risk management, including a summary risk profile. A summary risk profile is a graphical representation of information normally found in an existing risk register, and helps to increase the visibility of risks. For more information on summary risk profiles and other M_o_R techniques, see *Management of Risk: Guidance for Practitioners* (OGC, 2010).

## C.3   ISO 31000

ISO 31000 was published in November 2009 and is the first set of international guidelines for risk management, intended to be applicable and adaptable for 'any public, private or community enterprise, association, group or individual.' ISO 31000 is a process-oriented rather than a control-oriented approach to risk management, and provides guidance on a broader, more conceptual basis, rather than specifying all aspects of an organization's risk assessment and management approach. For example, ISO 31000 does not define how an organization will create risk data or measure risk, nor does it ensure that an organization will include a review of all risk areas relevant to the achievement of their objectives. ISO 31000 was published as a standard without certification.

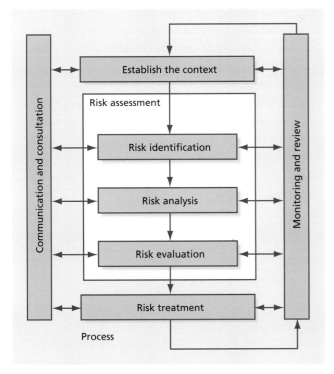

*Figure C.2 ISO 31000 risk management process flow*

ISO 31000 defines risk as 'the effect of uncertainty on objectives'. Risk management should be performed within a framework that provides the foundations and provisions which will embed the management of risk throughout all levels of the organization. ISO 31000 identifies the necessary components of such a framework as:

- Mandate and commitment
- Design of framework for managing risk
- Understanding the organization and its context
- Establishing risk management policy
- Accountability
- Integration into organizational processes
- Resources
- Establishing internal communication and reporting mechanisms
- Establishing external communication and reporting mechanisms
- Implementing risk management
- Monitoring and review of the framework
- Continual improvement of the framework.

Within this context the risk management process is seen at a high level in Figure C.2.

Once the framework has been established and the context understood, risk assessment is undertaken.

This consists of three steps: risk identification, risk analysis and risk evaluation. The risk identification step is intended to create a comprehensive list of risks based on those events that might create, enhance, prevent, degrade, accelerate or delay the achievement of the organization's objectives. Risk analysis involves developing a full understanding of the risks as an input to risk evaluation and the decisions regarding the plan for treating the risks. Risk evaluation is to make decisions about which risks require treatment and the relative priorities amongst them.

Risk treatment involves the modification of risks using one or more approaches. These approaches are not necessarily mutually exclusive and may include:

- Avoiding the risk by deciding not to start or continue with the activity that gives rise to the risk
- Taking or increasing the risk in order to pursue an opportunity
- Removing the risk source
- Changing the likelihood
- Changing the consequences
- Sharing the risk with another party or parties (including contracts and risk financing)
- Retaining the risk by informed decision.

The approach described in ISO 31000 provides broad scope for each organization to adopt the high-level principles and adapt them to their specific needs and circumstances.

## C.4 ISO/IEC 27001

ISO/IEC 27001 was published in October 2005 and is an information security management system (ISMS) standard which formally specifies a management system that is intended to bring information security under explicit management control. While ISO/IEC 27001 is a security standard, not a risk management standard, it mandates specific requirements for security, including requirements relating to risk management. The risk management methods described in this context may be applied to general risk management activities as well.

ISO/IEC 27001 requires that management:

- Systematically examines the organization's information security risks, taking account of the threats, vulnerabilities and impacts

- Designs and implements a coherent and comprehensive suite of information security controls and/or other forms of risk treatment (such as risk avoidance or risk transfer) to address those risks that are deemed unacceptable
- Adopts an overarching management process to ensure that the information security controls continue to meet the organization's information security needs on an ongoing basis.

The key risk management-related steps described in ISO/IEC 27001 include:

- Define the risk assessment approach of the organization
- Identify a risk assessment methodology that is suited to the ISMS, and the identified business information security, legal and regulatory requirements
- Develop criteria for accepting risks and identify acceptable levels of risk
- Identify the risks
- Identify the assets within the scope of the ISMS, and the owners of these assets
- Identify the threats to these assets
- Identify the vulnerabilities that might be exploited by the threats
- Identify the impact that losses of confidentiality, integrity and availability may have on these assets
- Analyse and evaluate the risks
- Assess the business impacts on the organization that might result from security failures, taking into account the consequences of a loss of confidentiality, integrity or availability of the assets
- Assess the realistic likelihood of security failures occurring in the light of prevailing threats and vulnerabilities, and impacts associated with these assets, and the controls currently implemented
- Estimate the levels of risk
- Determine whether the risks are acceptable or require treatment using the previously established criteria for accepting risks
- Identify and evaluate options for the treatment of risks. Possible actions may include:
  - Applying appropriate controls

- Knowingly and objectively accepting risks, providing they clearly satisfy the organization's policies and the criteria for accepting risks
- Avoiding risks
- Transferring the associated business risks to other parties, e.g. insurers, suppliers
- Select control objectives and controls for the treatment of risks
- Obtain management approval of the proposed residual risks
- Obtain management authorization to implement and operate the ISMS.

During the implementation and operation of the ISMS, a plan for risk treatment is formulated (identifying the appropriate management action, resources, responsibilities and priorities for managing information security risks) and implemented. ISO/IEC 27001 also calls for the ongoing monitoring and reviewing of the risks and risk treatment and the formal maintenance of the ISMS to ensure that the organization's goals are met.

This approach is focused specifically on the assets involved in organizational information security, but the general principles can be applied to overall service provision.

## C.5 RISK IT

Risk IT is part of the IT governance product portfolio of ISACA that provides a framework for effective governance and management of IT risk, based on a set of guiding principles. Risk IT is about IT risk, including business risk related to the use of IT. The publications in which Risk IT is documented include *The Risk IT Framework* (ISACA, 2009) and *The Risk IT Practitioner Guide* (ISACA, 2009) (available from www.isaca.org).

The key principles in Risk IT are that effective enterprise governance and management of IT risk:

- Always connect to the business objectives
- Align the management of IT-related business risk with overall enterprise risk management
- Balance the costs and benefits of managing IT risk
- Promote fair and open communication of IT risk

- Establish the right tone from the top while defining and enforcing personal accountability for operating within acceptable and well-defined tolerance levels
- Are continuous processes and part of daily activities.

The framework provides for three domains, each containing three processes, as shown in Figure C.3. *The Risk IT Framework* describes the key activities of each process, the responsibilities for the process, information flows between the processes and the performance management of each process.

Risk governance ensures that IT risk management practices are embedded in the enterprise, enabling it to secure optimal risk-adjusted return. Risk evaluation ensures that IT-related risks and opportunities are identified, analysed and presented in business terms. Risk response ensures that IT-related risk issues, opportunities and events are addressed in a cost-effective manner and in line with business priorities.

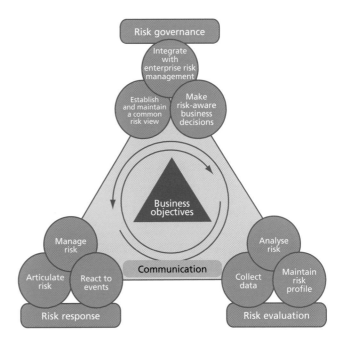

*Figure C.3 ISACA Risk IT process framework*

Appendix D:
Examples of inputs
and outputs across
the service lifecycle

D

# Appendix D: Examples of inputs and outputs across the service lifecycle

This appendix identifies some of the major inputs and outputs between each stage of the service lifecycle. This is not an exhaustive list and is designed to help understand how the different lifecycle stages interact. See Table 3.1 for more detail on the inputs and outputs of the CSI stage.

| Lifecycle stage | Examples of inputs from other service lifecycle stages | Examples of outputs to other service lifecycle stages |
|---|---|---|
| Service strategy | Information and feedback for business cases and service portfolio<br>Requirements for strategies and plans<br>Inputs and feedback on strategies and policies<br>Financial reports, service reports, dashboards, and outputs of service review meetings<br>Response to change proposals<br>Service portfolio updates including the service catalogue<br>Change schedule<br>Knowledge and information in the service knowledge management system (SKMS) | Vision and mission<br>Strategies, strategic plans and policies<br>Financial information and budgets<br>Service portfolio<br>Change proposals<br>Service charters including service packages, service models, and details of utility and warranty<br>Patterns of business activity and demand forecasts<br>Updated knowledge and information in the SKMS<br>Achievements against metrics, KPIs and CSFs<br>Feedback to other lifecycle stages<br>Improvement opportunities logged in the CSI register |
| Service design | Vision and mission<br>Strategies, strategic plans and policies<br>Financial information and budgets<br>Service portfolio<br>Service charters including service packages, service models, and details of utility and warranty<br>Feedback on all aspects of service design and service design packages<br>Requests for change (RFCs) for designing changes and improvements<br>Input to design requirements from other lifecycle stages<br>Service reports, dashboards, and outputs of service review meetings<br>Knowledge and information in the SKMS | Service portfolio updates including the service catalogue<br>Service design packages, including:<br>■ Details of utility and warranty<br>■ Acceptance criteria<br>■ Updated service models<br>■ Designs and interface specifications<br>■ Transition plans<br>■ Operation plans and procedures<br>Information security policies<br>Designs for new or changed services, management information systems and tools, technology architectures, processes, measurement methods and metrics<br>SLAs, OLAs and underpinning contracts<br>RFCs to transition or deploy new or changed services<br>Financial reports<br>Updated knowledge and information in the SKMS<br>Achievements against metrics, KPIs and CSFs<br>Feedback to other lifecycle stages<br>Improvement opportunities logged in the CSI register |

| Lifecycle stage | Examples of inputs from other service lifecycle stages | Examples of outputs to other service lifecycle stages |
|---|---|---|
| Service transition | Vision and mission<br>Strategies, strategic plans and policies<br>Financial information and budgets<br>Service portfolio<br>Change proposals, including utility and warranty requirements and expected timescales<br>RFCs for implementing changes and improvements<br>Service design packages, including:<br><ul><li>Details of utility and warranty</li><li>Acceptance criteria</li><li>Service models</li><li>Designs and interface specifications</li><li>Transition plans</li><li>Operation plans and procedures</li></ul>Input to change evaluation and change advisory board (CAB) meetings<br>Knowledge and information in the SKMS | New or changed services, management information systems and tools, technology architectures, processes, measurement methods and metrics<br>Responses to change proposals and RFCs<br>Change schedule<br>Known errors<br>Standard changes for use in request fulfilment<br>Knowledge and information in the SKMS (including the configuration management system)<br>Financial reports<br>Updated knowledge and information in the SKMS<br>Achievements against metrics, KPIs and CSFs<br>Feedback to other lifecycle stages<br>Improvement opportunities logged in the CSI register |
| Service operation | Vision and mission<br>Strategies, strategic plans and policies<br>Financial information and budgets<br>Service portfolio<br>Service reports, dashboards, and outputs of service review meetings<br>Service design packages, including:<br><ul><li>Details of utility and warranty</li><li>Operations plans and procedures</li><li>Recovery procedures</li></ul>Service level agreements (SLAs), operational level agreements (OLAs) and underpinning contracts<br>Known errors<br>Standard changes for use in request fulfilment<br>Information security policies<br>Change schedule<br>Patterns of business activity and demand forecasts<br>Knowledge and information in the SKMS | Achievement of agreed service levels to deliver value to the business<br>Operational requirements<br>Operational performance data and service records<br>RFCs to resolve operational issues<br>Financial reports<br>Updated knowledge and information in the SKMS<br>Achievements against metrics, KPIs and CSFs<br>Feedback to other lifecycle stages<br>Improvement opportunities logged in the CSI register |
| Continual service improvement | Vision and mission<br>Strategies, strategic plans and policies<br>Financial information and budgets<br>Service portfolio<br>Achievements against metrics, key performance indicators (KPIs) and critical success factors (CSFs) from each lifecycle stage<br>Operational performance data and service records<br>Improvement opportunities logged in the CSI register<br>Knowledge and information in the SKMS | RFCs for implementing improvements across all lifecycle stages<br>Business cases for significant improvements<br>Updated CSI register<br>Service improvement plans<br>Results of customer and user satisfaction surveys<br>Service reports, dashboards, and outputs of service review meetings<br>Financial reports<br>Updated knowledge and information in the SKMS<br>Achievements against metrics, KPIs and CSFs<br>Feedback to other lifecycle stages |

# Abbreviations and
glossary

# Abbreviations

| | | | |
|---|---|---|---|
| ACD | automatic call distribution | eSCM-CL | eSourcing Capability Model for Client Organizations |
| AM | availability management | eSCM-SP | eSourcing Capability Model for Service Providers |
| AMIS | availability management information system | FTA | fault tree analysis |
| ASP | application service provider | IRR | internal rate of return |
| AST | agreed service time | ISG | IT steering group |
| BCM | business continuity management | ISM | information security management |
| BCP | business continuity plan | ISMS | information security management system |
| BIA | business impact analysis | ISO | International Organization for Standardization |
| BMP | Best Management Practice | | |
| BRM | business relationship manager | ISP | internet service provider |
| BSI | British Standards Institution | IT | information technology |
| CAB | change advisory board | ITSCM | IT service continuity management |
| CAPEX | capital expenditure | ITSM | IT service management |
| CCM | component capacity management | itSMF | IT Service Management Forum |
| CFIA | component failure impact analysis | IVR | interactive voice response |
| CI | configuration item | KEDB | known error database |
| CMDB | configuration management database | KPI | key performance indicator |
| CMIS | capacity management information system | LOS | line of service |
| | | MIS | management information system |
| CMM | capability maturity model | M_o_R | Management of Risk |
| CMMI | Capability Maturity Model Integration | MTBF | mean time between failures |
| CMS | configuration management system | MTBSI | mean time between service incidents |
| COBIT | Control OBjectives for Information and related Technology | MTRS | mean time to restore service |
| | | MTTR | mean time to repair |
| COTS | commercial off the shelf | NPV | net present value |
| CSF | critical success factor | OLA | operational level agreement |
| CSI | continual service improvement | OPEX | operational expenditure |
| CTI | computer telephony integration | PBA | pattern of business activity |
| DIKW | Data-to-Information-to-Knowledge-to-Wisdom | PDCA | Plan-Do-Check-Act |
| DML | definitive media library | PFS | prerequisite for success |
| ECAB | emergency change advisory board | PIR | post-implementation review |
| ELS | early life support | | |

| | |
|---|---|
| PMBOK | Project Management Body of Knowledge |
| PMI | Project Management Institute |
| PMO | project management office |
| PRINCE2 | PRojects IN Controlled Environments |
| PSO | projected service outage |
| QA | quality assurance |
| QMS | quality management system |
| RACI | responsible, accountable, consulted and informed |
| RCA | root cause analysis |
| RFC | request for change |
| ROA | return on assets |
| ROI | return on investment |
| RPO | recovery point objective |
| RTO | recovery time objective |
| SAC | service acceptance criteria |
| SACM | service asset and configuration management |
| SAM | software asset management |
| SCM | service capacity management |
| SCMIS | supplier and contract management information system |
| SDP | service design package |
| SFA | service failure analysis |
| SIP | service improvement plan |
| SKMS | service knowledge management system |

| | |
|---|---|
| SLA | service level agreement |
| SLM | service level management |
| SLP | service level package |
| SLR | service level requirement |
| SMART | specific, measurable, achievable, relevant and time-bound |
| SMIS | security management information system |
| SMO | service maintenance objective |
| SoC | separation of concerns |
| SOP | standard operating procedure |
| SOR | statement of requirements |
| SOX | Sarbanes-Oxley (US law) |
| SPI | service provider interface |
| SPM | service portfolio management |
| SPOF | single point of failure |
| TCO | total cost of ownership |
| TCU | total cost of utilization |
| TO | technical observation |
| TOR | terms of reference |
| TQM | total quality management |
| UC | underpinning contract |
| UP | user profile |
| VBF | vital business function |
| VOI | value on investment |
| WIP | work in progress |

# Glossary

The core ITIL publications (*ITIL Service Strategy, ITIL Service Design, ITIL Service Operation, ITIL Service Transition, ITIL Continual Service Improvement*) referred to in parentheses at the beginning of a definition indicate where a reader can find more information. Terms without such a reference may either be used generically across all five core publications, or simply may not be explained in any greater detail elsewhere in the ITIL series. In other words, readers are only directed to other sources where they can expect to expand on their knowledge or to see a greater context.

## acceptance

Formal agreement that an IT service, process, plan or other deliverable is complete, accurate, reliable and meets its specified requirements. Acceptance is usually preceded by change evaluation or testing and is often required before proceeding to the next stage of a project or process. *See also* service acceptance criteria.

## access management

(*ITIL Service Operation*) The process responsible for allowing users to make use of IT services, data or other assets. Access management helps to protect the confidentiality, integrity and availability of assets by ensuring that only authorized users are able to access or modify them. Access management implements the policies of information security management and is sometimes referred to as rights management or identity management.

## accounting

(*ITIL Service Strategy*) The process responsible for identifying the actual costs of delivering IT services, comparing these with budgeted costs, and managing variance from the budget.

## accredited

Officially authorized to carry out a role. For example, an accredited body may be authorized to provide training or to conduct audits.

## activity

A set of actions designed to achieve a particular result. Activities are usually defined as part of processes or plans, and are documented in procedures.

## agreement

A document that describes a formal understanding between two or more parties. An agreement is not legally binding, unless it forms part of a contract. *See also* operational level agreement; service level agreement.

## alert

(*ITIL Service Operation*) A notification that a threshold has been reached, something has changed, or a failure has occurred. Alerts are often created and managed by system management tools and are managed by the event management process.

## analytical modelling

(*ITIL Continual Service Improvement*) (*ITIL Service Design*) (*ITIL Service Strategy*) A technique that uses mathematical models to predict the behaviour of IT services or other configuration items. Analytical models are commonly used in capacity management and availability management. *See also* modelling; simulation modelling.

## application

Software that provides functions which are required by an IT service. Each application may be part of more than one IT service. An application runs on one or more servers or clients. *See also* application management; application portfolio.

## application management

(*ITIL Service Operation*) The function responsible for managing applications throughout their lifecycle.

**application portfolio**

(*ITIL Service Design*) A database or structured document used to manage applications throughout their lifecycle. The application portfolio contains key attributes of all applications. The application portfolio is sometimes implemented as part of the service portfolio, or as part of the configuration management system.

**application sizing**

(*ITIL Service Design*) The activity responsible for understanding the resource requirements needed to support a new application, or a major change to an existing application. Application sizing helps to ensure that the IT service can meet its agreed service level targets for capacity and performance.

**architecture**

(*ITIL Service Design*) The structure of a system or IT service, including the relationships of components to each other and to the environment they are in. Architecture also includes the standards and guidelines that guide the design and evolution of the system.

**assessment**

Inspection and analysis to check whether a standard or set of guidelines is being followed, that records are accurate, or that efficiency and effectiveness targets are being met. *See also* audit.

**asset**

(*ITIL Service Strategy*) Any resource or capability. The assets of a service provider include anything that could contribute to the delivery of a service. Assets can be one of the following types: management, organization, process, knowledge, people, information, applications, infrastructure or financial capital. *See also* customer asset; service asset; strategic asset.

**asset management**

(*ITIL Service Transition*) A generic activity or process responsible for tracking and reporting the value and ownership of assets throughout their lifecycle. *See also* service asset and configuration management; fixed asset management; software asset management.

**attribute**

(*ITIL Service Transition*) A piece of information about a configuration item. Examples are name, location, version number and cost. Attributes of CIs are recorded in a configuration management database (CMDB) and maintained as part of a configuration management system (CMS). *See also* relationship; configuration management system.

**audit**

Formal inspection and verification to check whether a standard or set of guidelines is being followed, that records are accurate, or that efficiency and effectiveness targets are being met. An audit may be carried out by internal or external groups. *See also* assessment; certification.

**authority matrix**

*See* RACI.

**automatic call distribution (ACD)**

(*ITIL Service Operation*) Use of information technology to direct an incoming telephone call to the most appropriate person in the shortest possible time. ACD is sometimes called automated call distribution.

**availability**

(*ITIL Service Design*) Ability of an IT service or other configuration item to perform its agreed function when required. Availability is determined by reliability, maintainability, serviceability, performance and security. Availability is usually calculated as a percentage. This calculation is often based on agreed service time and downtime. It is best practice to calculate availability of an IT service using measurements of the business output.

**availability management (AM)**

(*ITIL Service Design*) The process responsible for ensuring that IT services meet the current and future availability needs of the business in a cost-effective and timely manner. Availability management defines, analyses, plans, measures and improves all aspects of the availability of IT services, and ensures that all IT infrastructures, processes, tools, roles etc. are appropriate for the agreed service level targets for availability. *See also* availability management information system.

## availability management information system (AMIS)

(*ITIL Service Design*) A set of tools, data and information that is used to support availability management. *See also* service knowledge management system.

## availability plan

(*ITIL Service Design*) A plan to ensure that existing and future availability requirements for IT services can be provided cost-effectively.

## balanced scorecard

(*ITIL Continual Service Improvement*) A management tool developed by Drs Robert Kaplan (Harvard Business School) and David Norton. A balanced scorecard enables a strategy to be broken down into key performance indicators. Performance against the KPIs is used to demonstrate how well the strategy is being achieved. A balanced scorecard has four major areas, each of which has a small number of KPIs. The same four areas are considered at different levels of detail throughout the organization.

## baseline

(*ITIL Continual Service Improvement*) (*ITIL Service Transition*) A snapshot that is used as a reference point. Many snapshots may be taken and recorded over time but only some will be used as baselines. For example:

- An ITSM baseline can be used as a starting point to measure the effect of a service improvement plan
- A performance baseline can be used to measure changes in performance over the lifetime of an IT service
- A configuration baseline can be used as part of a back-out plan to enable the IT infrastructure to be restored to a known configuration if a change or release fails.

*See also* benchmark.

## benchmark

(*ITIL Continual Service Improvement*) (*ITIL Service Transition*) A baseline that is used to compare related data sets as part of a benchmarking exercise. For example, a recent snapshot of a process can be compared to a previous baseline of that process, or a current baseline can be compared to industry data or best practice. *See also* benchmarking; baseline.

## benchmarking

(*ITIL Continual Service Improvement*) The process responsible for comparing a benchmark with related data sets such as a more recent snapshot, industry data or best practice. The term is also used to mean creating a series of benchmarks over time, and comparing the results to measure progress or improvement. This process is not described in detail within the core ITIL publications.

## Best Management Practice (BMP)

The Best Management Practice portfolio is owned by the Cabinet Office, part of HM Government. Formerly owned by CCTA and then OGC, the BMP functions moved to the Cabinet Office in June 2010. The BMP portfolio includes guidance on IT service management and project, programme, risk, portfolio and value management. There is also a management maturity model as well as related glossaries of terms.

## best practice

Proven activities or processes that have been successfully used by multiple organizations. ITIL is an example of best practice.

## billing

(*ITIL Service Strategy*) Part of the charging process. Billing is the activity responsible for producing an invoice or a bill and recovering the money from customers. *See also* pricing.

## British Standards Institution (BSI)

The UK national standards body, responsible for creating and maintaining British standards. *See* www.bsi-global.com for more information. *See also* International Organization for Standardization.

### budget

A list of all the money an organization or business unit plans to receive, and plans to pay out, over a specified period of time. *See also* budgeting; planning.

### budgeting

The activity of predicting and controlling the spending of money. Budgeting consists of a periodic negotiation cycle to set future budgets (usually annual) and the day-to-day monitoring and adjusting of current budgets.

### build

(*ITIL Service Transition*) The activity of assembling a number of configuration items to create part of an IT service. The term is also used to refer to a release that is authorized for distribution – for example, server build or laptop build. *See also* configuration baseline.

### business

(*ITIL Service Strategy*) An overall corporate entity or organization formed of a number of business units. In the context of ITSM, the term includes public sector and not-for-profit organizations, as well as companies. An IT service provider provides IT services to a customer within a business. The IT service provider may be part of the same business as its customer (internal service provider), or part of another business (external service provider).

### business capacity management

(*ITIL Continual Service Improvement*) (*ITIL Service Design*) In the context of ITSM, business capacity management is the sub-process of capacity management responsible for understanding future business requirements for use in the capacity plan. *See also* service capacity management; component capacity management.

### business case

(*ITIL Service Strategy*) Justification for a significant item of expenditure. The business case includes information about costs, benefits, options, issues, risks and possible problems. *See also* cost benefit analysis.

### business continuity management (BCM)

(*ITIL Service Design*) The business process responsible for managing risks that could seriously affect the business. Business continuity management safeguards the interests of key stakeholders, reputation, brand and value-creating activities. The process involves reducing risks to an acceptable level and planning for the recovery of business processes should a disruption to the business occur. Business continuity management sets the objectives, scope and requirements for IT service continuity management.

### business customer

(*ITIL Service Strategy*) A recipient of a product or a service from the business. For example, if the business is a car manufacturer, then the business customer is someone who buys a car.

### business objective

(*ITIL Service Strategy*) The objective of a business process, or of the business as a whole. Business objectives support the business vision, provide guidance for the IT strategy, and are often supported by IT services.

### business operations

(*ITIL Service Strategy*) The day-to-day execution, monitoring and management of business processes.

### business perspective

(*ITIL Continual Service Improvement*) An understanding of the service provider and IT services from the point of view of the business, and an understanding of the business from the point of view of the service provider.

### business process

A process that is owned and carried out by the business. A business process contributes to the delivery of a product or service to a business customer. For example, a retailer may have a purchasing process that helps to deliver services to its business customers. Many business processes rely on IT services.

## business relationship management

(*ITIL Service Strategy*) The process responsible for maintaining a positive relationship with customers. Business relationship management identifies customer needs and ensures that the service provider is able to meet these needs with an appropriate catalogue of services. This process has strong links with service level management.

## business relationship manager (BRM)

(*ITIL Service Strategy*) A role responsible for maintaining the relationship with one or more customers. This role is often combined with the service level manager role.

## business service

A service that is delivered to business customers by business units. For example, delivery of financial services to customers of a bank, or goods to the customers of a retail store. Successful delivery of business services often depends on one or more IT services. A business service may consist almost entirely of an IT service – for example, an online banking service or an external website where product orders can be placed by business customers. *See also* customer-facing service.

## business service management

The management of business services delivered to business customers. Business service management is performed by business units.

## business unit

(*ITIL Service Strategy*) A segment of the business that has its own plans, metrics, income and costs. Each business unit owns assets and uses these to create value for customers in the form of goods and services.

## call

(*ITIL Service Operation*) A telephone call to the service desk from a user. A call could result in an incident or a service request being logged.

## capability

(*ITIL Service Strategy*) The ability of an organization, person, process, application, IT service or other configuration item to carry out an activity. Capabilities are intangible assets of an organization. *See also* resource.

## Capability Maturity Model Integration (CMMI)

(*ITIL Continual Service Improvement*) A process improvement approach developed by the Software Engineering Institute (SEI) of Carnegie Mellon University, US. CMMI provides organizations with the essential elements of effective processes. It can be used to guide process improvement across a project, a division or an entire organization. CMMI helps integrate traditionally separate organizational functions, set process improvement goals and priorities, provide guidance for quality processes, and provide a point of reference for appraising current processes. *See* www.sei.cmu.edu/cmmi for more information. *See also* maturity.

## capacity

(*ITIL Service Design*) The maximum throughput that a configuration item or IT service can deliver. For some types of CI, capacity may be the size or volume – for example, a disk drive.

## capacity management

(*ITIL Continual Service Improvement*) (*ITIL Service Design*) The process responsible for ensuring that the capacity of IT services and the IT infrastructure is able to meet agreed capacity- and performance-related requirements in a cost-effective and timely manner. Capacity management considers all resources required to deliver an IT service, and is concerned with meeting both the current and future capacity and performance needs of the business. Capacity management includes three sub-processes: business capacity management, service capacity management, and component capacity management. *See also* capacity management information system.

## capacity management information system (CMIS)

(*ITIL Service Design*) A set of tools, data and information that is used to support capacity management. *See also* service knowledge management system.

## capacity plan

(*ITIL Service Design*) A plan used to manage the resources required to deliver IT services. The plan contains details of current and historic usage of IT services and components, and any issues that need to be addressed (including related improvement activities). The plan also contains scenarios for different predictions of business demand and costed options to deliver the agreed service level targets.

## capacity planning

(*ITIL Service Design*) The activity within capacity management responsible for creating a capacity plan.

## capital cost

(*ITIL Service Strategy*) The cost of purchasing something that will become a financial asset – for example, computer equipment and buildings. The value of the asset depreciates over multiple accounting periods. *See also* operational cost.

## capital expenditure (CAPEX)

*See* capital cost.

## category

A named group of things that have something in common. Categories are used to group similar things together. For example, cost types are used to group similar types of cost. Incident categories are used to group similar types of incident, while CI types are used to group similar types of configuration item.

## certification

Issuing a certificate to confirm compliance to a standard. Certification includes a formal audit by an independent and accredited body. The term is also used to mean awarding a certificate to provide evidence that a person has achieved a qualification.

## change

(*ITIL Service Transition*) The addition, modification or removal of anything that could have an effect on IT services. The scope should include changes to all architectures, processes, tools, metrics and documentation, as well as changes to IT services and other configuration items.

## change advisory board (CAB)

(*ITIL Service Transition*) A group of people that support the assessment, prioritization, authorization and scheduling of changes. A change advisory board is usually made up of representatives from: all areas within the IT service provider; the business; and third parties such as suppliers.

## change evaluation

(*ITIL Service Transition*) The process responsible for formal assessment of a new or changed IT service to ensure that risks have been managed and to help determine whether to authorize the change.

## change management

(*ITIL Service Transition*) The process responsible for controlling the lifecycle of all changes, enabling beneficial changes to be made with minimum disruption to IT services.

## change model

(*ITIL Service Transition*) A repeatable way of dealing with a particular category of change. A change model defines specific agreed steps that will be followed for a change of this category. Change models may be very complex with many steps that require authorization (e.g. major software release) or may be very simple with no requirement for authorization (e.g. password reset). *See also* change advisory board; standard change.

## change proposal

(*ITIL Service Strategy*) (*ITIL Service Transition*) A document that includes a high level description of a potential service introduction or significant change, along with a corresponding business case and an expected implementation schedule. Change proposals are normally created by the service portfolio management process and are passed to change management for authorization. Change management will review the potential impact on other services, on shared resources, and on the overall change schedule. Once the change proposal has been authorized, service portfolio management will charter the service.

## change record

(*ITIL Service Transition*) A record containing the details of a change. Each change record documents the lifecycle of a single change. A change record is created for every request for change that is received, even those that are subsequently rejected. Change records should reference the configuration items that are affected by the change. Change records may be stored in the configuration management system, or elsewhere in the service knowledge management system.

## change request

*See* request for change.

## change schedule

(*ITIL Service Transition*) A document that lists all authorized changes and their planned implementation dates, as well as the estimated dates of longer-term changes. A change schedule is sometimes called a forward schedule of change, even though it also contains information about changes that have already been implemented.

## charging

(*ITIL Service Strategy*) Requiring payment for IT services. Charging for IT services is optional, and many organizations choose to treat their IT service provider as a cost centre. *See also* charging process; charging policy.

## charging policy

(*ITIL Service Strategy*) A policy specifying the objective of the charging process and the way in which charges will be calculated. *See also* cost.

## charging process

(*ITIL Service Strategy*) The process responsible for deciding how much customers should pay (pricing) and recovering money from them (billing). This process is not described in detail within the core ITIL publications.

## charter

(*ITIL Service Strategy*) A document that contains details of a new service, a significant change or other significant project. Charters are typically authorized by service portfolio management or by a project management office. The term charter is also used to describe the act of authorizing the work required to complete the service change or project. *See also* change proposal; service charter; project portfolio.

## client

A generic term that means a customer, the business or a business customer. For example, client manager may be used as a synonym for business relationship manager. The term is also used to mean:

- A computer that is used directly by a user – for example, a PC, a handheld computer or a work station
- The part of a client server application that the user directly interfaces with – for example, an email client.

## closed

(*ITIL Service Operation*) The final status in the lifecycle of an incident, problem, change etc. When the status is closed, no further action is taken.

## closure

(*ITIL Service Operation*) The act of changing the status of an incident, problem, change etc. to closed.

## COBIT

(*ITIL Continual Service Improvement*) Control OBjectives for Information and related Technology (COBIT) provides guidance and best practice for the management of IT processes. COBIT is published by ISACA in conjunction with the IT Governance Institute (ITGI). *See* www.isaca.org for more information.

## code of practice

A guideline published by a public body or a standards organization, such as ISO or BSI. Many standards consist of a code of practice and a specification. The code of practice describes recommended best practice.

## commercial off the shelf (COTS)

(*ITIL Service Design*) Pre-existing application software or middleware that can be purchased from a third party.

## compliance

Ensuring that a standard or set of guidelines is followed, or that proper, consistent accounting or other practices are being employed.

## component

A general term that is used to mean one part of something more complex. For example, a computer system may be a component of an IT service; an application may be a component of a release unit. Components that need to be managed should be configuration items.

## component capacity management (CCM)

(*ITIL Continual Service Improvement*) (*ITIL Service Design*) The sub-process of capacity management responsible for understanding the capacity, utilization and performance of configuration items. Data is collected, recorded and analysed for use in the capacity plan. *See also* business capacity management; service capacity management.

## component CI

(*ITIL Service Transition*) A configuration item that is part of an assembly. For example, a CPU or memory CI may be part of a server CI.

## component failure impact analysis (CFIA)

(*ITIL Service Design*) A technique that helps to identify the impact of configuration item failure on IT services and the business. A matrix is created with IT services on one axis and CIs on the other. This enables the identification of critical CIs (that could cause the failure of multiple IT services) and fragile IT services (that have multiple single points of failure).

## confidentiality

(*ITIL Service Design*) A security principle that requires that data should only be accessed by authorized people.

## configuration

(*ITIL Service Transition*) A generic term used to describe a group of configuration items that work together to deliver an IT service, or a recognizable part of an IT service. Configuration is also used to describe the parameter settings for one or more configuration items.

## configuration baseline

(*ITIL Service Transition*) The baseline of a configuration that has been formally agreed and is managed through the change management process. A configuration baseline is used as a basis for future builds, releases and changes.

## configuration item (CI)

(*ITIL Service Transition*) Any component or other service asset that needs to be managed in order to deliver an IT service. Information about each configuration item is recorded in a configuration record within the configuration management system and is maintained throughout its lifecycle by service asset and configuration management. Configuration items are under the control of change management. They typically include IT services, hardware, software, buildings, people and formal documentation such as process documentation and service level agreements.

## configuration management

*See* service asset and configuration management.

## configuration management database (CMDB)

(*ITIL Service Transition*) A database used to store configuration records throughout their lifecycle. The configuration management system maintains one or more configuration management databases, and each database stores attributes of configuration items, and relationships with other configuration items.

## configuration management system (CMS)

(*ITIL Service Transition*) A set of tools, data and information that is used to support service asset and configuration management. The CMS is part of an overall service knowledge management system and includes tools for collecting, storing, managing, updating, analysing and presenting data about all configuration items and their relationships. The CMS may also include information about incidents, problems, known errors, changes and releases. The CMS is maintained by service asset and configuration management and is used by all IT service management processes. *See also* configuration management database.

## continual service improvement (CSI)

(*ITIL Continual Service Improvement*) A stage in the lifecycle of a service. Continual service improvement ensures that services are aligned with changing business needs by identifying and implementing improvements to IT services that support business processes. The performance of the IT service provider is continually measured and improvements are made to processes, IT services and IT infrastructure in order to increase efficiency, effectiveness and cost effectiveness. Continual service improvement includes the seven-step improvement process. Although this process is associated with continual service improvement, most processes have activities that take place across multiple stages of the service lifecycle. *See also* Plan-Do-Check-Act.

## contract

A legally binding agreement between two or more parties.

## control

A means of managing a risk, ensuring that a business objective is achieved or that a process is followed. Examples of control include policies, procedures, roles, RAID, door locks etc. A control is sometimes called a countermeasure or safeguard. Control also means to manage the utilization or behaviour of a configuration item, system or IT service.

## Control OBjectives for Information and related Technology

*See* COBIT.

## control perspective

(*ITIL Service Strategy*) An approach to the management of IT services, processes, functions, assets etc. There can be several different control perspectives on the same IT service, process etc., allowing different individuals or teams to focus on what is important and relevant to their specific role. Examples of control perspective include reactive and proactive management within IT operations, or a lifecycle view for an application project team.

## core service

(*ITIL Service Strategy*) A service that delivers the basic outcomes desired by one or more customers. A core service provides a specific level of utility and warranty. Customers may be offered a choice of utility and warranty through one or more service options. *See also* enabling service; enhancing service; IT service; service package.

## cost

The amount of money spent on a specific activity, IT service or business unit. Costs consist of real cost (money), notional cost (such as people's time) and depreciation.

## cost benefit analysis

An activity that analyses and compares the costs and the benefits involved in one or more alternative courses of action. *See also* business case; internal rate of return; net present value; return on investment; value on investment.

## cost centre

(*ITIL Service Strategy*) A business unit or project to which costs are assigned. A cost centre does not charge for services provided. An IT service provider can be run as a cost centre or a profit centre.

## cost element

(*ITIL Service Strategy*) The middle level of category to which costs are assigned in budgeting and accounting. The highest-level category is cost type. For example, a cost type of 'people' could have cost elements of payroll, staff benefits, expenses, training, overtime etc. Cost elements can be further broken down to give cost units. For example, the cost element 'expenses' could include cost units of hotels, transport, meals etc.

### cost management

(*ITIL Service Strategy*) A general term that is used to refer to budgeting and accounting, and is sometimes used as a synonym for financial management.

### cost model

(*ITIL Service Strategy*) A framework used in budgeting and accounting in which all known costs can be recorded, categorized and allocated to specific customers, business units or projects. *See also* cost type; cost element; cost unit.

### cost type

(*ITIL Service Strategy*) The highest level of category to which costs are assigned in budgeting and accounting – for example, hardware, software, people, accommodation, external and transfer. *See also* cost element; cost unit.

### cost unit

(*ITIL Service Strategy*) The lowest level of category to which costs are assigned, cost units are usually things that can be easily counted (e.g. staff numbers, software licences) or things easily measured (e.g. CPU usage, electricity consumed). Cost units are included within cost elements. For example, a cost element of 'expenses' could include cost units of hotels, transport, meals etc. *See also* cost type.

### cost effectiveness

A measure of the balance between the effectiveness and cost of a service, process or activity. A cost-effective process is one that achieves its objectives at minimum cost. *See also* key performance indicator; return on investment; value for money.

### countermeasure

Can be used to refer to any type of control. The term is most often used when referring to measures that increase resilience, fault tolerance or reliability of an IT service.

### course corrections

Changes made to a plan or activity that has already started to ensure that it will meet its objectives. Course corrections are made as a result of monitoring progress.

### crisis management

Crisis management is the process responsible for managing the wider implications of business continuity. A crisis management team is responsible for strategic issues such as managing media relations and shareholder confidence, and decides when to invoke business continuity plans.

### critical success factor (CSF)

Something that must happen if an IT service, process, plan, project or other activity is to succeed. Key performance indicators are used to measure the achievement of each critical success factor. For example, a critical success factor of 'protect IT services when making changes' could be measured by key performance indicators such as 'percentage reduction of unsuccessful changes', 'percentage reduction in changes causing incidents' etc.

### CSI register

(*ITIL Continual Service Improvement*) A database or structured document used to record and manage improvement opportunities throughout their lifecycle.

### culture

A set of values that is shared by a group of people, including expectations about how people should behave, their ideas, beliefs and practices. *See also* vision.

### customer

Someone who buys goods or services. The customer of an IT service provider is the person or group who defines and agrees the service level targets. The term is also sometimes used informally to mean user – for example, 'This is a customer-focused organization.'

### customer asset

Any resource or capability of a customer. *See also* asset.

## customer agreement portfolio

(*ITIL Service Strategy*) A database or structured document used to manage service contracts or agreements between an IT service provider and its customers. Each IT service delivered to a customer should have a contract or other agreement that is listed in the customer agreement portfolio. *See also* customer-facing service; service catalogue; service portfolio.

## customer-facing service

(*ITIL Service Design*) An IT service that is visible to the customer. These are normally services that support the customer's business processes and facilitate one or more outcomes desired by the customer. All live customer-facing services, including those available for deployment, are recorded in the service catalogue along with customer-visible information about deliverables, prices, contact points, ordering and request processes. Other information such as relationships to supporting services and other CIs will also be recorded for internal use by the IT service provider.

## dashboard

(*ITIL Service Operation*) A graphical representation of overall IT service performance and availability. Dashboard images may be updated in real time, and can also be included in management reports and web pages. Dashboards can be used to support service level management, event management and incident diagnosis.

## Data-to-Information-to-Knowledge-to-Wisdom (DIKW)

(*ITIL Service Transition*) A way of understanding the relationships between data, information, knowledge and wisdom. DIKW shows how each of these builds on the others.

## definitive media library (DML)

(*ITIL Service Transition*) One or more locations in which the definitive and authorized versions of all software configuration items are securely stored. The definitive media library may also contain associated configuration items such as licences and documentation. It is a single logical storage area even if there are multiple locations. The definitive media library is controlled by service asset and configuration management and is recorded in the configuration management system.

## deliverable

Something that must be provided to meet a commitment in a service level agreement or a contract. It is also used in a more informal way to mean a planned output of any process.

## demand management

(*ITIL Service Design*) (*ITIL Service Strategy*) The process responsible for understanding, anticipating and influencing customer demand for services. Demand management works with capacity management to ensure that the service provider has sufficient capacity to meet the required demand. At a strategic level, demand management can involve analysis of patterns of business activity and user profiles, while at a tactical level, it can involve the use of differential charging to encourage customers to use IT services at less busy times, or require short-term activities to respond to unexpected demand or the failure of a configuration item.

## Deming Cycle

*See* Plan-Do-Check-Act.

## dependency

The direct or indirect reliance of one process or activity on another.

## deployment

(*ITIL Service Transition*) The activity responsible for movement of new or changed hardware, software, documentation, process etc. to the live environment. Deployment is part of the release and deployment management process.

## design

(*ITIL Service Design*) An activity or process that identifies requirements and then defines a solution that is able to meet these requirements. *See also* service design.

## design coordination

(*ITIL Service Design*) The process responsible for coordinating all service design activities, processes and resources. Design coordination ensures the consistent and effective design of new or changed IT services, service management information systems, architectures, technology, processes, information and metrics.

### detection

(*ITIL Service Operation*) A stage in the expanded incident lifecycle. Detection results in the incident becoming known to the service provider. Detection can be automatic or the result of a user logging an incident.

### development

(*ITIL Service Design*) The process responsible for creating or modifying an IT service or application ready for subsequent release and deployment. Development is also used to mean the role or function that carries out development work. This process is not described in detail within the core ITIL publications.

### development environment

(*ITIL Service Design*) An environment used to create or modify IT services or applications. Development environments are not typically subjected to the same degree of control as test or live environments. *See also* development.

### diagnosis

(*ITIL Service Operation*) A stage in the incident and problem lifecycles. The purpose of diagnosis is to identify a workaround for an incident or the root cause of a problem.

### document

Information in readable form. A document may be paper or electronic – for example, a policy statement, service level agreement, incident record or diagram of a computer room layout. *See also* record.

### downtime

(*ITIL Service Design*) (*ITIL Service Operation*) The time when an IT service or other configuration item is not available during its agreed service time. The availability of an IT service is often calculated from agreed service time and downtime.

### driver

Something that influences strategy, objectives or requirements – for example, new legislation or the actions of competitors.

### early life support (ELS)

(*ITIL Service Transition*) A stage in the service lifecycle that occurs at the end of deployment and before the service is fully accepted into operation. During early life support, the service provider reviews key performance indicators, service levels and monitoring thresholds and may implement improvements to ensure that service targets can be met. The service provider may also provide additional resources for incident and problem management during this time.

### economies of scale

(*ITIL Service Strategy*) The reduction in average cost that is possible from increasing the usage of an IT service or asset. *See also* economies of scope.

### economies of scope

(*ITIL Service Strategy*) The reduction in cost that is allocated to an IT service by using an existing asset for an additional purpose. For example, delivering a new IT service from an existing IT infrastructure. *See also* economies of scale.

### effectiveness

(*ITIL Continual Service Improvement*) A measure of whether the objectives of a process, service or activity have been achieved. An effective process or activity is one that achieves its agreed objectives. *See also* key performance indicator.

### efficiency

(*ITIL Continual Service Improvement*) A measure of whether the right amount of resource has been used to deliver a process, service or activity. An efficient process achieves its objectives with the minimum amount of time, money, people or other resources. *See also* key performance indicator.

### emergency change

(*ITIL Service Transition*) A change that must be introduced as soon as possible – for example, to resolve a major incident or implement a security patch. The change management process will normally have a specific procedure for handling emergency changes. *See also* emergency change advisory board.

## emergency change advisory board (ECAB)

(*ITIL Service Transition*) A subgroup of the change advisory board that makes decisions about emergency changes. Membership may be decided at the time a meeting is called, and depends on the nature of the emergency change.

## enabling service

(*ITIL Service Strategy*) A service that is needed in order to deliver a core service. Enabling services may or may not be visible to the customer, but they are not offered to customers in their own right. *See also* enhancing service.

## enhancing service

(*ITIL Service Strategy*) A service that is added to a core service to make it more attractive to the customer. Enhancing services are not essential to the delivery of a core service but are used to encourage customers to use the core services or to differentiate the service provider from its competitors. *See also* enabling service; excitement factor.

## enterprise financial management

(*ITIL Service Strategy*) The function and processes responsible for managing the overall organization's budgeting, accounting and charging requirements. Enterprise financial management is sometimes referred to as the 'corporate' financial department. *See also* financial management for IT services.

## environment

(*ITIL Service Transition*) A subset of the IT infrastructure that is used for a particular purpose – for example, live environment, test environment, build environment. Also used in the term 'physical environment' to mean the accommodation, air conditioning, power system etc. Environment is used as a generic term to mean the external conditions that influence or affect something.

## error

(*ITIL Service Operation*) A design flaw or malfunction that causes a failure of one or more IT services or other configuration items. A mistake made by a person or a faulty process that impacts a configuration item is also an error.

## escalation

(*ITIL Service Operation*) An activity that obtains additional resources when these are needed to meet service level targets or customer expectations. Escalation may be needed within any IT service management process, but is most commonly associated with incident management, problem management and the management of customer complaints. There are two types of escalation: functional escalation and hierarchic escalation.

## eSourcing Capability Model for Client Organizations (eSCM-CL)

(*ITIL Service Strategy*) A framework to help organizations in their analysis and decision-making on service sourcing models and strategies. It was developed by Carnegie Mellon University in the US. *See also* eSourcing Capability Model for Service Providers.

## eSourcing Capability Model for Service Providers (eSCM-SP)

(*ITIL Service Strategy*) A framework to help IT service providers develop their IT service management capabilities from a service sourcing perspective. It was developed by Carnegie Mellon University in the US. *See also* eSourcing Capability Model for Client Organizations.

## event

(*ITIL Service Operation*) A change of state that has significance for the management of an IT service or other configuration item. The term is also used to mean an alert or notification created by any IT service, configuration item or monitoring tool. Events typically require IT operations personnel to take actions, and often lead to incidents being logged.

## event management

(*ITIL Service Operation*) The process responsible for managing events throughout their lifecycle. Event management is one of the main activities of IT operations.

## excitement factor

(*ITIL Service Strategy*) An attribute added to something to make it more attractive or more exciting to the customer. For example, a restaurant may provide a free drink with every meal. *See also* enhancing service.

### expanded incident lifecycle

(*ITIL Continual Service Improvement*) (*ITIL Service Design*) Detailed stages in the lifecycle of an incident. The stages are detection, diagnosis, repair, recovery and restoration. The expanded incident lifecycle is used to help understand all contributions to the impact of incidents and to plan for how these could be controlled or reduced.

### external customer

A customer who works for a different business from the IT service provider. *See also* external service provider; internal customer.

### external service provider

(*ITIL Service Strategy*) An IT service provider that is part of a different organization from its customer. An IT service provider may have both internal and external customers. *See also* outsourcing; Type III service provider.

### facilities management

(*ITIL Service Operation*) The function responsible for managing the physical environment where the IT infrastructure is located. Facilities management includes all aspects of managing the physical environment – for example, power and cooling, building access management, and environmental monitoring.

### failure

(*ITIL Service Operation*) Loss of ability to operate to specification, or to deliver the required output. The term may be used when referring to IT services, processes, activities, configuration items etc. A failure often causes an incident.

### fault

*See* error.

### fault tolerance

(*ITIL Service Design*) The ability of an IT service or other configuration item to continue to operate correctly after failure of a component part. *See also* countermeasure; resilience.

### fault tree analysis (FTA)

(*ITIL Continual Service Improvement*) (*ITIL Service Design*) A technique that can be used to determine a chain of events that has caused an incident, or may cause an incident in the future. Fault tree analysis represents a chain of events using Boolean notation in a diagram.

### financial management

(*ITIL Service Strategy*) A generic term used to describe the function and processes responsible for managing an organization's budgeting, accounting and charging requirements. Enterprise financial management is the specific term used to describe the function and processes from the perspective of the overall organization. Financial management for IT services is the specific term used to describe the function and processes from the perspective of the IT service provider.

### financial management for IT services

(*ITIL Service Strategy*) The function and processes responsible for managing an IT service provider's budgeting, accounting and charging requirements. Financial management for IT services secures an appropriate level of funding to design, develop and deliver services that meet the strategy of the organization in a cost-effective manner. *See also* enterprise financial management.

### fit for purpose

(*ITIL Service Strategy*) The ability to meet an agreed level of utility. Fit for purpose is also used informally to describe a process, configuration item, IT service etc. that is capable of meeting its objectives or service levels. Being fit for purpose requires suitable design, implementation, control and maintenance.

### fit for use

(*ITIL Service Strategy*) The ability to meet an agreed level of warranty. Being fit for use requires suitable design, implementation, control and maintenance.

### fixed asset management

(*ITIL Service Transition*) The process responsible for tracking and reporting the value and ownership of fixed assets throughout their lifecycle. Fixed asset management maintains the asset register and is usually carried out by the overall business, rather than by the IT organization. Fixed asset management is sometimes called financial asset management and is not described in detail within the core ITIL publications.

### fulfilment

Performing activities to meet a need or requirement – for example, by providing a new IT service, or meeting a service request.

### function

A team or group of people and the tools or other resources they use to carry out one or more processes or activities – for example, the service desk. The term also has two other meanings:

■ An intended purpose of a configuration item, person, team, process or IT service. For example, one function of an email service may be to store and forward outgoing mails, while the function of a business process may be to despatch goods to customers.
■ To perform the intended purpose correctly, as in 'The computer is functioning.'

### gap analysis

(*ITIL Continual Service Improvement*) An activity that compares two sets of data and identifies the differences. Gap analysis is commonly used to compare a set of requirements with actual delivery. *See also* benchmarking.

### governance

Ensures that policies and strategy are actually implemented, and that required processes are correctly followed. Governance includes defining roles and responsibilities, measuring and reporting, and taking actions to resolve any issues identified.

### guideline

A document describing best practice, which recommends what should be done. Compliance with a guideline is not normally enforced. *See also* standard.

### impact

(*ITIL Service Operation*) (*ITIL Service Transition*) A measure of the effect of an incident, problem or change on business processes. Impact is often based on how service levels will be affected. Impact and urgency are used to assign priority.

### incident

(*ITIL Service Operation*) An unplanned interruption to an IT service or reduction in the quality of an IT service. Failure of a configuration item that has not yet affected service is also an incident – for example, failure of one disk from a mirror set.

### incident management

(*ITIL Service Operation*) The process responsible for managing the lifecycle of all incidents. Incident management ensures that normal service operation is restored as quickly as possible and the business impact is minimized.

### incident record

(*ITIL Service Operation*) A record containing the details of an incident. Each incident record documents the lifecycle of a single incident.

### indirect cost

(*ITIL Service Strategy*) The cost of providing an IT service which cannot be allocated in full to a specific customer – for example, the cost of providing shared servers or software licences. Also known as overhead. *See also* direct cost.

### information security management (ISM)

(*ITIL Service Design*) The process responsible for ensuring that the confidentiality, integrity and availability of an organization's assets, information, data and IT services match the agreed needs of the business. Information security management supports business security and has a wider scope than that of the IT service provider, and includes handling of paper, building access, phone calls etc. for the entire organization. *See also* security management information system.

### information security management system (ISMS)

(*ITIL Service Design*) The framework of policy, processes, functions, standards, guidelines and tools that ensures an organization can achieve its information security management objectives. *See also* security management information system.

### information security policy

(*ITIL Service Design*) The policy that governs the organization's approach to information security management.

### information system

*See* management information system.

### information technology (IT)

The use of technology for the storage, communication or processing of information. The technology typically includes computers, telecommunications, applications and other software. The information may include business data, voice, images, video etc. Information technology is often used to support business processes through IT services.

### insourcing

(*ITIL Service Strategy*) Using an internal service provider to manage IT services. The term insourcing is also used to describe the act of transferring the provision of an IT service from an external service provider to an internal service provider. *See also* service sourcing.

### integrity

(*ITIL Service Design*) A security principle that ensures data and configuration items are modified only by authorized personnel and activities. Integrity considers all possible causes of modification, including software and hardware failure, environmental events, and human intervention.

### internal customer

A customer who works for the same business as the IT service provider. *See also* external customer; internal service provider.

### internal rate of return (IRR)

(*ITIL Service Strategy*) A technique used to help make decisions about capital expenditure. It calculates a figure that allows two or more alternative investments to be compared. A larger internal rate of return indicates a better investment. *See also* net present value; return on investment.

### internal service provider

(*ITIL Service Strategy*) An IT service provider that is part of the same organization as its customer. An IT service provider may have both internal and external customers. *See also* insourcing; Type I service provider; Type II service provider.

### International Organization for Standardization (ISO)

The International Organization for Standardization (ISO) is the world's largest developer of standards. ISO is a non-governmental organization that is a network of the national standards institutes of 156 countries. *See* www.iso.org for further information about ISO.

### International Standards Organization

*See* International Organization for Standardization.

### internet service provider (ISP)

An external service provider that provides access to the internet. Most ISPs also provide other IT services such as web hosting.

### Ishikawa diagram

(*ITIL Continual Service Improvement*) (*ITIL Service Operation*) A technique that helps a team to identify all the possible causes of a problem. Originally devised by Kaoru Ishikawa, the output of this technique is a diagram that looks like a fishbone.

### ISO 9000

A generic term that refers to a number of international standards and guidelines for quality management systems. *See* www.iso.org for more information. *See also* International Organization for Standardization.

## ISO 9001

An international standard for quality management systems. *See also* ISO 9000; standard.

## ISO/IEC 20000

An international standard for IT service management.

## ISO/IEC 27001

(*ITIL Continual Service Improvement*) (*ITIL Service Design*) An international specification for information security management. The corresponding code of practice is ISO/IEC 27002. *See also* standard.

## ISO/IEC 27002

(*ITIL Continual Service Improvement*) An international code of practice for information security management. The corresponding specification is ISO/IEC 27001. *See also* standard.

## IT infrastructure

All of the hardware, software, networks, facilities etc. that are required to develop, test, deliver, monitor, control or support applications and IT services. The term includes all of the information technology but not the associated people, processes and documentation.

## IT operations

(*ITIL Service Operation*) Activities carried out by IT operations control, including console management/ operations bridge, job scheduling, backup and restore, and print and output management. IT operations is also used as a synonym for service operation.

## IT operations control

(*ITIL Service Operation*) The function responsible for monitoring and control of the IT services and IT infrastructure. *See also* operations bridge.

## IT operations management

(*ITIL Service Operation*) The function within an IT service provider that performs the daily activities needed to manage IT services and the supporting IT infrastructure. IT operations management includes IT operations control and facilities management.

## IT service

A service provided by an IT service provider. An IT service is made up of a combination of information technology, people and processes. A customer-facing IT service directly supports the business processes of one or more customers and its service level targets should be defined in a service level agreement. Other IT services, called supporting services, are not directly used by the business but are required by the service provider to deliver customer-facing services. *See also* core service; enabling service; enhancing service; service; service package.

## IT service continuity management (ITSCM)

(*ITIL Service Design*) The process responsible for managing risks that could seriously affect IT services. IT service continuity management ensures that the IT service provider can always provide minimum agreed service levels, by reducing the risk to an acceptable level and planning for the recovery of IT services. IT service continuity management supports business continuity management.

## IT service management (ITSM)

The implementation and management of quality IT services that meet the needs of the business. IT service management is performed by IT service providers through an appropriate mix of people, process and information technology. *See also* service management.

## IT service provider

(*ITIL Service Strategy*) A service provider that provides IT services to internal or external customers.

### ITIL

A set of best-practice publications for IT service management. Owned by the Cabinet Office (part of HM Government), ITIL gives guidance on the provision of quality IT services and the processes, functions and other capabilities needed to support them. The ITIL framework is based on a service lifecycle and consists of five lifecycle stages (service strategy, service design, service transition, service operation and continual service improvement), each of which has its own supporting publication. There is also a set of complementary ITIL publications providing guidance specific to industry sectors, organization types, operating models and technology architectures. *See* www.itil-officialsite. com for more information.

### job description

A document that defines the roles, responsibilities, skills and knowledge required by a particular person. One job description can include multiple roles – for example, the roles of configuration manager and change manager may be carried out by one person.

### key performance indicator (KPI)

(*ITIL Continual Service Improvement*) (*ITIL Service Design*) A metric that is used to help manage an IT service, process, plan, project or other activity. Key performance indicators are used to measure the achievement of critical success factors. Many metrics may be measured, but only the most important of these are defined as key performance indicators and used to actively manage and report on the process, IT service or activity. They should be selected to ensure that efficiency, effectiveness and cost effectiveness are all managed.

### knowledge base

(*ITIL Service Transition*) A logical database containing data and information used by the service knowledge management system.

### knowledge management

(*ITIL Service Transition*) The process responsible for sharing perspectives, ideas, experience and information, and for ensuring that these are available in the right place and at the right time. The knowledge management process enables informed decisions, and improves efficiency by reducing the need to rediscover knowledge. *See also* Data-to-Information-to-Knowledge-to-Wisdom; service knowledge management system.

### known error

(*ITIL Service Operation*) A problem that has a documented root cause and a workaround. Known errors are created and managed throughout their lifecycle by problem management. Known errors may also be identified by development or suppliers.

### lifecycle

The various stages in the life of an IT service, configuration item, incident, problem, change etc. The lifecycle defines the categories for status and the status transitions that are permitted. For example:

- The lifecycle of an application includes requirements, design, build, deploy, operate, optimize
- The expanded incident lifecycle includes detection, diagnosis, repair, recovery and restoration
- The lifecycle of a server may include: ordered, received, in test, live, disposed etc.

### live

(*ITIL Service Transition*) Refers to an IT service or other configuration item that is being used to deliver service to a customer.

### live environment

(*ITIL Service Transition*) A controlled environment containing live configuration items used to deliver IT services to customers.

## maintainability

(*ITIL Service Design*) A measure of how quickly and effectively an IT service or other configuration item can be restored to normal working after a failure. Maintainability is often measured and reported as MTRS. Maintainability is also used in the context of software or IT service development to mean ability to be changed or repaired easily.

## major incident

(*ITIL Service Operation*) The highest category of impact for an incident. A major incident results in significant disruption to the business.

## management information

Information that is used to support decision making by managers. Management information is often generated automatically by tools supporting the various IT service management processes. Management information often includes the values of key performance indicators, such as 'percentage of changes leading to incidents' or 'first-time fix rate'.

## management information system (MIS)

(*ITIL Service Design*) A set of tools, data and information that is used to support a process or function. Examples include the availability management information system and the supplier and contract management information system. *See also* service knowledge management system.

## Management of Risk (M_o_R)

M_o_R includes all the activities required to identify and control the exposure to risk, which may have an impact on the achievement of an organization's business objectives. *See* www.mor-officialsite.com for more details.

## management system

The framework of policy, processes, functions, standards, guidelines and tools that ensures an organization or part of an organization can achieve its objectives. This term is also used with a smaller scope to support a specific process or activity – for example, an event management system or risk management system. *See also* system.

## manual workaround

(*ITIL Continual Service Improvement*) A workaround that requires manual intervention. Manual workaround is also used as the name of a recovery option in which the business process operates without the use of IT services. This is a temporary measure and is usually combined with another recovery option.

## market space

(*ITIL Service Strategy*) Opportunities that an IT service provider could exploit to meet the business needs of customers. Market spaces identify the possible IT services that an IT service provider may wish to consider delivering.

## maturity

(*ITIL Continual Service Improvement*) A measure of the reliability, efficiency and effectiveness of a process, function, organization etc. The most mature processes and functions are formally aligned to business objectives and strategy, and are supported by a framework for continual improvement.

## maturity level

A named level in a maturity model, such as the Carnegie Mellon Capability Maturity Model Integration.

## mean time between failures (MTBF)

(*ITIL Service Design*) A metric for measuring and reporting reliability. MTBF is the average time that an IT service or other configuration item can perform its agreed function without interruption. This is measured from when the configuration item starts working, until it next fails.

## mean time to repair (MTTR)

The average time taken to repair an IT service or other configuration item after a failure. MTTR is measured from when the configuration item fails until it is repaired. MTTR does not include the time required to recover or restore. It is sometimes incorrectly used instead of mean time to restore service.

## mean time to restore service (MTRS)

The average time taken to restore an IT service or other configuration item after a failure. MTRS is measured from when the configuration item fails until it is fully restored and delivering its normal functionality. *See also* maintainability; mean time to repair.

## metric

(*ITIL Continual Service Improvement*) Something that is measured and reported to help manage a process, IT service or activity. *See also* key performance indicator.

## middleware

(*ITIL Service Design*) Software that connects two or more software components or applications. Middleware is usually purchased from a supplier, rather than developed within the IT service provider. *See also* commercial off the shelf.

## mission

A short but complete description of the overall purpose and intentions of an organization. It states what is to be achieved, but not how this should be done. *See also* vision.

## model

A representation of a system, process, IT service, configuration item etc. that is used to help understand or predict future behaviour.

## modelling

A technique that is used to predict the future behaviour of a system, process, IT service, configuration item etc. Modelling is commonly used in financial management, capacity management and availability management.

## monitoring

(*ITIL Service Operation*) Repeated observation of a configuration item, IT service or process to detect events and to ensure that the current status is known.

## net present value (NPV)

(*ITIL Service Strategy*) A technique used to help make decisions about capital expenditure. It compares cash inflows with cash outflows. Positive net present value indicates that an investment is worthwhile. *See also* internal rate of return; return on investment.

## objective

The outcomes required from a process, activity or organization in order to ensure that its purpose will be fulfilled. Objectives are usually expressed as measurable targets. The term is also informally used to mean a requirement.

## Office of Government Commerce (OGC)

OGC (former owner of Best Management Practice) and its functions have moved into the Cabinet Office as part of HM Government. *See* www.cabinetoffice.gov.uk

## operate

To perform as expected. A process or configuration item is said to operate if it is delivering the required outputs. Operate also means to perform one or more operations. For example, to operate a computer is to do the day-to-day operations needed for it to perform as expected.

## operation

(*ITIL Service Operation*) Day-to-day management of an IT service, system or other configuration item. Operation is also used to mean any predefined activity or transaction – for example, loading a magnetic tape, accepting money at a point of sale, or reading data from a disk drive.

## operational

The lowest of three levels of planning and delivery (strategic, tactical, operational). Operational activities include the day-to-day or short-term planning or delivery of a business process or IT service management process. The term is also a synonym for live.

## operational cost

The cost resulting from running the IT services, which often involves repeating payments – for example, staff costs, hardware maintenance and electricity (also known as current expenditure or revenue expenditure). *See also* capital expenditure.

## operational expenditure (OPEX)

*See* operational cost.

## operational level agreement (OLA)

(*ITIL Continual Service Improvement*) (*ITIL Service Design*) An agreement between an IT service provider and another part of the same organization. It supports the IT service provider's delivery of IT services to customers and defines the goods or services to be provided and the responsibilities of both parties. For example, there could be an operational level agreement:

■ Between the IT service provider and a procurement department to obtain hardware in agreed times

■ Between the service desk and a support group to provide incident resolution in agreed times.

*See also* service level agreement.

## operations control

*See* IT operations control.

## operations management

*See* IT operations management.

## optimize

Review, plan and request changes, in order to obtain the maximum efficiency and effectiveness from a process, configuration item, application etc.

## organization

A company, legal entity or other institution. The term is sometimes used to refer to any entity that has people, resources and budgets – for example, a project or business unit.

## outcome

The result of carrying out an activity, following a process, or delivering an IT service etc. The term is used to refer to intended results as well as to actual results. *See also* objective.

## outsourcing

(*ITIL Service Strategy*) Using an external service provider to manage IT services. *See also* service sourcing.

## overhead

*See* indirect cost.

## Pareto principle

(*ITIL Service Operation*) A technique used to prioritize activities. The Pareto principle says that 80% of the value of any activity is created with 20% of the effort. Pareto analysis is also used in problem management to prioritize possible problem causes for investigation.

## partnership

A relationship between two organizations that involves working closely together for common goals or mutual benefit. The IT service provider should have a partnership with the business and with third parties who are critical to the delivery of IT services. *See also* value network.

## pattern of business activity (PBA)

(*ITIL Service Strategy*) A workload profile of one or more business activities. Patterns of business activity are used to help the IT service provider understand and plan for different levels of business activity. *See also* user profile.

## performance

A measure of what is achieved or delivered by a system, person, team, process or IT service.

## performance management

Activities to ensure that something achieves its expected outcomes in an efficient and consistent manner.

## pilot

(*ITIL Service Transition*) A limited deployment of an IT service, a release or a process to the live environment. A pilot is used to reduce risk and to gain user feedback and acceptance. *See also* change evaluation; test.

## plan

A detailed proposal that describes the activities and resources needed to achieve an objective – for example, a plan to implement a new IT service or process. ISO/IEC 20000 requires a plan for the management of each IT service management process.

## Plan-Do-Check-Act (PDCA)

(*ITIL Continual Service Improvement*) A four-stage cycle for process management, attributed to Edward Deming. Plan-Do-Check-Act is also called the Deming Cycle. **Plan** – design or revise processes that support the IT services; **Do** – implement the plan and manage the processes; **Check** – measure the processes and IT services, compare with objectives and produce reports; **Act** – plan and implement changes to improve the processes.

## planning

An activity responsible for creating one or more plans – for example, capacity planning.

## policy

Formally documented management expectations and intentions. Policies are used to direct decisions, and to ensure consistent and appropriate development and implementation of processes, standards, roles, activities, IT infrastructure etc.

## post-implementation review (PIR)

A review that takes place after a change or a project has been implemented. It determines if the change or project was successful, and identifies opportunities for improvement.

## practice

A way of working, or a way in which work must be done. Practices can include activities, processes, functions, standards and guidelines. *See also* best practice.

## pricing

(*ITIL Service Strategy*) Pricing is the activity for establishing how much customers will be charged.

## PRINCE2

*See* PRojects IN Controlled Environments.

## priority

(*ITIL Service Operation*) (*ITIL Service Transition*) A category used to identify the relative importance of an incident, problem or change. Priority is based on impact and urgency, and is used to identify required times for actions to be taken. For example, the service level agreement may state that Priority 2 incidents must be resolved within 12 hours.

## proactive problem management

(*ITIL Service Operation*) Part of the problem management process. The objective of proactive problem management is to identify problems that might otherwise be missed. Proactive problem management analyses incident records, and uses data collected by other IT service management processes to identify trends or significant problems.

## problem

(*ITIL Service Operation*) A cause of one or more incidents. The cause is not usually known at the time a problem record is created, and the problem management process is responsible for further investigation.

## problem management

(*ITIL Service Operation*) The process responsible for managing the lifecycle of all problems. Problem management proactively prevents incidents from happening and minimizes the impact of incidents that cannot be prevented.

## problem record

(*ITIL Service Operation*) A record containing the details of a problem. Each problem record documents the lifecycle of a single problem.

## procedure

A document containing steps that specify how to achieve an activity. Procedures are defined as part of processes. *See also* work instruction.

## process

A structured set of activities designed to accomplish a specific objective. A process takes one or more defined inputs and turns them into defined outputs. It may include any of the roles, responsibilities, tools and management controls required to reliably deliver the outputs. A process may define policies, standards, guidelines, activities and work instructions if they are needed.

## process control

The activity of planning and regulating a process, with the objective of performing the process in an effective, efficient and consistent manner.

## process manager

A role responsible for the operational management of a process. The process manager's responsibilities include planning and coordination of all activities required to carry out, monitor and report on the process. There may be several process managers for one process – for example, regional change managers or IT service continuity managers for each data centre. The process manager role is often assigned to the person who carries out the process owner role, but the two roles may be separate in larger organizations.

## process owner

The person who is held accountable for ensuring that a process is fit for purpose. The process owner's responsibilities include sponsorship, design, change management and continual improvement of the process and its metrics. This role can be assigned to the same person who carries out the process manager role, but the two roles may be separate in larger organizations.

## production environment

*See* live environment.

## programme

A number of projects and activities that are planned and managed together to achieve an overall set of related objectives and other outcomes.

## project

A temporary organization, with people and other assets, that is required to achieve an objective or other outcome. Each project has a lifecycle that typically includes initiation, planning, execution, and closure. Projects are usually managed using a formal methodology such as PRojects IN Controlled Environments (PRINCE2) or the Project Management Body of Knowledge (PMBOK). *See also* charter; project management office; project portfolio.

## Project Management Body of Knowledge (PMBOK)

A project management standard maintained and published by the Project Management Institute. *See* www.pmi.org for more information. *See also* PRojects IN Controlled Environments (PRINCE2).

## Project Management Institute (PMI)

A membership association that advances the project management profession through globally recognized standards and certifications, collaborative communities, an extensive research programme, and professional development opportunities. PMI is a not-for-profit membership organization with representation in many countries around the world. PMI maintains and publishes the Project Management Body of Knowledge (PMBOK). *See* www.pmi.org for more information. *See also* PRojects IN Controlled Environments (PRINCE2).

## project management office (PMO)

(*ITIL Service Design*) (*ITIL Service Strategy*) A function or group responsible for managing the lifecycle of projects. *See also* charter; project portfolio.

## project portfolio

(*ITIL Service Design*) (*ITIL Service Strategy*) A database or structured document used to manage projects throughout their lifecycle. The project portfolio is used to coordinate projects and ensure that they meet their objectives in a cost-effective and timely manner. In larger organizations, the project portfolio is typically defined and maintained by a project management office. The project portfolio is important to service portfolio management as new services and significant changes are normally managed as projects. *See also* charter.

## projected service outage (PSO)

(*ITIL Service Transition*) A document that identifies the effect of planned changes, maintenance activities and test plans on agreed service levels.

## PRojects IN Controlled Environments (PRINCE2)

The standard UK government methodology for project management. *See* www.prince-officialsite.com for more information. *See also* Project Management Body of Knowledge (PMBOK).

## qualification

(*ITIL Service Transition*) An activity that ensures that the IT infrastructure is appropriate and correctly configured to support an application or IT service. *See also* validation.

## quality

The ability of a product, service or process to provide the intended value. For example, a hardware component can be considered to be of high quality if it performs as expected and delivers the required reliability. Process quality also requires an ability to monitor effectiveness and efficiency, and to improve them if necessary. *See also* quality management system.

## quality assurance (QA)

(*ITIL Service Transition*) The process responsible for ensuring that the quality of a service, process or other service asset will provide its intended value. Quality assurance is also used to refer to a function or team that performs quality assurance. This process is not described in detail within the core ITIL publications. *See also* service validation and testing.

## quality management system (QMS)

(*ITIL Continual Service Improvement*) The framework of policy, processes, functions, standards, guidelines and tools that ensures an organization is of a suitable quality to reliably meet business objectives or service levels. *See also* ISO 9000.

## quick win

(*ITIL Continual Service Improvement*) An improvement activity that is expected to provide a return on investment in a short period of time with relatively small cost and effort. *See also* Pareto principle.

## RACI

(*ITIL Service Design*) A model used to help define roles and responsibilities. RACI stands for responsible, accountable, consulted and informed.

## record

A document containing the results or other output from a process or activity. Records are evidence of the fact that an activity took place and may be paper or electronic – for example, an audit report, an incident record or the minutes of a meeting.

## recovery

(*ITIL Service Design*) (*ITIL Service Operation*) Returning a configuration item or an IT service to a working state. Recovery of an IT service often includes recovering data to a known consistent state. After recovery, further steps may be needed before the IT service can be made available to the users (restoration).

## relationship

A connection or interaction between two people or things. In business relationship management, it is the interaction between the IT service provider and the business. In service asset and configuration management, it is a link between two configuration items that identifies a dependency or connection between them. For example, applications may be linked to the servers they run on, and IT services have many links to all the configuration items that contribute to that IT service.

## release

(*ITIL Service Transition*) One or more changes to an IT service that are built, tested and deployed together. A single release may include changes to hardware, software, documentation, processes and other components.

## release and deployment management

(*ITIL Service Transition*) The process responsible for planning, scheduling and controlling the build, test and deployment of releases, and for delivering new functionality required by the business while protecting the integrity of existing services.

## release management

*See* release and deployment management.

## release record

(*ITIL Service Transition*) A record that defines the content of a release. A release record has relationships with all configuration items that are affected by the release. Release records may be in the configuration management system or elsewhere in the service knowledge management system.

## reliability

(*ITIL Continual Service Improvement*) (*ITIL Service Design*) A measure of how long an IT service or other configuration item can perform its agreed function without interruption. Usually measured as MTBF or MTBSI. The term can also be used to state how likely it is that a process, function etc. will deliver its required outputs. *See also* availability.

## repair

(*ITIL Service Operation*) The replacement or correction of a failed configuration item.

## request for change (RFC)

(*ITIL Service Transition*) A formal proposal for a change to be made. It includes details of the proposed change, and may be recorded on paper or electronically. The term is often misused to mean a change record, or the change itself.

## request fulfilment

(*ITIL Service Operation*) The process responsible for managing the lifecycle of all service requests.

## requirement

(*ITIL Service Design*) A formal statement of what is needed – for example, a service level requirement, a project requirement or the required deliverables for a process. *See also* statement of requirements.

## resilience

(*ITIL Service Design*) The ability of an IT service or other configuration item to resist failure or to recover in a timely manner following a failure. For example, an armoured cable will resist failure when put under stress. *See also* fault tolerance.

## resolution

(*ITIL Service Operation*) Action taken to repair the root cause of an incident or problem, or to implement a workaround. In ISO/IEC 20000, resolution processes is the process group that includes incident and problem management.

## resource

(*ITIL Service Strategy*) A generic term that includes IT infrastructure, people, money or anything else that might help to deliver an IT service. Resources are considered to be assets of an organization. *See also* capability; service asset.

## response time

A measure of the time taken to complete an operation or transaction. Used in capacity management as a measure of IT infrastructure performance, and in incident management as a measure of the time taken to answer the phone, or to start diagnosis.

## responsiveness

A measurement of the time taken to respond to something. This could be response time of a transaction, or the speed with which an IT service provider responds to an incident or request for change etc.

## restoration of service

*See* restore.

## restore

(*ITIL Service Operation*) Taking action to return an IT service to the users after repair and recovery from an incident. This is the primary objective of incident management.

## retire

(*ITIL Service Transition*) Permanent removal of an IT service, or other configuration item, from the live environment. Being retired is a stage in the lifecycle of many configuration items.

## return on investment (ROI)

(*ITIL Continual Service Improvement*) (*ITIL Service Strategy*) A measurement of the expected benefit of an investment. In the simplest sense, it is the net profit of an investment divided by the net worth of the assets invested. *See also* net present value; value on investment.

## review

An evaluation of a change, problem, process, project etc. Reviews are typically carried out at predefined points in the lifecycle, and especially after closure. The purpose of a review is to ensure that all deliverables have been provided, and to identify opportunities for improvement. *See also* change evaluation; post-implementation review.

**risk**

A possible event that could cause harm or loss, or affect the ability to achieve objectives. A risk is measured by the probability of a threat, the vulnerability of the asset to that threat, and the impact it would have if it occurred. Risk can also be defined as uncertainty of outcome, and can be used in the context of measuring the probability of positive outcomes as well as negative outcomes.

**risk assessment**

The initial steps of risk management: analysing the value of assets to the business, identifying threats to those assets, and evaluating how vulnerable each asset is to those threats. Risk assessment can be quantitative (based on numerical data) or qualitative.

**risk management**

The process responsible for identifying, assessing and controlling risks. Risk management is also sometimes used to refer to the second part of the overall process after risks have been identified and assessed, as in 'risk assessment and management'. This process is not described in detail within the core ITIL publications. *See also* risk assessment.

**role**

A set of responsibilities, activities and authorities assigned to a person or team. A role is defined in a process or function. One person or team may have multiple roles – for example, the roles of configuration manager and change manager may be carried out by a single person. Role is also used to describe the purpose of something or what it is used for.

**root cause**

(*ITIL Service Operation*) The underlying or original cause of an incident or problem.

**root cause analysis (RCA)**

(*ITIL Service Operation*) An activity that identifies the root cause of an incident or problem. Root cause analysis typically concentrates on IT infrastructure failures. *See also* service failure analysis.

**Sarbanes-Oxley (SOX)**

US law that regulates financial practice and corporate governance.

**scope**

The boundary or extent to which a process, procedure, certification, contract etc. applies. For example, the scope of change management may include all live IT services and related configuration items; the scope of an ISO/IEC 20000 certificate may include all IT services delivered out of a named data centre.

**security**

*See* information security management.

**security management**

*See* information security management.

**security management information system (SMIS)**

(*ITIL Service Design*) A set of tools, data and information that is used to support information security management. The security management information system is part of the information security management system. *See also* service knowledge management system.

**security policy**

*See* information security policy.

**server**

(*ITIL Service Operation*) A computer that is connected to a network and provides software functions that are used by other computers.

**service**

A means of delivering value to customers by facilitating outcomes customers want to achieve without the ownership of specific costs and risks. The term 'service' is sometimes used as a synonym for core service, IT service or service package. *See also* utility; warranty.

**service acceptance criteria (SAC)**

(*ITIL Service Transition*) A set of criteria used to ensure that an IT service meets its functionality and quality requirements and that the IT service provider is ready to operate the new IT service when it has been deployed. *See also* acceptance.

## service asset

Any resource or capability of a service provider. *See also* asset.

## service asset and configuration management (SACM)

(*ITIL Service Transition*) The process responsible for ensuring that the assets required to deliver services are properly controlled, and that accurate and reliable information about those assets is available when and where it is needed. This information includes details of how the assets have been configured and the relationships between assets. *See also* configuration management system.

## service capacity management (SCM)

(*ITIL Continual Service Improvement*) (*ITIL Service Design*) The sub-process of capacity management responsible for understanding the performance and capacity of IT services. Information on the resources used by each IT service and the pattern of usage over time are collected, recorded and analysed for use in the capacity plan. *See also* business capacity management; component capacity management.

## service catalogue

(*ITIL Service Design*) (*ITIL Service Strategy*) A database or structured document with information about all live IT services, including those available for deployment. The service catalogue is part of the service portfolio and contains information about two types of IT service: customer-facing services that are visible to the business; and supporting services required by the service provider to deliver customer-facing services. *See also* customer agreement portfolio; service catalogue management.

## service catalogue management

(*ITIL Service Design*) The process responsible for providing and maintaining the service catalogue and for ensuring that it is available to those who are authorized to access it.

## service charter

(*ITIL Service Design*) (*ITIL Service Strategy*) A document that contains details of a new or changed service. New service introductions and significant service changes are documented in a charter and authorized by service portfolio management. Service charters are passed to the service design lifecycle stage where a new or modified service design package will be created. The term charter is also used to describe the act of authorizing the work required by each stage of the service lifecycle with respect to the new or changed service. *See also* change proposal; service portfolio; service catalogue.

## service continuity management

*See* IT service continuity management.

## service culture

A customer-oriented culture. The major objectives of a service culture are customer satisfaction and helping customers to achieve their business objectives.

## service design

(*ITIL Service Design*) A stage in the lifecycle of a service. Service design includes the design of the services, governing practices, processes and policies required to realize the service provider's strategy and to facilitate the introduction of services into supported environments. Service design includes the following processes: design coordination, service catalogue management, service level management, availability management, capacity management, IT service continuity management, information security management, and supplier management. Although these processes are associated with service design, most processes have activities that take place across multiple stages of the service lifecycle. *See also* design.

## service design package (SDP)

(*ITIL Service Design*) Document(s) defining all aspects of an IT service and its requirements through each stage of its lifecycle. A service design package is produced for each new IT service, major change or IT service retirement.

### service desk

(*ITIL Service Operation*) The single point of contact between the service provider and the users. A typical service desk manages incidents and service requests, and also handles communication with the users.

### service failure analysis (SFA)

(*ITIL Service Design*) A technique that identifies underlying causes of one or more IT service interruptions. Service failure analysis identifies opportunities to improve the IT service provider's processes and tools, and not just the IT infrastructure. It is a time-constrained, project-like activity, rather than an ongoing process of analysis.

### service improvement plan (SIP)

(*ITIL Continual Service Improvement*) A formal plan to implement improvements to a process or IT service.

### service knowledge management system (SKMS)

(*ITIL Service Transition*) A set of tools and databases that is used to manage knowledge, information and data. The service knowledge management system includes the configuration management system, as well as other databases and information systems. The service knowledge management system includes tools for collecting, storing, managing, updating, analysing and presenting all the knowledge, information and data that an IT service provider will need to manage the full lifecycle of IT services. *See also* knowledge management.

### service level

Measured and reported achievement against one or more service level targets. The term is sometimes used informally to mean service level target.

### service level agreement (SLA)

(*ITIL Continual Service Improvement*) (*ITIL Service Design*) An agreement between an IT service provider and a customer. A service level agreement describes the IT service, documents service level targets, and specifies the responsibilities of the IT service provider and the customer. A single agreement may cover multiple IT services or multiple customers. *See also* operational level agreement.

### service level management (SLM)

(*ITIL Service Design*) The process responsible for negotiating achievable service level agreements and ensuring that these are met. It is responsible for ensuring that all IT service management processes, operational level agreements and underpinning contracts are appropriate for the agreed service level targets. Service level management monitors and reports on service levels, holds regular service reviews with customers, and identifies required improvements.

### service level package (SLP)

*See* service option.

### service level requirement (SLR)

(*ITIL Continual Service Improvement*) (*ITIL Service Design*) A customer requirement for an aspect of an IT service. Service level requirements are based on business objectives and used to negotiate agreed service level targets.

### service level target

(*ITIL Continual Service Improvement*) (*ITIL Service Design*) A commitment that is documented in a service level agreement. Service level targets are based on service level requirements, and are needed to ensure that the IT service is able to meet business objectives. They should be SMART, and are usually based on key performance indicators.

### service lifecycle

An approach to IT service management that emphasizes the importance of coordination and control across the various functions, processes and systems necessary to manage the full lifecycle of IT services. The service lifecycle approach considers the strategy, design, transition, operation and continual improvement of IT services. Also known as service management lifecycle.

### service management

A set of specialized organizational capabilities for providing value to customers in the form of services.

### service management lifecycle

*See* service lifecycle.

**service manager**

A generic term for any manager within the service provider. Most commonly used to refer to a business relationship manager, a process manager or a senior manager with responsibility for IT services overall.

**service model**

(*ITIL Service Strategy*) A model that shows how service assets interact with customer assets to create value. Service models describe the structure of a service (how the configuration items fit together) and the dynamics of the service (activities, flow of resources and interactions). A service model can be used as a template or blueprint for multiple services.

**service operation**

(*ITIL Service Operation*) A stage in the lifecycle of a service. Service operation coordinates and carries out the activities and processes required to deliver and manage services at agreed levels to business users and customers. Service operation also manages the technology that is used to deliver and support services. Service operation includes the following processes: event management, incident management, request fulfilment, problem management, and access management. Service operation also includes the following functions: service desk, technical management, IT operations management, and application management. Although these processes and functions are associated with service operation, most processes and functions have activities that take place across multiple stages of the service lifecycle. *See also* operation.

**service option**

(*ITIL Service Design*) (*ITIL Service Strategy*) A choice of utility and warranty offered to customers by a core service or service package. Service options are sometimes referred to as service level packages.

**service owner**

(*ITIL Service Strategy*) A role responsible for managing one or more services throughout their entire lifecycle. Service owners are instrumental in the development of service strategy and are responsible for the content of the service portfolio. *See also* business relationship management.

**service package**

(*ITIL Service Strategy*) Two or more services that have been combined to offer a solution to a specific type of customer need or to underpin specific business outcomes. A service package can consist of a combination of core services, enabling services and enhancing services. A service package provides a specific level of utility and warranty. Customers may be offered a choice of utility and warranty through one or more service options. *See also* IT service.

**service pipeline**

(*ITIL Service Strategy*) A database or structured document listing all IT services that are under consideration or development, but are not yet available to customers. The service pipeline provides a business view of possible future IT services and is part of the service portfolio that is not normally published to customers.

**service portfolio**

(*ITIL Service Strategy*) The complete set of services that is managed by a service provider. The service portfolio is used to manage the entire lifecycle of all services, and includes three categories: service pipeline (proposed or in development), service catalogue (live or available for deployment), and retired services. *See also* customer agreement portfolio; service portfolio management.

**service portfolio management (SPM)**

(*ITIL Service Strategy*) The process responsible for managing the service portfolio. Service portfolio management ensures that the service provider has the right mix of services to meet required business outcomes at an appropriate level of investment. Service portfolio management considers services in terms of the business value that they provide.

**service provider**

(*ITIL Service Strategy*) An organization supplying services to one or more internal customers or external customers. Service provider is often used as an abbreviation for IT service provider. *See also* Type I service provider; Type II service provider; Type III service provider.

## service reporting

(*ITIL Continual Service Improvement*) Activities that produce and deliver reports of achievement and trends against service levels. The format, content and frequency of reports should be agreed with customers.

## service request

(*ITIL Service Operation*) A formal request from a user for something to be provided – for example, a request for information or advice; to reset a password; or to install a workstation for a new user. Service requests are managed by the request fulfilment process, usually in conjunction with the service desk. Service requests may be linked to a request for change as part of fulfilling the request.

## service sourcing

(*ITIL Service Strategy*) The strategy and approach for deciding whether to provide a service internally, to outsource it to an external service provider, or to combine the two approaches. Service sourcing also means the execution of this strategy. *See also* insourcing; internal service provider; outsourcing.

## service strategy

(*ITIL Service Strategy*) A stage in the lifecycle of a service. Service strategy defines the perspective, position, plans and patterns that a service provider needs to execute to meet an organization's business outcomes. Service strategy includes the following processes: strategy management for IT services, service portfolio management, financial management for IT services, demand management, and business relationship management. Although these processes are associated with service strategy, most processes have activities that take place across multiple stages of the service lifecycle.

## service transition

(*ITIL Service Transition*) A stage in the lifecycle of a service. Service transition ensures that new, modified or retired services meet the expectations of the business as documented in the service strategy and service design stages of the lifecycle. Service transition includes the following processes: transition planning and support, change management, service asset and configuration management, release and deployment management, service validation and testing, change evaluation, and knowledge management. Although these processes are associated with service transition, most processes have activities that take place across multiple stages of the service lifecycle. *See also* transition.

## service validation and testing

(*ITIL Service Transition*) The process responsible for validation and testing of a new or changed IT service. Service validation and testing ensures that the IT service matches its design specification and will meet the needs of the business.

## serviceability

(*ITIL Continual Service Improvement*) (*ITIL Service Design*) The ability of a third-party supplier to meet the terms of its contract. This contract will include agreed levels of reliability, maintainability and availability for a configuration item.

## seven-step improvement process

(*ITIL Continual Service Improvement*) The process responsible for defining and managing the steps needed to identify, define, gather, process, analyse, present and implement improvements. The performance of the IT service provider is continually measured by this process and improvements are made to processes, IT services and IT infrastructure in order to increase efficiency, effectiveness and cost effectiveness. Opportunities for improvement are recorded and managed in the CSI register.

## shift

(*ITIL Service Operation*) A group or team of people who carry out a specific role for a fixed period of time. For example, there could be four shifts of IT operations control personnel to support an IT service that is used 24 hours a day.

## simulation modelling

(*ITIL Continual Service Improvement*) (*ITIL Service Design*) A technique that creates a detailed model to predict the behaviour of an IT service or other configuration item. A simulation model is often created by using the actual configuration items that are being modelled with artificial workloads or transactions. They are used in capacity management when accurate results are important. A simulation model is sometimes called a performance benchmark. *See also* analytical modelling; modelling.

## single point of contact

(*ITIL Service Operation*) Providing a single consistent way to communicate with an organization or business unit. For example, a single point of contact for an IT service provider is usually called a service desk.

## single point of failure (SPOF)

(*ITIL Service Design*) Any configuration item that can cause an incident when it fails, and for which a countermeasure has not been implemented. A single point of failure may be a person or a step in a process or activity, as well as a component of the IT infrastructure. *See also* failure.

## SLAM chart

(*ITIL Continual Service Improvement*) A service level agreement monitoring chart is used to help monitor and report achievements against service level targets. A SLAM chart is typically colour-coded to show whether each agreed service level target has been met, missed or nearly missed during each of the previous 12 months.

## SMART

(*ITIL Continual Service Improvement*) (*ITIL Service Design*) An acronym for helping to remember that targets in service level agreements and project plans should be specific, measurable, achievable, relevant and time-bound.

## snapshot

(*ITIL Continual Service Improvement*) (*ITIL Service Transition*) The current state of a configuration item, process or any other set of data recorded at a specific point in time. Snapshots can be captured by discovery tools or by manual techniques such as an assessment. *See also* baseline; benchmark.

## software asset management (SAM)

(*ITIL Service Transition*) The process responsible for tracking and reporting the use and ownership of software assets throughout their lifecycle. Software asset management is part of an overall service asset and configuration management process. This process is not described in detail within the core ITIL publications.

## source

*See* service sourcing.

## specification

A formal definition of requirements. A specification may be used to define technical or operational requirements, and may be internal or external. Many public standards consist of a code of practice and a specification. The specification defines the standard against which an organization can be audited.

## stakeholder

A person who has an interest in an organization, project, IT service etc. Stakeholders may be interested in the activities, targets, resources or deliverables. Stakeholders may include customers, partners, employees, shareholders, owners etc. *See also* RACI.

## standard

A mandatory requirement. Examples include ISO/IEC 20000 (an international standard), an internal security standard for Unix configuration, or a government standard for how financial records should be maintained. The term is also used to refer to a code of practice or specification published by a standards organization such as ISO or BSI. *See also* guideline.

## standard change

(*ITIL Service Transition*) A pre-authorized change that is low risk, relatively common and follows a procedure or work instruction – for example, a password reset or provision of standard equipment to a new employee. Requests for change are not required to implement a standard change, and they are logged and tracked using a different mechanism, such as a service request. *See also* change model.

**standby**

(*ITIL Service Design*) Used to refer to resources that are not required to deliver the live IT services, but are available to support IT service continuity plans. For example, a standby data centre may be maintained to support hot standby, warm standby or cold standby arrangements.

**statement of requirements (SOR)**

(*ITIL Service Design*) A document containing all requirements for a product purchase, or a new or changed IT service. *See also* terms of reference.

**status**

The name of a required field in many types of record. It shows the current stage in the lifecycle of the associated configuration item, incident, problem etc.

**storage management**

(*ITIL Service Operation*) The process responsible for managing the storage and maintenance of data throughout its lifecycle.

**strategic**

(*ITIL Service Strategy*) The highest of three levels of planning and delivery (strategic, tactical, operational). Strategic activities include objective setting and long-term planning to achieve the overall vision.

**strategic asset**

(*ITIL Service Strategy*) Any asset that provides the basis for core competence, distinctive performance or sustainable competitive advantage, or which allows a business unit to participate in business opportunities. Part of service strategy is to identify how IT can be viewed as a strategic asset rather than an internal administrative function.

**strategy**

(*ITIL Service Strategy*) A strategic plan designed to achieve defined objectives.

**strategy management for IT services**

(*ITIL Service Strategy*) The process responsible for defining and maintaining an organization's perspective, position, plans and patterns with regard to its services and the management of those services. Once the strategy has been defined, strategy management for IT services is also responsible for ensuring that it achieves its intended business outcomes.

**supplier**

(*ITIL Service Design*) (*ITIL Service Strategy*) A third party responsible for supplying goods or services that are required to deliver IT services. Examples of suppliers include commodity hardware and software vendors, network and telecom providers, and outsourcing organizations. *See also* supply chain; underpinning contract.

**supplier and contract management information system (SCMIS)**

(*ITIL Service Design*) A set of tools, data and information that is used to support supplier management. *See also* service knowledge management system.

**supplier management**

(*ITIL Service Design*) The process responsible for obtaining value for money from suppliers, ensuring that all contracts and agreements with suppliers support the needs of the business, and that all suppliers meet their contractual commitments. *See also* supplier and contract management information system.

**supply chain**

(*ITIL Service Strategy*) The activities in a value chain carried out by suppliers. A supply chain typically involves multiple suppliers, each adding value to the product or service. *See also* value network.

**support group**

(*ITIL Service Operation*) A group of people with technical skills. Support groups provide the technical support needed by all of the IT service management processes. *See also* technical management.

**supporting service**

(*ITIL Service Design*) An IT service that is not directly used by the business, but is required by the IT service provider to deliver customer-facing services (for example, a directory service or a backup service). Supporting services may also include IT services only used by the IT service provider. All live supporting services, including those available for deployment, are recorded in the service catalogue along with information about their relationships to customer-facing services and other CIs.

**SWOT analysis**

(*ITIL Continual Service Improvement*) A technique that reviews and analyses the internal strengths and weaknesses of an organization and the external opportunities and threats that it faces. SWOT stands for strengths, weaknesses, opportunities and threats.

**system**

A number of related things that work together to achieve an overall objective. For example:

- A computer system including hardware, software and applications
- A management system, including the framework of policy, processes, functions, standards, guidelines and tools that are planned and managed together – for example, a quality management system
- A database management system or operating system that includes many software modules which are designed to perform a set of related functions.

**tactical**

The middle of three levels of planning and delivery (strategic, tactical, operational). Tactical activities include the medium-term plans required to achieve specific objectives, typically over a period of weeks to months.

**technical management**

(*ITIL Service Operation*) The function responsible for providing technical skills in support of IT services and management of the IT infrastructure. Technical management defines the roles of support groups, as well as the tools, processes and procedures required.

**technical observation (TO)**

(*ITIL Continual Service Improvement*) (*ITIL Service Operation*) A technique used in service improvement, problem investigation and availability management. Technical support staff meet to monitor the behaviour and performance of an IT service and make recommendations for improvement.

**technical support**

*See* technical management.

**tension metrics**

(*ITIL Continual Service Improvement*) A set of related metrics, in which improvements to one metric have a negative effect on another. Tension metrics are designed to ensure that an appropriate balance is achieved.

**terms of reference (TOR)**

(*ITIL Service Design*) A document specifying the requirements, scope, deliverables, resources and schedule for a project or activity.

**test**

(*ITIL Service Transition*) An activity that verifies that a configuration item, IT service, process etc. meets its specification or agreed requirements. *See also* acceptance; service validation and testing.

**third party**

A person, organization or other entity that is not part of the service provider's own organization and is not a customer – for example, a software supplier or a hardware maintenance company. Requirements for third parties are typically specified in contracts that underpin service level agreements. *See also* underpinning contract.

**threat**

A threat is anything that might exploit a vulnerability. Any potential cause of an incident can be considered a threat. For example, a fire is a threat that could exploit the vulnerability of flammable floor coverings. This term is commonly used in information security management and IT service continuity management, but also applies to other areas such as problem and availability management.

**threshold**

The value of a metric that should cause an alert to be generated or management action to be taken. For example, 'Priority 1 incident not solved within four hours', 'More than five soft disk errors in an hour', or 'More than 10 failed changes in a month'.

**throughput**

(*ITIL Service Design*) A measure of the number of transactions or other operations performed in a fixed time – for example, 5,000 e-mails sent per hour, or 200 disk I/Os per second.

**total cost of ownership (TCO)**

(*ITIL Service Strategy*) A methodology used to help make investment decisions. It assesses the full lifecycle cost of owning a configuration item, not just the initial cost or purchase price. *See also* total cost of utilization.

**total cost of utilization (TCU)**

(*ITIL Service Strategy*) A methodology used to help make investment and service sourcing decisions. Total cost of utilization assesses the full lifecycle cost to the customer of using an IT service. *See also* total cost of ownership.

**total quality management (TQM)**

(*ITIL Continual Service Improvement*) A methodology for managing continual improvement by using a quality management system. Total quality management establishes a culture involving all people in the organization in a process of continual monitoring and improvement.

**transaction**

A discrete function performed by an IT service – for example, transferring money from one bank account to another. A single transaction may involve numerous additions, deletions and modifications of data. Either all of these are completed successfully or none of them is carried out.

**transition**

(*ITIL Service Transition*) A change in state, corresponding to a movement of an IT service or other configuration item from one lifecycle status to the next.

**transition planning and support**

(*ITIL Service Transition*) The process responsible for planning all service transition processes and coordinating the resources that they require.

**trend analysis**

(*ITIL Continual Service Improvement*) Analysis of data to identify time-related patterns. Trend analysis is used in problem management to identify common failures or fragile configuration items, and in capacity management as a modelling tool to predict future behaviour. It is also used as a management tool for identifying deficiencies in IT service management processes.

**tuning**

The activity responsible for planning changes to make the most efficient use of resources. Tuning is most commonly used in the context of IT services and components. Tuning is part of capacity management, which also includes performance monitoring and implementation of the required changes. Tuning is also called optimization, particularly in the context of processes and other non-technical resources.

**Type I service provider**

(*ITIL Service Strategy*) An internal service provider that is embedded within a business unit. There may be several Type I service providers within an organization.

**Type II service provider**

(*ITIL Service Strategy*) An internal service provider that provides shared IT services to more than one business unit. Type II service providers are also known as shared service units.

**Type III service provider**

(*ITIL Service Strategy*) A service provider that provides IT services to external customers.

**underpinning contract (UC)**

(*ITIL Service Design*) A contract between an IT service provider and a third party. The third party provides goods or services that support delivery of an IT service to a customer. The underpinning contract defines targets and responsibilities that are required to meet agreed service level targets in one or more service level agreements.

## unit cost

(*ITIL Service Strategy*) The cost to the IT service provider of providing a single component of an IT service. For example, the cost of a single desktop PC, or of a single transaction.

## urgency

(*ITIL Service Design*) (*ITIL Service Transition*) A measure of how long it will be until an incident, problem or change has a significant impact on the business. For example, a high-impact incident may have low urgency if the impact will not affect the business until the end of the financial year. Impact and urgency are used to assign priority.

## usability

(*ITIL Service Design*) The ease with which an application, product or IT service can be used. Usability requirements are often included in a statement of requirements.

## user

A person who uses the IT service on a day-to-day basis. Users are distinct from customers, as some customers do not use the IT service directly.

## user profile (UP)

(*ITIL Service Strategy*) A pattern of user demand for IT services. Each user profile includes one or more patterns of business activity.

## utility

(*ITIL Service Strategy*) The functionality offered by a product or service to meet a particular need. Utility can be summarized as 'what the service does', and can be used to determine whether a service is able to meet its required outcomes, or is 'fit for purpose'. The business value of an IT service is created by the combination of utility and warranty. *See also* service validation and testing.

## validation

(*ITIL Service Transition*) An activity that ensures a new or changed IT service, process, plan or other deliverable meets the needs of the business. Validation ensures that business requirements are met even though these may have changed since the original design. *See also* acceptance; qualification; service validation and testing; verification.

## value chain

(*ITIL Service Strategy*) A sequence of processes that creates a product or service that is of value to a customer. Each step of the sequence builds on the previous steps and contributes to the overall product or service. *See also* value network.

## value for money

An informal measure of cost effectiveness. Value for money is often based on a comparison with the cost of alternatives. *See also* cost benefit analysis.

## value network

(*ITIL Service Strategy*) A complex set of relationships between two or more groups or organizations. Value is generated through exchange of knowledge, information, goods or services. *See also* partnership; value chain.

## value on investment (VOI)

(*ITIL Continual Service Improvement*) A measurement of the expected benefit of an investment. Value on investment considers both financial and intangible benefits. *See also* return on investment.

## variance

The difference between a planned value and the actual measured value. Commonly used in financial management, capacity management and service level management, but could apply in any area where plans are in place.

## verification

(*ITIL Service Transition*) An activity that ensures that a new or changed IT service, process, plan or other deliverable is complete, accurate, reliable and matches its design specification. *See also* acceptance; validation; service validation and testing.

## version

(*ITIL Service Transition*) A version is used to identify a specific baseline of a configuration item. Versions typically use a naming convention that enables the sequence or date of each baseline to be identified. For example, payroll application version 3 contains updated functionality from version 2.

### vision

A description of what the organization intends to become in the future. A vision is created by senior management and is used to help influence culture and strategic planning. *See also* mission.

### vital business function (VBF)

(*ITIL Service Design*) Part of a business process that is critical to the success of the business. Vital business functions are an important consideration of business continuity management, IT service continuity management and availability management.

### vulnerability

A weakness that could be exploited by a threat – for example, an open firewall port, a password that is never changed, or a flammable carpet. A missing control is also considered to be a vulnerability.

### warranty

(*ITIL Service Strategy*) Assurance that a product or service will meet agreed requirements. This may be a formal agreement such as a service level agreement or contract, or it may be a marketing message or brand image. Warranty refers to the ability of a service to be available when needed, to provide the required capacity, and to provide the required reliability in terms of continuity and security. Warranty can be summarized as 'how the service is delivered', and can be used to determine whether a service is 'fit for use'. The business value of an IT service is created by the combination of utility and warranty. *See also* service validation and testing.

### work instruction

A document containing detailed instructions that specify exactly what steps to follow to carry out an activity. A work instruction contains much more detail than a procedure and is only created if very detailed instructions are needed.

### workaround

(*ITIL Service Operation*) Reducing or eliminating the impact of an incident or problem for which a full resolution is not yet available – for example, by restarting a failed configuration item. Workarounds for problems are documented in known error records. Workarounds for incidents that do not have associated problem records are documented in the incident record.

### workload

The resources required to deliver an identifiable part of an IT service. Workloads may be categorized by users, groups of users, or functions within the IT service. This is used to assist in analysing and managing the capacity, performance and utilization of configuration items and IT services. The term is sometimes used as a synonym for throughput.

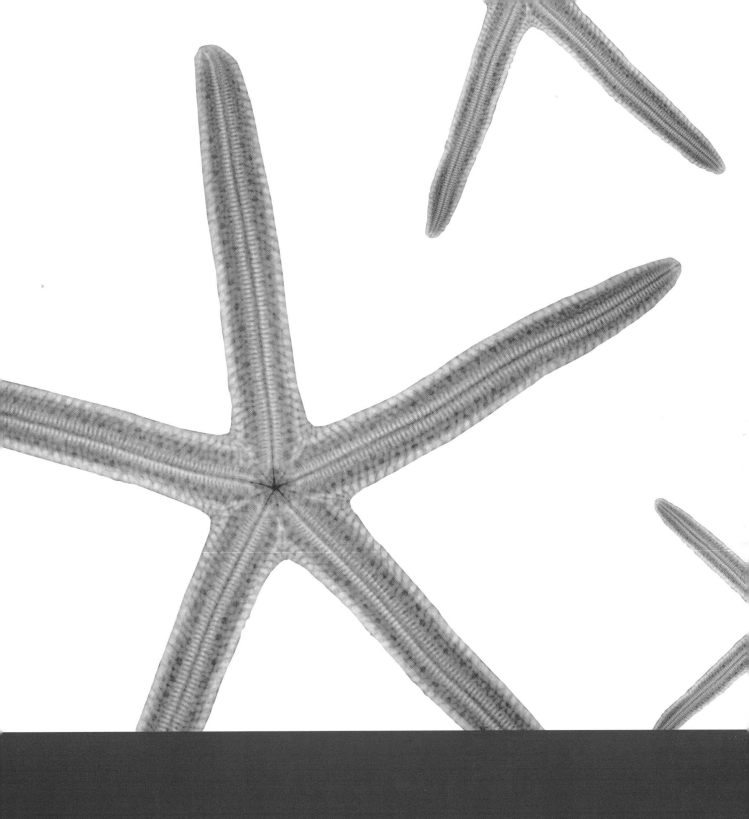

Index

# Index

Page numbers in *italic* refer to figures and tables.

analytical modelling  119
application management  23
application monitoring  149–50
approach
    assessment, pros and cons  *76*
    benchmarking  84–5
    CSI  35–6, *35*
    functional group  156
    lifecycle  155–6
    *Management of Risk* (M_o_R)  189–90
    service  155
assessments  74–6
advantages and risks of  76–8
    gap analysis  79
    processes, services and systems relationship  *77*
    pros and cons of assessment processes  *76*
    value of processes versus maturity of processes  78, *79*
assets  20
automated incident/problem resolution  148
availability management  66–8, 112–15, 131
availability reporting  *86*

balanced scorecard  *see* scorecards
baseline models  119
behaviours
    customer  118
    employee  161–2
    organizational  23
benchmarking  79–85
benefits
    of benchmarking  81
    measuring achieved  110–11
    of trend analysis  60
Best Management Practice (BMP) publications  8, *9*, 175
business capacity growth model  *117*
business capacity management  115, *116, 117*
business cases  108–10
business continuity management (BCM)  119–20, 123
business drivers  156
business impact  52
business intelligence  152
business relationship managers  30, 130, 136, *137–8*
business reporting  152

capabilities  20, *21*
Capability Maturity Model Integration (CMMI)  75, *84*, 180
capacity management  66–8, 115, 118–19, *120*, 131
Carnegie Mellon University  180
categories
    benchmarking  81
    of evaluation of CSI initiatives  74
    KPI  90
challenges when implementing CSI  70, 155–6, *157*, 167–8
change
    investigation of  146
    organizational, and CSI  36, 157–62, *158*, 179–80
    process changes  156
change management  69, 120–1, 131
coalitions, forming guiding  159
COBIT  75, 91, 176–7
communication
    plans, defining  162–3, *163*
    strategy  162
    transformation  163–4
    of vision  159
competencies  *see* skills
component capacity management  115–18, *117*
component failure impact analysis (CFIA)  112
concepts
    of knowledge management  121–2
    of M_o_R framework  189–90, *190*
    of organizational culture  23, 161–2
    of service management  20–5
    of seven-step improvement process  49
configuration data  146
continual service improvement  *see* CSI
Control OBjectives for Information and related Technology  *see* COBIT
core services  14
cost(s)
    benchmarking  80
    and effort  73
    management  150–1
    of ownership (total)  84
    and return on investment  106, 108
Covey, Stephen  61
CSFs (critical success factors)  69–70, 91–2, 167
CSI (continual service improvement)
    challenges, risks and success factors  167–8

CSI (continual service improvement) *continued*
    implementation of 70, 73–4, 155–64, 167–8
    methods and techniques 73–125
    and organizational change 36, 157–62, *158*, 179–80
    organizing for 129–41
    overview 3–5
    principles 35–44
    processes 47–70
    register 36–7, *185*
    and the service lifecycle *31*
    tools to support activities 145–52
CSI manager role 132–3, *137–8*
customer behaviour 118
customer engagement 138, *139*
customer-facing services 24
customer satisfaction surveys 52
customers
    and assets 20
    and benchmarking 82
    and information 61
    and services 13–18

data
    analysis 40, 58–60, 67–8, 83, 135, *136*
    configuration 146
    data-poor environment 109–10
    defining 41
    gathering 39, 53–5, *55*, 65–7, 83, 134, *135*
    layers 24–5, *26*, *147*
    management, example of poor data 56
    processing 39, 55–8, *57*, 65–7, 83, 135
Data-to-Information-to-Knowledge-to-Wisdom (DIKW) 38, 47
Deming Cycle 38, 175–6
    *see also* Plan-Do-Check-Act (PDCA) cycle
Deming, W. Edwards 38
departmental requirements *116*
departments and divisions 22
drivers
    business 156
    external and internal 37
    first- to fourth-order *64*

effort and cost 73
employee behaviour 161–2
enabling and enhancing services 14
environmental management 177–8
eSCM framework 180
evaluation 73–4
event management 67, 148
expanded incident lifecycle 113–15, *114*
external service providers 82, 85, 98

fault tree analysis 112–13
financial management for IT services 67, 131, 150–1
frameworks 42, 44
    designing a service measurement 86–7
    eSCM 180
    ITIL 3
    *Management of Risk* (M_o_R) 189–90, *190*
    public 19–20
    Risk IT process 192–3, *193*
functional groups 48, 156
functions 22–3, 129

gap analysis 79
goals
    deriving measurements and metrics from *99*
    high-level and KPIs *91*
    and metrics 93–5, 177
governance 25, 156
    enterprise *42*
    of IT 42, 176
    of risk 193
groups 22
    *see also* functional groups

implementation of CSI
    communication strategy and plan 163–4
    considerations and challenges 70, 155–6, *157*, 167–8
    cost and effort 73
    governance 156
    and organizational change 157–62
    review and evaluation 73–4
    starting approaches 155–6
incident management 67, 68, 69, 131
industry norms, comparison with 74, 83–4
information analysis 58–60, 67–8
information management 69
information presentation and use 60–2, *62*, 68–9
information security management 67, 68, 131, 150
inputs
    across service lifecycle *197–8*
    and CSI roles *164*
    definition 21
    to identify improvement strategy 50
    by lifecycle stage *43*
    to measurement 52
    to monitoring process 64–5
interfaces 65
internal service providers 82, 85, 98
interpretation of metrics 95–7

ISO 31000  190–1, *191*
   *see also* risk management
ISO/IEC 20000  3, 27, 44, 177
   *see also* IT service management
ISO/IEC 27001  191–2
   *see also* information security management
ISO standards  177–8
IT
   balanced scorecard  *104*
   financial management for  67, 131, 150–1
   governance  42, 176
   green  177–8
   managers  98
   operations management  22
   publications  178
   Risk IT  192–3, *193*
IT service continuity management (ITSCM)  119–20,
   131
IT service definition  13
IT service management (ITSM)  16, 146–8
ITIL
   guidance and web services  175
   introduction to framework  3
   and the OSI framework  178–9
   qualification scheme  141
   reasons for success  8–9
   relationship with other BMP guides  8, *9*
   service lifecycle  *3*
ITIL publications  6, 28, 83, 175
   *ITIL Continual Service Improvement*  3–5, 7, 10,
     *29*, 140
   *ITIL Service Design*  6–7, *29*, 38, 53, 65, 85, 112,
     118, 132, 139, 178
   *ITIL Service Operation*  7, 22–3, *29*, 118, 120, 129,
     178
   *ITIL Service Strategy*  6, 13, 17, 22, 24, 25, *29*, 42,
     118, 129, 132, 145, 176
   *ITIL Service Transition*  7, *29*, 38, 121, 122, 179

key performance indicators  *see* KPIs
knowledge management
   concepts  121–2
   as CSI support tool  38, 121, 148–9
   and IT decisions  *38*
   and the SKMS  24–5
KPIs (key performance indicators)
   and high-level goals  *91*
   number of  91–2
   qualitative and quantitative  92
   samples of, for different processes  *102*
   suitability for purpose  93
   of value of service management processes  *90*

lifecycle approach  155–6

*Management of Risk* (M_o_R)  189–90, *190*
   *see also* risk management
management systems  25–7
market performance  52
maturity assessments  74, 84
measurement and metrics
   balanced scorecard  103–5
   creating scorecards and reports  98–100
   CSFs and KPIs  91–3
   defining what to measure  50–3
   framework for effort and cost  73
   and goals  93–5, *99*
   interpreting metrics  95–7
   measuring benefits  110–11
   organizational metrics  95
   service quality metrics examples  *94*
   SWOT analysis  105–6
   target setting  100, 103
   tension metrics  93
   types of metrics  91
   usage of  97–8
   from vision to measurement  *50, 92*
   *see also* service measurement
measurement-based management  104–5
modelling  118–19
models  42, 44
   baseline  119
   business capacity growth  *117*
   CMMI (Capability Maturity Model Integration)
     75, *84*, 180
   process  *21*
   responsibility (RACI)  138–9, *140*
   service management  *90*
   service measurement  *88*
monitoring
   of application and service performance  149–50
   of CSI  53–6
   detection of incident  114
   procedures  *55*
   reasons for  39

objectives
   of CSI  4
   deriving measurements and metrics from  *99*
   of seven-step improvement process  47
organizational behaviour  23
organizational capabilities  15
organizational change  36, 157–62, *158*, 179–80
organizational culture  23, 161–2
organizational metrics  95

organizing for CSI
    competence and training 139–41
    customer engagement 138, *139*
    functions 129
    organizational development 129
    responsibility model (RACI) 138–9, *140*
    roles 129–38
organizing for service management
    competence and skills 139–40
    functions 22–3
    organizational culture and behaviour 23, 161–2
    roles 23
OSI (Open Systems Interconnection) framework
        178–9
outages 62, *100–1*
outputs
    across service lifecycle *197–8*
    definition 21
    by lifecycle stage *43*
    to monitoring process 64–5

performance 54, 90
performance indicators *see* KPIs
performance management 149
performance monitoring 149–50
Plan-Do-Check-Act (PDCA) cycle 26–7, *27*, 38, 47,
        78, 175–6
policy
    reporting 111
    seven-step improvement process 48
    template example *49*
portfolio management 150
post-implementation review (PIR) 121
presentation layer 24, *147*
PRINCE2 (PRojects IN Controlled Environments, V2)
        8, *9*, 179
principles
    of CSI 35–44
    of *Management of Risk* (M_o_R) 189–90
    of seven-step improvement process 48–9
problem management 68, 69, 120, 131
process assessments *84*, 178
process changes 156, *157*
process compliance 54
process maturity comparison 84
process metrics 53, 91
process re-engineering *157*
process roles
    process managers 133
    process owners 80, 130, 131–2, 133
    process practitioners 132
processes

CSI *see* seven-step improvement process
    service management 20–2
programme management 179
project management 150, 179
proprietary knowledge 19
public frameworks and standards 19–20

quality 54, 90
quality management systems 175–6
quality metrics *94*
quality systems 42, 44

registers
    CSI 36–7, *185*
    risk *125*
release and deployment management 120–1, 131
releases 146–7
reporting
    availability *86*
    business 152
    levels of 87–8
    service 111–12
reporting analysts 133
reports
    creation of 98–100
    examples of *100, 101*
requesting services 149
requests for change (RFCs) 69, 89
resources 20, *21*
responsibility model (RACI) 138–9, *140*
retired services 24
return on investment (ROI)
    business cases in a data-poor environment 109–10
    creating 106, 108
    establishing the business case 108–9
    and expectations 109
    measuring benefits achieved 110–11
risk management 122–3, 176
    business perspective on 123–4
    definition of 189
    ISO 31000 190–1, *191*
    ISO/IEC 27001 191–2
    *Management of Risk* (M_o_R) 189–90, *190*
    profiles and responsibilities 124–5
    reasons for *124*
    relation to safety, security and business
    continuity 123
    Risk IT 192–3, *193*
    risk register *125*
roles 23, 129–38

Sarbanes-Oxley 109
scorecards
    balanced 103–5, 180
    creation of 98–9
    IT balanced *104*
    service desk example *105*
service approach 155
service capacity management 115, *116*
service catalogue 24, 149
service desk 22, 67, 68, 69
    measurement *96–7, 104–5*
service failure analysis (SFA) 113
service level agreements (SLAs) 16
service level management (SLM) 37–8, 131
    as CSI support tool 147–8
    and information 65–6, 67, 68, 69
service levels 52
    achievement chart *62*
service lifecycle 27–8
    and continual service improvement *31*
    integration across *30*
    ITIL *3*
    processes through 28–31, *29*
    specialization and coordination across 28
service management 15–16
    assets, capabilities and resources 20, *21*
    best practices 18–20, *19*
    competence and skills for 139–41
    functions and roles 22–3
    governance 25
    ISO/IEC 20000 series 3, 27, 44, 177
    IT service management (ITSM) 16, 146–8
    knowledge management and the SKMS 24–5, *26*
    management systems 25–7
    model *90*
    organizational culture and behaviour 23
    Plan-Do-Check-Act cycle *27*
    process measurement 89–90, *90*
    processes 20–2, 112–25
    roles and customer engagement *139*
    service lifecycle 27–31
    service portfolio 23–4, *25*
    service providers 16–17
    services 13–15
    stakeholders 17
    versus technology domain *89*
    utility and warranty 17–18
service managers 130
service measurement 85–6
    baselines 38–9
    creating a measurement framework grid 90, 91
    design and development of 86–7

levels of 87–8
    model *88*
    reasons for measuring 39
    seven-step improvement process 39–42, *40, 41*
    *see also* measurement and metrics
service metrics 53, 91
service owners 130–1
service performance monitoring 149–50
service pipeline 24
service portfolio 23–4, *25*
service providers 82, 85, 98
service quality metrics *94*
service reporting
    content 111–12
    policy and rules 111
services 13–15
    customer-facing 24
    requesting 149
    types of 14
    utility and warranty of 17–18
*Seven Habits of Highly Effective People* 61
seven-step improvement process 39–42, *40*
    challenges and risks 70
    concepts 49
    CSFs and KPIs 69–70
    data and information analysis 58–60, 67–8
    data gathering 53–5, *55*, 65–7
    data processing 55–8, *57*, 65–7
    defining what to measure 50–3
    identifying strategy for improvement 49–50, *50*
    implementing improvement 62–4, *64*, 69
    information management 69
    information presentation and use 60–2, *62*, 68–9
    policies 48, *49*
    principles 48–9
    purpose and objectives 47
    scope 47–8
    triggers, inputs, outputs and interfaces 64–5
    value to business 48
SFIA (skills framework for the information age) 140, 180
Shewhart Cycle *see* Plan-Do-Check-Act (PDCA) cycle
simulation modelling 119
Six Sigma 180–1
skills
    benchmarking 80
    and competence framework 140
    for CSI *134, 135–6, 138*
    framework for the information age 140, 180
    for service management 139–40
SKMS (service knowledge management system) 24–5, *26, 123, 147*

software configuration management 150
software test management 150
software version control 150
standards 19–20, 26–7, 42, 44, 177–8
statistical analysis tools 150
strategic business units (SBUs) 104
supplier performance 52
suppliers 17, 61
supporting services 24
SWOT analysis 105–6, *107*
systems and network management 148

target setting 100, 103
teams 22
technical management 22, 30
technical observation (TO) 113
technology 145
    application of architectural layers of CMS *147*
    service-centric view of the IT enterprise *151*
    versus service management *89*
    tools to support CSI activities 146–52
technology metrics 53, 91
tension metrics 93
time cost 80
total cost of ownership (TCO) 84
total quality management (TQM) 175
training 141
training cost 73
trend analysis 58–60, 95–7, 118
triggers 64–5

urgency, creating a sense of 157
usage
    of information 60–2, *62*, 68–9
    of *ITIL Continual Service Improvement* 5
    of measurement and metrics 95–8
users *see* customers
utility of services 17–18

value
    of benchmarking 81
    of CSI to business 5
    *Management of Value* (MoV) 8
    of process versus maturity of process 78, *79*
    of service 17–18, *18*
    of seven-step improvement process 48
vision *50*, *92*, 159–60, *163*
volume 54

warranty of services 17–18
wins, planning for and creating 160
wisdom 41
workflow 149
workload management 118